DOCTOR WHO
THE SIXTIES

David J. Howe
Mark Stammers
Stephen James Walker

First published in 1992 by
Doctor Who Books
an imprint of Virgin Publishing Ltd
338 Ladbroke Grove
London W10 5AH

Copyright © David J. Howe, Mark Stammers & Stephen James Walker 1992
'Doctor Who' copyright
© British Broadcasting Corporation 1992

Certain photographic illustrations
© BBC Photographs, © Barry Newbery
© Raymond P. Cusick, © Christopher Barry
© John Wood, © Topham's Picture Source
© Alexandra Tynan, © Sue Willis
© Jennie Linden

This book is published by arrangement with BBC Books, a division of
BBC Enterprises Ltd. 'Doctor Who' is a registered trade mark of The
British Broadcasting Corporation

Cover and internal layout
designed by Mark Stammers
Typeset by
D&S Design
1 Edith Grove
London SW10 0JY

Printed and bound by
Singapore National Printers

ISBN 1 852 27420 4

Acknowledgements

No factual book of this nature is produced in complete isolation and over the years we have been indebted to a large number of people who have given their time to speak to us and to share their knowledge of *Doctor Who*. We would like to thank in particular the following:

John Ainsworth, Carole Ann Ford, Clive Banks, Morris Barry, June Barry, Christopher Barry, Irene Basterfield and Alison Turner of the BBC TV Drama Script Unit, Dave Baston, Jeremy Bentham, British Film Institute, Anthony Brown, Peter Bryant, Tony Clark, Shirley Cooklin, Shirley Coward, Raymond P. Cusick, Guy Daniels, Daphne Dare, Emma Darrell of Roger Hancock Ltd, Kevin Davies, Gerry Davis, Terrance Dicks, Monica Erickson, Sandra Exelby, Michael Ferguson, Gordon Flemyng, John Freeman and *Doctor Who Magazine* (Marvel Comics UK), David Gibbes-Auger, Mick Hall, Michealjohn Harris, Peter Hawkins, Richard Hollis of BBC Enterprises, Gary Hopkins, Rosemary Howe, Waris Hussein, Garry Kennard, A. J. 'Mitch' Mitchell, Paul James, Susan James, Dallas Jones, Robert Jewell, Ian K. McLachlan, Bobbie Mitchell and Alison Kenvin of BBC Photographs, Robert Kew, Verity Lambert, Richard Landen, Andrew Lane, Gary Leigh and *Dream Watch Bulletin*, Barry Letts, Ian Levine, Jennie Linden, Innes Lloyd, Bernard Lodge, Derek Martinus, Anthony McKay and *Time Screen*, Barry Newbery, Sydney Newman, John Peel, Victor Pemberton, Andrew Pixley, Marc Platt, Nicholas Ratcliffe and BBC Registry, Steve Roberts, Tim Robins, Gordon Roxburgh, Gary Russell, Derrick Sherwin, Rex Tucker, Alexandra Tynan, Julian Vince, Jan Vincent-Rudzki, Chris Weller and Julia Howe of BBC Books, Trevor Wells, Martin Wiggins, Anneke Wills, Sue Willis, Graeme Wood, John Wood and Peter Wylde.

Thanks also to our editor, Peter Darvill-Evans, for his confidence in this project, to everyone who has ever helped or contributed to *The Frame*, and to anyone else we might have inadvertently missed. All your help and enthusiasm is greatly appreciated.

Contents

For all our friends and families,
but especially:

Rosemary and James - DJH

Helen Topley - SJW

Susan, Ron and Jean - MS

Introduction

Doctor Who. What impressions does that name conjure up for you?

Most likely, it brings to mind an image of a man. He might be tall and athletic with silver hair and a deeply lined face, wearing a ruffled shirt and a velvet jacket, or a flamboyant bohemian with a battered felt hat and a long, trailing scarf. Maybe you picture a somewhat younger-looking, fair-haired man in old-fashioned cricket attire, or an unpre-dictable maverick with twinkling eyes and a garish, multicoloured coat. You might even think of a diminutive fellow with a faint Scots accent and sporting a paisley-patterned scarf, a question-mark pullover and a brolly.

The fact is, depending on when they first encountered him, people have widely differing perceptions of that stranger known as the Doctor, for he has the extraordinary ability, unique amongst popular fictional heroes, to take on a new physical form whenever his old one wears

DOCTOR WHO?

There is some evidence to suggest that 'Doctor Who' is the Doctor's full name as well as being the title of the series. For example, the closing credits of every episode up to the end of Season 18 in 1981 refer to the character as 'Doctor Who', as do the scripts and other BBC documentation; in **The War Machines**, *the computer WOTAN identifies him as 'Doctor Who' and several other people during the story call him by that name; and the camera script of* **The Underwater Menace** *clearly indicates that he signs his own name as 'Doctor Who' in that story. In this book we refer to the character as 'the Doctor' throughout, as this has become the accepted norm.*

◀ **The first Doctor and his grand-daughter Susan, played by William Hartnell and Carole Ann Ford.** *The Keys of Marinus.*

SEASONS

When discussing Doctor Who's history, fans and media researchers generally divide it up into a number of separate seasons, each corresponding to a regular run of episodes in the original UK transmission sequence. The term 'season' is in fact an Americanism which gained currency in the UK only in the late seventies; before that, the word 'series' was used. For the sake of clarity, this book follows the standard convention.

The second Doctor, ▶
Patrick Troughton. *The
Abominable Snowmen.*

The Doctor's faithful ▶
TARDIS, a time ship capable
of taking its occupants
anywhere in time and space.
Marco Polo.

out. How that idea evolved is just one of the many things described in this book, which covers the first six years of *Doctor Who*'s history, from 1963 to 1969 – the period when the Doctor first appeared as an elderly man with long white hair and Edwardian clothes and then as a short, dark-haired figure, scruffily dressed in an old frock coat and baggy checked trousers.

In this book we will be examining the genesis of *Doctor Who*, presenting a detailed behind-the-scenes account of its first six years; recalling the Doctor's early companions and his many monstrous adversaries; looking at the various spin-offs and the wealth of associated merchandise; exploding many myths which have grown up amongst fans of the series; and, perhaps most important of all, trying to recapture some of the feeling and spirit of the era.

The sixties was a time when watching *Doctor Who* meant gathering around the family's small black-and-white TV set on a Saturday evening, waiting impatiently for *Grandstand* to finish as the late football results chattered up on the teleprinter, savouring the smells of your favourite tea being prepared in the kitchen and feeling the tingle of excitement as the unique theme tune reverberated around the room and the eerie patterns of the title sequence made their unearthly progress across the screen. It was a time when youngsters watched through their fingers, from behind the sofa or even through the crack in the door. Those too frightened to watch would later listen wide-eyed as elder siblings recounted tales of silver giants, death-dealing Daleks, furry Yeti and other fearsome creatures which had temporarily invaded their sitting room.

Doctor Who has always been good, escapist entertainment, but at its best it can be much more than that. Its stories contain a great deal that could be considered educational, often conveying factual information about science and history, dealing with important moral and philosophical questions or commenting on issues of direct relevance to our own everyday lives. The central character, the Doctor, stands for compassion, justice, peace, love and understanding. In essence, he represents a role model for the millions of viewers who follow his adventures.

Certainly *Doctor Who* is a phenomenon which can be appreciated on many different levels. From its humble beginnings as a Saturday teatime TV show for adults and children alike, it has featured in the worlds of film, stage, literature, recording and merchandise. It has crossed language barriers and continents and has inspired many to great artistic and charitable endeavours. Such a concept is surely almost unique, and certainly worthy of celebration.

Join us on a trip back in time, to re-live, remember and, above all, enjoy a little slice of history.

David, Stephen and Mark

December 1991

CHAPTER ONE

Origins

The vital spark of inspiration for *Doctor Who* came from the BBC's Head of Drama, distinguished Canadian producer Sydney Newman, who had just joined the Corporation in December 1962 on a five-year contract. Previously he had worked in a similar capacity at ABC TV, under Managing Director Howard Thomas. Thomas has since claimed in his autobiography, *With an Independent Air*, that Newman thought up the idea for *Doctor Who* while still at ABC but failed to get it off the ground as it was felt that the regulatory body for independent television, the ITA, would consider it unsuitable for children. Newman, however, strongly maintains that 'the whole notion of *Doctor Who* was dreamed up entirely at the BBC.'

As Newman tells it, the need for a new series arose in the first place because the BBC's programme planners decided that there was a gap to be filled in their Saturday evening line-up between the end of the afternoon's sports coverage and the start of the pop music show *Juke Box Jury* at around six o'clock. What Newman was after was 'a new programme which would bridge the state of mind of sports fans and the teenage pop music audience', but which would also appeal to children.

Having identified his target audience, Newman's next concern was to decide on the subject matter of the new series. He did not think specifically in terms of a science-fiction concept but considered a wide range of ideas, including one about two pupils in a boys' school which he rejected as he felt it would not appeal to the adult sports fans. Science fiction had, however, been a lifelong interest of his and seemed a logical choice.

Earlier in his career, Newman had supervised a children's science-fiction series, based partly on *Twenty Thousand Leagues under the Sea*, at CBC in Canada; then, at ABC, he had produced *Pathfinders In Space* and its sequels, about the interplanetary exploits of a space-age family. These comic-book-style adventures followed the same tradition of 'cliffhanger' serials which the BBC itself had previously tapped with such productions as *Stranger from Space* (1951/2) and *The Lost Planet* (1954) – a tradition which would no doubt have been at the back of Newman's mind when he devised his new Saturday teatime serial for the BBC.

Inspired partly by H. G. Wells's *The Time Machine*, he came up with the idea of a time-travel adventure exploring scientific and historical themes and which could be described as educational, or at least mind-opening, for the children watching. Although space travel would obviously come into it, he was keen that the programme should avoid the 'bug-eyed monsters' he saw as the lowest form of science fiction.

SYDNEY NEWMAN
HEAD OF DRAMA

*Sydney Newman came to the UK in 1958 after a successful career in his native Canada. He was working as supervisor of drama production at the Canadian Broadcasting Corporation (CBC) when he accepted an invitation to take up a similar post at ABC Television in England. There, he produced the Sunday night single play anthology series **Armchair Theatre**, which focused on issues of interest to working-class people in the fifties – a style which critics quickly dubbed 'kitchen sink drama'. He also helped create **The Avengers** before moving to the BBC in December 1962. As Head of Drama Group at the BBC he was in charge of programmes from children's shows to opera, as well as popular series like **Z Cars, Doctor Finlay's Casebook** and his own brainchild **Doctor Who**. He left the BBC in 1967 and took up a post as Head of Production for the Associated British Picture Film Corporation at Elstree before returning to Canada to become Chairman and Chief Executive of the National Film Board. In 1985 he came back to England, where he has since undertaken projects as an independent producer while also working on his memoirs.*

◀ **Sydney Newman, Head of Drama at the BBC during the mid-sixties.**

PRODUCTION TEAMS

Based on the North American model – already followed by most ITV companies when Sydney Newman introduced it at the BBC – production teams usually consisted of a producer and a story editor (later renamed script editor), working full time on a particular programme. The producer would have overall artistic and financial responsibility for the programme and oversee the work of individual directors brought in to handle particular episodes or stories, while the relatively junior story editor would find and work with writers to provide the scripts, a task previously performed by the Script Department.

School teachers Ian and ▶ Barbara as they eventually appeared on screen. *Marco Polo.*

DONALD WILSON
HEAD OF SERIALS

*Born in Scotland in 1910, Donald Wilson entered the film industry as a script writer in 1932. After the War he went on to produce and direct feature films for the Rank Organisation and by 1953 had also written his first television script, a thriller called **Stand By to Shoot**. In 1955 he joined the BBC as Script Supervisor Television, responsible for the running of the Central Script Section. Then, in 1959, when the Section was expanded to become the Script Department, he became Head of Output Programmes, directly responsible to the BBC Controller for all script matters. When Sydney Newman re-organised Drama in 1963 the department was abolished and Wilson was asked by Newman to become the first Head of Serials. In 1965, Wilson returned to writing and producing for the BBC and was responsible for, amongst many others, **The Forsyte Saga** (1967) (for which he won a BAFTA award) and **Anna Karenina** (1977), shortly after which he retired.*

For the time machine itself Newman hit upon the concept of a ship larger inside than out, which he thought should be disguised as an everyday object so that viewers would be encouraged not to take things for granted. He devised the character of a crotchety old man, senile but with extraordinary flashes of brilliance, who had escaped in terror to Earth with his ship from an advanced civilisation on a far-distant planet. This old man would not be fully in control of the ship, and his attempts to return his human companions home would always lead them into new adventures in space and time.

Some time early in 1963, Newman put all these ideas into a two- or three-page memo which he gave to Donald Wilson, the Head of the BBC's Script Department. At first, as Newman recalls, Wilson was a little sceptical, but agreed to take the proposal away and have some further work done on it. Progress was not as smooth as it might have been, though, because the whole of the BBC Drama Group was in a state of some upheaval at that time following some of Newman's important changes. One of these was the splitting up of Drama into three separate departments – Series, Serials and Plays – each with its own Head who would exercise direct control and be answerable to Newman. Another was the establishment of production teams to take charge of making particular programmes, something that had normally been the responsibility of individual producer/directors.

Naturally, these changes did not take place overnight and the embryonic *Doctor Who* was caught up in them. Donald Wilson himself was in the process of transferring from the Script Department (which was to be abolished as a result of the switch to the production-team system) to become Head of the new Serials Department (the department which would produce *Doctor Who*), and one of the first people with whom Sydney Newman discussed his ideas for the new show was an old-style producer/director: Rex Tucker.

Today, Newman only vaguely recalls Tucker's name as one of a number of possible candidates, none of whom he approved of, put forward by Donald Wilson for the producer's job. However, there is no doubt that Tucker did actually take on that responsibility for several weeks around March 1963. His role as he saw it was very much a temporary one; he was to get things started on the right track until the new-style production team could be set up. But he was more than just a caretaker. For one thing, it may well have been he who came up with the title *Doctor Who* – although he has denied this, giving the credit to Sydney Newman. Undoubtedly he helped to develop Newman's original idea and the basic dramatic structure of the series. He was also initially responsible for setting up the technical side of the production and for taking decisions on the scripting.

At this stage the actual job of providing scripts was still the responsibility of the Script Department, and the man asked to handle the new project was C. E. Webber (known to all at the BBC as 'Bunny'), a mutual friend of Donald Wilson's and Rex Tucker's. Webber's task was twofold: first, he had to flesh out the basic idea handed down to him and produce a more detailed format for the series, and secondly he had to write the scripts intended to comprise the first televised story.

By this time, Sydney Newman no longer had any day-to-day involvement with the programme – as Head of the whole Drama Group he had far more weighty responsibilities – and although Webber would certainly have discussed his ideas quite extensively with Donald Wilson (and probably also with Rex Tucker), he himself devised a number of important elements of *Doctor Who*. In particular, he thought up the detailed characters of the Doctor's fellow travellers: two teachers, Ian and Barbara, and Susan, a pupil at their school – Sydney Newman was keen that there should be a young girl or boy in the story to help with audience identification. On screen these characters did not turn out quite as he had envisaged. Originally, Ian and Barbara were to have been somewhat younger than they eventually appeared – Barbara, for example, was described as an inexperienced student teacher in her early twen-

The police box exterior of the TARDIS as seen in the season one story *Marco Polo*.

ties. Susan, on the other hand, was intended to be somewhat like Andromeda, the otherworldly character from *A for Andromeda* and *The Andromeda Breakthrough*, two BBC science-fiction serials from 1961 and 1962.

According to Irene Basterfield, the Script Department employee who typed up his hand-written script, Webber even had some early casting ideas, thinking that Ian could be played by pop star Cliff Richard and one of the girls – presumably Barbara – by Susan Hampshire. However, these ideas were never pursued.

In Webber's original story, the Doctor was to have taken the other three characters on a journey in his time-space machine and landed them in an adventure where they were all reduced to just an inch in height, an idea later re-used in the transmitted story *Planet of Giants*.

As Irene Basterfield recalls, the title of the series may not have been fixed as *Doctor Who* even at this late stage, but as no copies of Webber's script have survived, the full details may never be known. In any event, the fact is that when the script was presented to Rex Tucker, he decided to reject it, something he now explains by saying that Webber was 'too good a writer to write down to the level required.' Although very much part of the BBC old guard himself, Tucker felt that what his friend had written was basically too cerebral and was the sort of old-fashioned children's drama he

knew Sydney Newman was anxious to get away from.

Following the rejection of Webber's script, Donald Wilson asked another in-house writer, Australian Anthony Coburn, to try his hand at writing a suitable opening story based on the existing format. He also appointed David Whitaker, again an established BBC staffer, to be the series' first story editor under the new production-team regime.

By the end of April 1963 Coburn had completed a first draft script and he and Whitaker had begun to discuss it. The first episode was based in part on Webber's rejected draft, but the other three, set in the Stone Age, were completely new. Whitaker requested a number of amendments, specifically to tone down the educational content and to make the story more exciting, but he was happy enough with what he had seen to ask Coburn to produce a storyline for the second serial, intended to be a six-parter. In addition, he readily accepted Coburn's suggestions that the Doctor's ship should be disguised as a police box – and, later, that it should be called TARDIS – and that Susan should be his grand-daughter rather than just a young travelling companion, something which might have had sexual connotations.

In the meantime, Tucker had been having his own ideas about casting. He had found a young unknown Australian actress for the part of Susan

REX TUCKER
DIRECTOR

*Rex Tucker first set out to be a businessman after leaving Cambridge University but disliked the commercial world so much that he took up teaching and freelance writing instead. In the thirties he began writing scripts for radio and eventually joined the staff of the BBC to work on such programmes as the popular **Children's Hour**. After the War he became a drama producer specialising in plays for children and also, as a sideline, wrote children's books. Moving over to television in the fifties, he worked as writer and producer/director on numerous programmes, including his play **The Pretender** (in August 1962) and many classic serials. By the time he became involved with **Doctor Who** in 1963, he was already something of a veteran. Tucker was never comfortable with the idea of working on the series and quickly moved on – he was already writing a script for an episode of **Maigret** and shortly after that he directed a production of Gustave Flaubert's **Madame Bovary**, transmitted in March 1964. In 1966 he returned to **Doctor Who** to direct **The Gunfighters**.*

C. E. WEBBER
WRITER

*An accomplished radio and television writer, C. E. 'Bunny' Webber had been on the BBC Script Department staff for some time and penned many successful children's dramas – including some acclaimed adaptations of the **Just William** books – when he was asked to help develop **Doctor Who** and to script the first story. Following the rejection of his script, he left the dwindling Script Department to start a freelance career.*

VERITY LAMBERT
PRODUCER

Verity Lambert was educated at Roedean and attended the Sorbonne in Paris before returning to England and taking a secretarial course. She started work as a typist at ABC Television, then became a production assistant working for Sydney Newman on such shows as **Armchair Theatre**. *Subsequently she accepted a post as secretary-cum-aide to an American producer, gaining valuable experience of the TV industry in the States. Back in England, she followed Newman to the BBC in 1963 to produce* **Doctor Who**, *and then launched two more series,* **The Newcomers** *and* **Adam Adamant Lives!** *In the late sixties she moved to ITV and made, amongst other programmes,* **Budgie, Minder, Quatermass** *and* **Reilly, Ace of Spies**. *As Executive Producer of Euston Films, and more recently with her own company, Cinema Verity, Lambert has established herself as one of Britain's top TV producers and executives, responsible for such shows as* **May to December** *and* **GBH** *– winning the coveted Business Woman of the Year award, and many other accolades. In latter years she has also moved into production of films for the cinema.*

William Hartnell as Johnson from the film *This Sporting Life*. **Hartnell's performance impressed Verity Lambert and she later offered him the role of the Doctor.**

William Russell in his role as Sir Lancelot from the series *The Adventures of Sir Lancelot*. **Russell was chosen to play science teacher Ian Chesterton.**

and approached his friend Hugh David (later to direct the stories *The Highlanders* and *Fury from the Deep* but at that time working as an actor) to play the central role of the Doctor; David declined as he had only recently finished a year's stint as the lead in a Granada TV series, *Knight Errant*, and had disliked the high public profile it had brought him.

Other aspects of the production to which Rex Tucker turned his attention included the music; he invited composer Tristram Cary to write the signature tune and the incidentals for the first story.

Around April 1963, Tucker's stint on the series came to an end as he left to take a holiday and Sydney Newman appointed a permanent producer: Verity Lambert. Lambert had previously been Newman's production assistant on the ground-breaking *Armchair Theatre* plays he had produced for ABC TV and she was just the sort of sharp, young, forward-looking person he wanted in charge of *Doctor Who*.

'She was the one who realised it all,' Newman says today, 'although I had a hand in the casting. I helped her quite a bit in the very beginning because she was inexperienced as a producer, and she was frightened to death coming to the BBC. However, she had worked with some of my best directors – like Ted Kotcheff and Philip Saville – so she knew the production grass roots extremely well. And she turned out to be a real winner.

'I'm told there were quite a few rumblings within the BBC about Verity, because she had never been a director. Also, there were rumblings because Verity was a girl: she was tough, good-looking and stubborn. If she didn't like something she came out honestly and said so. It wasn't "I don't know why I don't like it"; she would say "I don't like it because of X, Y and Z – it ought to be A, B and C." She was very positive, as a good producer has to be.'

Like Newman, Lambert was keen that *Doctor Who* should be a radical departure from anything the BBC had done before, and she very quickly demonstrated this by overriding most of Rex Tucker's earlier decisions. Donald Wilson, however, still felt that there should be someone senior and experienced working on the series as an adviser, and consequently he persuaded Sydney Newman to agree to the appointment of an associate producer, Mervyn Pinfield (who the previous year had directed the four-part BBC science-fiction serial *The Monsters*).

During May and June 1963, Verity Lambert set about assembling her own regular cast for the series. Cyril Cusack was David Whitaker's suggestion for the part of the Doctor, while Mervyn Pinfield favoured another distinguished character actor, Leslie French. However, when they were approached, neither actor was interested. Lambert eventually decided to offer the job to William Hartnell, whose performances in the film *This Sporting Life* and the TV comedy show *The Army Game* had greatly impressed her.

Actress Jacqueline Hill was chosen to play Barbara Wright.

Carole Ann Ford as Jacky in the 1963 BBC *Suspense* play *The Man on a Bicycle.*

After an initial hesitation, Hartnell decided to accept the offer.

The role of Ian went to another performer Verity Lambert had admired for some time, Russell Enoch, who at that time used the stage name William Russell. Russell was a very well known television actor who had starred as Sir Lancelot in the ITV film series *The Adventures of Sir Lancelot.*

Jacqueline Hill, a former model whose BBC credits included *Maigret* and *The Six Proud Walkers* and whose husband, Alvin Rakoff, was an old friend of Verity Lambert's, was cast as Barbara.

A number of actresses, including Jackie Lane, who was later to play the Doctor's companion Dodo, were considered for the role of Susan but it was eventually won by Carole Ann Ford, who had been making film appearances since the age of eight and had previously featured on BBC television in, amongst other things, episodes of *Moonstrike* and *Dixon of Dock Green.*

David Whitaker, meanwhile, had been turning his mind to the task of finding more scripts, and as a first step he had prepared a six-page Writers' Guide to the series. This document – which represents a 'snapshot' of the series midway between its original conception and its final televised form – was drawn primarily from Webber's original format (and therefore Newman's initial memo), but the character outlines were modified somewhat to reflect the

changes Whitaker had agreed with Anthony Coburn. Describing *Doctor Who* as 'an exciting adventure-science fiction drama serial for children's Saturday viewing', it went on to say:

The serial will run for fifty-two weeks and will be a series of stories, each in themselves separate entities but linked to make up the continuity. Each story will run from between four to ten episodes and each episode will have its own title and be of twenty-five minutes in length. Every episode will reach a climax about halfway through and end with a strong cliff hanger.

The guide then set out the background to the stories and explained the approach writers should take in formulating their ideas:

The series is neither fantasy nor space travel nor science fiction. The basic premise is that four characters are projected into real environments based on the best factual information of situations in time and space and in any material state we can realise in practical terms.

Using unusual, exciting backgrounds or ordinary backgrounds seen unusually, each story will have a strong informational core based on fact. Our central characters, because of their 'ship', may find themselves on the shores of Britain when Caesar and his legionnaires landed in 44 BC, may find themselves in their own school laboratories but reduced to the size of a pinhead; or on the dying planet of Mars or some as yet undiscovered world in another galaxy which seems identical to Earth yet where certain values

DAVID WHITAKER
STORY EDITOR

*Born in Knebworth in 1928, David Whitaker started his career in the theatre, writing, acting and directing for a wide range of companies, including the York Repertory Group. There, one of his plays, **A Choice of Partners**, was seen by a member of the BBC Script Department and he was commissioned to adapt it for television. On the strength of this, in 1957, Donald Wilson invited him to join the department's staff. For the next few years, Whitaker's work covered plays, situation comedies, light entertainment features and spectaculars, musical biographies – the most notable being **Hello Ragtime** – and series such as **Compact** and **Garry Halliday**. After leaving the **Doctor Who** production team he maintained a successful writing career - including a period of work in Australia - until his death on 4 February 1980.*

ANTHONY COBURN
WRITER

*Anthony Coburn liaised closely with David Whitaker on the development and introduction of the original central characters in **Doctor Who**. He had been on the BBC Script Department staff ever since coming to the UK from his native Australia, where he had worked as a butcher's assistant before turning to writing. Following the rejection of his second story, **The Robots**, he vowed he would never work on **Doctor Who** again. In later years, he had a successful career as a freelance writer and producer – initiating the BBC series **Warship** – before his death from a heart attack in 1978.*

THE FIRST STORY

*It was Anthony Coburn's idea to set most of the first story in prehistoric times – he had been interested in the Stone Age for years and felt it would make an interesting contrast to the twentieth century. Although it was he who thought of making the Doctor's ship a police box after he happened to see one while out walking, he also suggested that it should change its appearance every story to conform with its surroundings. This was eventually ruled out as being too costly, so it was written into the script that it had 'stuck' in its police-box form. Verity Lambert recalls that, although a very good writer, Coburn's view of **Doctor Who** was rather different from hers and David Whitaker's. Director Waris Hussein agrees: 'I think he had a strong feeling about doing the series differently, but he wasn't really given the opportunity to. He felt he'd been misused and his talent had not been given enough credit.'*

THE ROBOTS

*In Anthony Coburn's rejected second story **The Robots** (aka **The Masters of Luxor**) – inspired by reports he had read about computers, which were just starting to be used in industry – the Doctor's ship was to have moved forward in time to the thirtieth century, to find the human race extinct after an atomic war and the world inhabited only by robots. There, it would have been learnt that the robots, used to a life of servitude, had built a master robot capable of original thought but, realising the dangers, had rendered their invention inoperative – even though this meant that they themselves sank into total inertia. Unaware of this situation at first, the travellers were to have brought the robots and then the new invention 'to life' and faced the dangers inherent in a pitiless computer. Eventually, they would have succeeded in putting the process into reverse in the hope that life might be regenerated on Earth just as it had begun at the dawn of time.*

Ian, the Doctor and Susan in a scene from *The Keys of Marinus*.

are altered, laughter being the worst possible insult and sneezing a criminal offence.

It was further emphasised that once in any given situation the travellers would have only their intelligence and ingenuity to rely on and would not be able to use 'ray guns' or other such gimmickry. Nor would they be able to make or change established history.

Following this, the guide gave a brief profile of each of the four main characters:

Doctor Who

A name given to him by his two unwilling fellow travellers, Barbara Wright and Ian Chesterton, simply because they don't know who he is and he is happy to extend the mystery surrounding him. They do know that he is a Doctor of Science and that he is over sixty. He is frail-looking but wiry and tough like an old turkey and this latter is amply demonstrated whenever he is forced to run away from danger. His watery blue eyes are continually looking around in bewilderment, and occasionally suspicion clouds his face when he assumes his decisions are being opposed by his earthly 'passengers'. He can be enormously cunning once he feels he is being conspired against and he sometimes acts with impulse more than reasoned intelligence. He can be quite considerate and wise and he responds to intelligence eagerly. His forgetfulness and vagueness alternate with flashes of brilliant thought and deduction. He has escaped from the Fiftieth Century because he has found life at that time to be unpleasant and he is searching for another existence into which he can

settle. Insofar as his operation of the 'ship' is concerned he is much like the average driver of a motor car in that he is its master when it works properly and its bewildered slave when it is temperamental. Because he is somewhat pathetic, his grand-daughter and the other two continually try to help him find 'home' but they are never sure of his motives.

Susan

The Doctor's grand-daughter, aged fifteen. She is a sharp, intelligent girl, quick and perky. She makes mistakes, however, due to her inexperience. Addicted to Twentieth Century contemporary slang and likes pop records – in fact, she admires the life teenagers enjoy in 1963. At the beginning of the story, she has persuaded her grandfather to stay in 1963 so that she can go to school and create at least one complete section of experience. Since she has been visiting all sorts of existences and places with her grandfather, Susan has a wide general knowledge and on some subjects can be brilliantly factual. On other matters, she is lamentably ignorant. She has something of a crush on Ian Chesterton.

Ian Chesterton

27, red-brick university type, a teacher of applied science at Susan's school. A good physical specimen, a gymnast, dexterous with his hands and fortunate to possess the patience to deal with Doctor Who and his irrational moods. He occasionally clashes with the Doctor on decisions but for all the Doctor's superior scientific knowledge, is

MERVYN PINFIELD
ASSOCIATE PRODUCER

*Mervyn Pinfield had worked in the BBC's television service since its earliest days and was particularly expert in technical matters. For a time, he had been one of the Langham Group of specialists charged with developing experimental forms of drama using the latest television techniques. His most successful invention was the Piniprompter (named after him), a hand-turned scroll from which presenters could read their script while speaking to camera. This has since evolved into the autocue, used by TV companies the world over. Pinfield retired shortly after completing his stint on **Doctor Who** and died not long after that.*

WARIS HUSSEIN
DIRECTOR

*Born in 1938, Anglo-Indian Waris Hussein joined the staff of the BBC as a trainee director at the age of 23, about a year after graduating from Cambridge University. He was still relatively inexperienced when he came to work on **Doctor Who**, his only previous directing credits being for a **Suspense** play (**One Step from the Pavement**), a Sunday play (**The Shadow of Mart**) and episodes of the soap opera **Compact** and the series **Moonstrike**. Having directed two stories for **Doctor Who** – **100,000 BC** and **Marco Polo** – Hussein went on to handle some major dramas for the BBC in the late sixties and early seventies. These included plays by Hugh Whitemore and Simon Grey, the original **A Passage to India** (a 1965 **Play of the Month**) and, in 1976, **The Glittering Prizes** with Tom Conti, shortly after which he left the BBC and went freelance. Since the early eighties he has spent most of his time in the USA, directing TV movies and miniseries.*

◀ **The first Doctor as he appeared in The Sensorites.**

THE POLICE BOX

The first experimental police boxes appeared in London as early as 1888, although the blue box shape was pioneered in Newcastle-upon-Tyne. The TARDIS-type box – introduced in 1929 – was designed by Metropolitan Police architect Mr G Mackenzie-Trench. The earliest ones were made from Burmese teak, and subsequently pre-cast concrete panels were adopted (although the doors were still teak). Each box had a blue light on top, which would flash to attract a patrolling policeman's attention when his station wanted to contact him. Messages would be passed on via the box's telephone, located inside a compartment behind the hinged instruction panel on the left-hand door. Connected directly to Scotland Yard, this phone could also be used by members of the public in an emergency. Inside each box were a small desk, a stool, a first-aid kit, a coat-hook and a power supply. It was in 1969 that the Home Secretary approved a scheme for the removal of London's 640 police boxes. Similar boxes remained in use for some time in other regions of the country until they too were rendered obsolete by two-way radios. In later years, the BBC actually bought the copyright of the police box design from the Metropolitan Police in recognition of the fact that it is now associated almost entirely with **Doctor Who.**

The entrance to the junkyard at Totter's Lane – the opening shot of *Doctor Who's* first episode. *100,000 BC.*

able to make intelligent enquiry and bring sound common sense to bear at moments of stress.

Barbara Wright

23, attractive. A history teacher at the same school. Timid but capable of sudden courage. Although there is no question of a developing love story between her and Ian, her admiration for him results in undercurrents of antagonism between her and Susan.

The guide then went on to describe the Doctor's 'ship', as follows:

The Ship

Doctor Who has a 'ship' which can travel through space, through time and through matter. It is a product of the year 5733 and cannot travel forward from that date (otherwise the Doctor and Sue could discover their own destinies) the authorities of the Fiftieth Century deeming forward sight unlawful. This still enables Ian and Barbara (and the audience) to see into environments and existences far beyond the present day. The ship, when first seen, has the outward appearance of a police box, but the inside reveals an extensive electronic contrivance and comfortable living quarters with occasional bric-a-brac acquired by the Doctor in his travels. Primarily, the machine has a yearometer, which allows the traveller to select his stopping place. In the first story, however, the controls are damaged and the ship becomes uncertain in performance, which explains why Ian

and Barbara, once set upon their journey, are never able to return to their own time and place in their natural forms.

Finally, by way of illustration, the guide gave a brief synopsis of the two Anthony Coburn stories which were to open the series, together with a list of credits that indicates directors were already being assigned to the show. The responsibility of handling the first story fell to Waris Hussein, while although he now denies having had any knowledge of this, maintaining that as he disliked the series he would never have agreed to it, Rex Tucker was scheduled to take on the second.

Although the Writers' Guide contained synopses of Coburn's stories, now bearing the titles *Dr Who and the Tribe of Gum* and *Dr Who and the Robots*, work on these was progressing far from smoothly. Even though Coburn had carried out the requested rewrites on *The Tribe of Gum*, Whitaker and Lambert were still unhappy with it. In fact, Lambert went so far as to contact a number of other writers with a view to finding a replacement. As Waris Hussein recalls, 'We just sat there, looking at each other, saying "What do we do with these scripts?" Then we had to start seriously getting underway with it, and of course there was a lot of confusion. In the end, we just had to go with the scripts we'd got, as there was a deadline to meet.'

There was another small hiccup in June 1963 when the demise of the Script Department forced Coburn to go freelance and he had to be formally commissioned to continue working on his scripts.

(Coburn signed his contract on 8 July and received a standard fee of £225 for each of his ten episodes.)

By this time, Whitaker had sent a copy of the Writers' Guide, and in some cases also a copy of the draft script for the first episode, to a number of other freelance writers and writers' agents. 'They were all friends,' he later recalled, 'or otherwise friends of friends who were then recommended to me. People I knew I could trust not only to produce a good story within the restrictions we had, but also to work to a tight deadline.'

Storylines soon started arriving on Whitaker's desk, and the first new writer to be commissioned, in mid-July 1963, was Canadian John Lucarotti, whose story, originally titled *Dr Who and a Journey to Cathay*, involved the Doctor and his three companions meeting the famous Venetian explorer Marco Polo. Next, at the end of July, Terry Nation was commissioned to contribute a six-part story concerning a race of creatures called Daleks, based on a storyline he had submitted entitled *The Survivors*.

As August and September 1963 went by and further storylines came in, David Whitaker began to assemble the package of stories which would make up the fifty-two week series. John Lucarotti and Terry Nation each had a second serial commissioned, while Dennis Spooner, a good friend of Nation's, was asked to contribute a historical segment. Storylines by other writers were also under consideration. However, when in mid-September Anthony Coburn delivered his first drafts for *The Robots*, now retitled *The Masters of Luxor*, the production team were dissatisfied with them and decided to drop the story in favour of Terry Nation's Dalek serial (now expanded to seven episodes and retitled *The Mutants*).

In the meantime, Coburn's other story, now given its final title of *100,000 BC*, was gradually progressing towards recording, despite the fact that the production team were facing some hostility from others in the BBC who resented Sydney Newman's 'new broom' approach. Even Donald Wilson had grave doubts when shown the scripts for *The Mutants*, feeling that the Daleks were precisely the sort of 'bug-eyed monsters' the series was supposed to be avoiding, a sentiment later shared by Sydney Newman when he saw the transmitted episodes. In the end, the only thing which saved this now legendary story was that as with *100,000 BC*, there simply wasn't time for a replacement to be commissioned.

Despite the various problems encountered, *Doctor Who* went into production as planned – and, what's more, on schedule – using the BBC's premises and facilities in the Shepherd's Bush area of London.

Like all other BBC drama serials of the period, *Doctor Who* was made in TV studios using electronic cameras; all, of course, in black and white. It was always intended that the episodes would be Ampexed – that is, pre-recorded on videotape – rather than transmitted live, which was still quite common practice for many less complex programmes. There would, however, be an opportunity for certain special effects, fight sequences and other particularly difficult scenes to be completed in advance on the more controllable medium of film and incorporated into an episode when it was recorded. These film inserts would be shot at the BBC's Television Film Studios in Ealing.

The first filming ever done for the series was the shooting of the innovative title sequence. This made use of a visual feedback effect known as howl-around – an idea put forward by Mervyn Pinfield who is reputed to have had a hand in devising the effect – and was accomplished by Bernard Lodge, a designer from the BBC's Graphics Unit. Lodge explains how it came about:

'Howl-around was created by pointing a black-and-white camera at a monitor which showed the image that the camera was taking. You start the sequence off by flashing a light at the screen. The camera sees the blob of light, sends that signal to the monitor and then continuously reads it. What happens is that every little distortion is magnified and amplified until the whole screen goes blank. Then you have to start the sequence over again by flashing another light at the screen, and so on.

'Quite a lot of howl-around footage already existed as a technical guy called Ben Palmer had been experimenting and had produced these patterns for a drama called *Amahl and the Night Visitors*. Although the pattern generation was a purely electronic process it had been recorded on film. They had yards and yards of this experimental footage and I was asked to go down to Ealing Film Studios and watch through it all with Verity Lambert.'

To start with, Lambert asked Lodge to create some animated lettering of the words 'Doctor Who' to be superimposed over the existing footage, but Lodge convinced her that the studio should be set up again so that the words could be fed into the picture electronically. This was done on 20 August 1963.

'What I didn't realise was that the simple shape of the words, the two lines of fairly symmetrical type, would actually generate its own feedback pattern. We shot a whole lot of new cloudy abstract stuff as well, but in the end I think we used one piece from the old *Amahl* footage – the very nice opening line which comes up the screen then breaks away. I can't take credit for that. I then took all the footage away and supervised the editing, mixing it all together.'

THE PILOT EPISODE

Doctor Who's pilot episode differs from the transmitted version in a number of respects: the Doctor seems more sinister and wears an ordinary suit rather than his familiar costume; Susan seems more alien and has a more futuristic costume for the TARDIS interior scenes; the dialogue is different in some places, specifying Susan's origin as the forty ninth century and giving a more intellectual reason for the two teachers not being released from the ship – that it would risk changing the course of history; there is an unfamiliar 'thunderclap' noise at the start of the opening theme music; the TARDIS has a more complex dematerialisation noise; and the whole production is generally less polished.

THE PILOT REHEARSAL SCRIPT

*The rehearsal script of the pilot episode (called **An Unearthly Child**, although the story itself is referred to by its earlier title **The Tribe of Gum**) differs in a number of ways from the version eventually recorded – particularly in terms of dialogue. An early example is that the pop record Susan listens to is not by John Smith and the Common Men but by Ollie Typhoon. Her line when Ian identifies Typhoon by his real name, Fred Grub, is 'Grub-dub. He's left it all behind. Oh, Mr Chesterton he teaches me to... throb.' When the Doctor arrives on the scene, his clothes are described as 'bizarre'. He uses his key to remove the entire lock from the TARDIS door (as seen on screen in the pilot), and then shines a small torch-like object into the hole. When Ian and Barbara enter the TARDIS – which is located inside a shed at the Totter's Lane junkyard – the interior is described as '...a large room, parts of which are covered with dials, machines, screens and apparatus.' The rest of the script is, however, much closer to what was recorded.*

1. Camera B feeds an image to the TV monitor via the vision mixer.

2. Camera A records the image on the TV monitor and then sends it back to the monitor again.

3. The image on the monitor continues to be displayed and re-recorded in a constant loop, which creates distortion (howl around).

4. The howl around image is recorded onto film by a film recorder attached to the vision mixer.

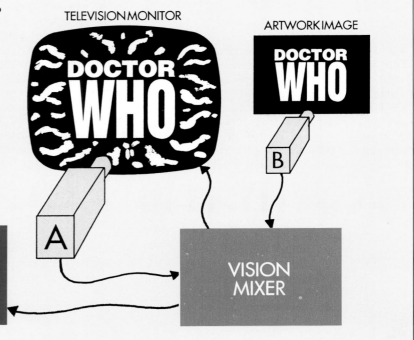

TELEVISION MONITOR

ARTWORK IMAGE

FILM RECORDER

VISION MIXER

The basic principle of howl-around as used by Bernard Lodge to create the title sequence.

RON GRAINER
COMPOSER

Ron Grainer came to Britain in 1952 from his native Australia. Unable to get work as a pianist he joined a variety act – Allen Brothers and June – and eventually, between tours of the variety act, landed a job playing piano for singers at a television company's auditions. This lead to sporadic composing work for television plays. His breakthrough came when he was asked to compose the music for **Maigret**, *having sent a demo tape in on spec. After this, his work was very much in demand. As well as the* **Doctor Who** *theme, he also wrote music for* **Steptoe and Son, Man in a Suitcase, The Prisoner, Detective, Paul Temple** *and* **Tales of the Unexpected**. *He died from cancer on 27 February 1981.*

Another essential component was the series' theme music. Verity Lambert's first idea was that this should be commissioned from an avant-garde French group called Les Structures Sonores, who created their music by playing glass rods mounted in steel. However, Head of TV Music Lionel Salter pointed her instead to the BBC's own Radiophonic Workshop. She visited its Maida Vale studios and spoke with its Head, Desmond Briscoe, explaining that what she was looking for was something radiophonic with a strong beat which would sound 'familiar but different'. She was also keen for it to be written by Ron Grainer, a top TV composer who had provided such famous signature tunes as those for *Maigret* and *Steptoe and Son*. As Grainer had only just finished working with the Workshop (on *Giants of Steam*, a programme about railways), Briscoe was able to arrange this easily.

Having agreed the timing of the sequence with Bernard Lodge, Grainer wrote a fairly simple score which he then discussed with Delia Derbyshire, the Workshop composer assigned the task of realising the theme. Grainer was naturally keen that the music should be in keeping with the visuals, and Derbyshire recalls that he used expressions like 'windbubble and clouds' when describing the sort of sounds he wanted. To create these effects, she and her assistant Dick Mills used sine and square-wave generators, a white-noise generator and a special beat frequency generator. The tune was put together virtually note by note – each 'swoop' in the music was a carefully timed hand adjustment of the oscillators – and the sounds were cut, shaped, filtered and manipu-

lated in various ways until the tracks were ready for mixing and synchronisation.

On Friday 13 September, an experimental session took place in the TV recording studio; getting the sets erected for a trial run to iron out any technical problems which might occur on this unusually complex show.

Pre-filming for the programme's debut episode – *An Unearthly Child*, the first instalment of *100,000 BC* – took place at the Ealing Studios on 19 September 1963, and the episode itself was recorded in Studio D, Lime Grove Studios, just eight days later. The intention was that if this recording proved successful it would be transmitted as the series' opening episode on Saturday 16 November; if not, it would be re-recorded on Friday 18 October and transmission would begin instead on 23 November. After seeing the pilot recording, Sydney Newman discussed it with Verity Lambert and Waris Hussein and decided that a number of changes needed to be made to dialogue and characterisation and a general tightening up of the direction. The episode would be re-recorded and broadcast on 23 November.

Despite the furore surrounding the assassination the previous day of US President John F. Kennedy, BBC documentation shows that *An Unearthly Child* was eventually broadcast at 5:16:20 on Saturday 23 November 1963 – only one minute and twenty seconds later than scheduled.

A legend had begun.

CHAPTER TWO

Who Was William Hartnell

Willi,am Hartnell was born on 8 January 1908, the only child of a dairy farmer in the village of Seaton in Devon. Breaking a centuries-old tradition in his family, he decided against a life on the land: he wanted to be an actor instead. Not surprisingly, his parents disapproved of this ambition, so in his early teens he ran away from home and went to London. For a time he worked as a stable boy and trained to be a jockey, and then spent a short period as a flyweight boxer. However, he was still keen to take up acting and an opportunity came at the age of sixteen when he was adopted by Hugh Blaker, a well-known art connoisseur, who helped him to get a job with Sir Frank Benson's Shakespearean Company. He started as a general dogsbody – call-boy, assistant stage manager, property master and assistant lighting director – but was occasionally allowed to play small walk-on parts.

Two years later, having gained a good grounding in the business, he left Sir Frank Benson's group and went off on tour, working for a number of different companies around Britain. He became known as an actor of farce and understudied renowned performers such as Lawrence Grossmith, Ernest Truex, Bud Flanagan and Charles Heslop. He played repertory in Richmond, Harrogate, Leeds and Sheffield and had a successful run as the lead in a touring production of *Charley's Aunt*. He also toured Canada in 1928–29, acquiring much valuable experience.

On his return to England, Hartnell married the actress Heather McIntyre and, as parts in the theatre were hard to come by, decided to try his luck in films. After a few dispiriting months when the only work he could get was in crowd scenes, he at last won a number of featured parts, often as a comedy lead, in 'quota quickies' – short films made very cheaply in two or three weeks of shooting. One of the earliest of these was *I'm an Explosive* (1933), in which he played a clerk who unwittingly swallows an explosive device and spends the rest of the film being chased by a group of people trying to rescue him. It was always to remain one of his favourite roles.

◀ **A 1930s publicity shot of William Hartnell.**

FAN MAIL

Over the years, William Hartnell received an enormous amount of correspondence from **Doctor Who** fans, and he tried to reply to every letter, enclosing a signed photograph when requested. Even when he was too ill to write, his wife Heather would take dictation for him. In July 1968, in a letter to fan Ian McLachlan, Hartnell wrote frankly about the artistic differences which had led to his departure from the series:

'Basically I left "Dr Who" because we did not see eye to eye over the stories and too much evil entered into the spirit of the thing. "Dr Who" was noted and spelled out to me as a children's programme, and I wanted it to stay as such, but I'm afraid the BBC had other ideas. So did I, so I left. I didn't willingly give up the part.'

THE FILMS OF WILLIAM HARTNELL

Say It With Music (1932); I'm An Explosive (1933); Follow The Lady (1933); The Lure (1933); Seeing Is Believing (1934); The Perfect Flaw (1934); Swinging The Lead (1934); While Parents Sleep (1935); Nothing Like Publicity (1936); Midnight At Madame Tussaud's (US title: Midnight At The Wax Museum) (1936); Farewell Again (US title: Troopship) (1937); They Drive By Night (1938); Too Dangerous To Live (1939); Murder Will Out (1939); They Came By Night (1940); They Flew Alone (US title: Wings And The Woman) (1942); Flying Fortress (1942); Suspected Person (1942); Sabotage at Sea (1942); The Goose Steps Out (1942); The Peterville Diamond (1942); The Bells Go Down (1943); The Dark Tower (1943); San Demetrio London (1943); Headline (1943); The Way Ahead (US title: Immortal Battalion) (1944); Strawberry Roan (1945); The Agitator (1945); Murder In Reverse (1945); Appointment With Crime (1946); Odd Man Out (US title: Gang War) (1946); Temptation Harbour (1947); Brighton Rock (US title: Young Scarface) (1947); Escape (1948); Now Barabbas... (aka Now Barabbas Was A Robber...) (1949); The Lost People (1949); Double Confession (1950); The Dark Man (1951); The Magic Box (1951)*; The Holly And The Ivy (1952); The Pickwick Papers (1952); The Ringer (1952); Will Any Gentleman? (1953)*; Footsteps In The Fog (1955)*; Josephine And Men (1955)*; Doublecross (1956); Private's Progress (1956); Tons Of Trouble (1956); The Yangtse Incident (US title: Battle Hell) (aka Escape of the Amethyst) (1957); Date With Disaster (1957); The Hypnotist (US title: Scotland Yard Dragnet) (1957); Hell Drivers (1957); On The Run (1958); Carry On Sergeant (1958); Shake Hands With The Devil (1959); The Mouse That Roared (1959)*; The Night We Dropped A Clanger (US title: Make Mine A Double) (1959); Strictly Confidential (1959); The Desperate Man (1959); And The Same To You (1960); Jackpot (1960); Piccadilly Third Stop (1960); Tomorrow At Ten (1962); This Sporting Life (1963); Heavens Above! (1963); The World Ten Times Over (US title: Pussycat Alley) (1963); To Have And To Hold (1963).

Notes: *Hartnell also appeared in crowd scenes in a few films in 1931 and 1932. In most of his films before 1946 he was credited as Billy Hartnell rather than as William Hartnell.*
* = colour film.

A young William Hartnell in the film *I'm an Explosive* released in 1933.

Despite this success, Hartnell's appearances in full-length feature films were still limited mainly to crowd scenes and extra work, and he returned to the theatre in the late thirties, understudying Ralph Lynn in London's West End.

Following the outbreak of the Second World War, he was drafted into the Royal Artillery Corps. However, some eleven months later he suffered a nervous breakdown and had to be invalided out, as he explained when interviewed by the *Sunday Mirror* in 1965:

'The strain of training was too much. I spent twelve weeks in an army hospital and came out with a terrible stutter. The Colonel said, "Better get back to the theatre. You're no bloody good here." I had to start all over again. I was still only a spit and a cough in the profession and now I had a stutter, which scared the life out of me!'

With perseverance he all but overcame his stutter and by 1941 he was starting to pick up the threads of his old life again. With the help of friends in the business, he managed to gain good parts in a number of films. However, his real breakthrough came in 1943 when director Carol Reed saw his performance as Dallow in a stage production of Graham Greene's *Brighton Rock* at the Garrick Theatre in London. So impressed was Reed that he offered Hartnell a screen test for the part of a tough army sergeant in his next film, *The Way Ahead* – a test which the 35 year-old actor came through with flying colours.

The Way Ahead proved to be an enormous hit, and Hartnell's performance was singled out for particular praise. He was now very much in the limelight, and a major studio, British National, signed him up to star in a series of pictures. Between 1944 and 1946 he was given top billing in four features – *Strawberry Roan*, *The Agitator*, *Murder in Reverse* and *Appointment with Crime* – and in each case his part was specially written for him. Sadly, though, these films did not do particularly well and British National decided not to renew his contract.

Despite this setback, the next few years saw Hartnell winning some excellent roles, including a reprise of his success as Dallow in *Brighton Rock*, this time for the Boulting Brothers' cinema version. His services were highly sought after by directors and the only problem was that he was now typecast in 'tough guy' roles – military men, prison officers, detectives, criminals and the like – and was no longer asked to play comedy. As early as 1950, in an interview to promote his new film *Double Confession*, he was expressing dissatisfaction with this state of affairs: 'I'm tired of being the eternal "tough guy" of British films. Asking me to play this type of role in the first place was about as practical as asking Danny Kaye to play Napoleon on Elba!'

However, as the years went by, he found himself quite unable to shake off his tough guy image. Even when he did manage to get a part in a comedy film, it was invariably as the straight man rather than as one of the comic characters. Much the same was true of his stage work (in the mid-fifties he had a very successful four year run in the play *Seagulls over Sorrento* at London's Apollo Theatre) and of his early television appearances. In 1957, Granada TV made him the star of their new situation comedy series *The Army Game*, but again he had to play a hectoring officer while the funny roles went to artists such as Alfie Bass, Bernard Bresslaw and Charles Hawtrey.

Indirectly, though, it was his part in *The Army Game*, along with his memorable portrayal of the hard-bitten rugby talent scout in Lindsay Anderson's 1963 film *This Sporting Life*, which gave Hartnell the opportunity he had been looking for. Having been greatly impressed by his performances in both these productions, Verity Lambert contacted his agent – Hartnell's own son-in-law, Terry Carney, of the Eric l'Epine Smith agency – to see if he would be interested in taking on the role of the Doctor.

Although a little reluctant to recommend a part in a 'children's programme', Carney realised that this might be just the thing the actor needed to break out of his type-casting. He went to the Hartnells' home near Mayfield in Sussex and discussed it with him, taking along a copy of the draft first script. As Heather Hartnell recalled, her husband's initial reaction was very positive; and certainly he was interested enough to agree to a meeting with Verity Lambert and director Waris Hussein. However, according to Hussein, he still had many doubts at this stage:

'We took him out to lunch one day and I had to talk literally non-stop to try to convince him. He had a number of worries. He had recently done a series – *The Army Game* – and didn't really want to get involved with something else which took up so much of his time. Also, he didn't quite know if he wanted to play such a peculiar character. He seemed to think that by asking him to play the part of an eccentric we were implying that he was eccentric himself – which of course he was! Ultimately, though, he agreed, and that was due largely to these diplomatic approaches from Verity and me.'

Hartnell's own perceptions of this meeting were different. As he later said, 'The moment this brilliant young producer, Miss Verity Lambert, started telling me about *Doctor Who*, I was hooked.' In any event, once he had accepted the role, he never doubted that he had made the right decision. He loved playing the Doctor, and revelled in his new-found popularity with children.

'Everyone calls me Doctor Who and I feel like him,' he told one reporter. 'I get letters addressed to me as "Mr Who" or even "Uncle Who". But I

love being this eccentric old man. I love it when my grand-daughter, Judith, calls me "barmy old grandad".'

'I'm the High Lama of the Planet,' he said on another occasion. 'Although I portray a mixed-up old man I have discovered I can hypnotise children. Hypnosis goes with the fear of the

◀ **William Hartnell in** *The Night We Dropped a Clanger*. **Hartnell became well known for his portrayal of gruff military types and heavies.**

HEATHER HARTNELL

*After William Hartnell's death, his wife Heather, who wrote under the name Heather McIntyre, gave a number of interviews about her husband's work and attended several **Doctor Who** conventions, where she spoke of his great love for the series. She died in December 1984.*

◀ **William Hartnell relaxes with a neighbour and his wife Heather, at their home near Hayling Island in 1947.**

After three years in the part William Hartnell began his last Dr. Who adventure last night. At the end of the month actor Patrick Troughton takes over. What happens to Hartnell?

His wife Heather, who comes from Glasgow and was once an actress, told me last night: 'Bill is going into a touring pantomime for the first time. He's playing the magic cobbler in Puss in Boots. He's a very good comedian – brilliant, in fact – and he's always wanted a panto part.'
From an unknown newspaper dated 9 October 1966

'Last year I was invited by Whitehall to be VIP guest of honour at a Battle of Britain display near Doncaster. I put on my Doctor Who clothes and appeared in a colourful battle of the Daleks-- with planes dropping bombs, etc. There were 110,000 people there. Kids smashed barriers to get near me. But the greatest moment for me was to be entertained afterwards by 150 of Britain's most famous fliers.'
William Hartnell, interviewed in 1965

The Yangtse Incident. ▲

With Bob Monkhouse in ▲
Carry On Sergeant.

unknown. I communicate fear to children because they don't know where I'm going to lead them. This frightens them and is the attraction of the series.'

To the local kids in Mayfield, Hartnell acquired the status of a Pied Piper. They would even follow him to the pub when he went for a drink, and wait outside for him to emerge. Throughout his time as the Doctor, he made frequent public appearances, opening fêtes, hospitals and shops and supporting many charity functions. Any appearance fee he was paid he always donated to his own favourite charity, Guide Dogs for the Blind.

Right from the start, Hartnell had enormous faith in *Doctor Who*, predicting that it would run for five years, and he soon developed a deep commitment to his role. But he did find coming to grips with the incredible concepts involved in some of the series' scripts difficult; while he was quite at home with the historical stories – and particularly with those containing a lot of humour – he was rather less comfortable with the science-based ones. As he told the weekly newspaper *Reveille* in a January 1965 interview, he was by nature a very down-to-earth man:

'Space travel? Quite honestly it scares me stiff.

'I haven't the slightest wish to get in a rocket and zoom through the stratosphere. Somebody else can be the first man on the moon. It doesn't interest me at all.

'If God had wanted us to live on Mars, he'd have put us up there in the first place. I prefer life on Earth.

'Everyone has to escape somehow. Some people do it through TV. My escape is the English countryside, which I love. Nothing would ever make me leave it to explore life on some other planet.'

In another interview, he explained how he coped with the more incredible stories:

'I am hypnotised by *Doctor Who*. When I look at a script I find it unbelievable, so I allow myself to be hypnotised by it. Otherwise I would have nothing to do with it.'

Hartnell always saw *Doctor Who* as a children's programme and, as he explained in his interview with *Reveille*, he disliked any elements which seemed to him to be at odds with this approach:

'The programme is a success because we keep it as a children's programme.

'The scriptwriters sometimes try to make Doc-

William Hartnell in the 1955 film *Footsteps in the Fog.*

tor Who use expressions like "centrifugal force", but I refuse. If it all gets too technical, the children don't understand and they lose interest. After all, it's an adventure story, not a scientific documentary. And Doctor Who isn't a scientist. He's a wizard.'

It was a bitter disappointment to Hartnell when Verity Lambert decided to relinquish the producer's job, and he strongly opposed the efforts made by her successor, John Wiles, to bring a greater degree of sophistication to the series. He also regretted the departure of his original co-stars, Carole Ann Ford, William Russell and Jacqueline Hill, and disliked the subsequent trend towards more short-term companions. Although a better working relationship developed when Innes Lloyd took over from John Wiles as producer, Hartnell was no less disapproving of his attempts to reduce the series' historical content and to make the stories more 'gutsy'.

There were other factors, too, which compounded the actor's increasing dissatisfaction with the way *Doctor Who* was being made. For one thing, the gruelling production schedule which allowed him only a short break each year was gradually wearing him down. As a countryman whose hobbies included fishing and ornithology and whose favourite form of exercise was chopping wood, he found it irksome to have to spend five days a week in London, away from his wife, his home and his family. Although he would often take his co-stars out to dinner at the end of the week, he disliked 'talking shop' and would rarely mix socially with other actors. Consequently he tended to lead a rather lonely existence. His favourite 'digs' were at a little pub near Ealing Broadway, where he could relax by sharing a round of drinks and a game of darts with the regulars.

The strain of sustaining such a long run in a virtually year-round weekly show would have taken its toll on any actor, particularly when coupled with the extra workload and responsibility inevitably borne by the star. In Hartnell's case, there was the added difficulty that he was not in the best of health: he was suffering from arteriosclerosis – a hardening of the artery walls which leads to poor blood circulation.

Partly as a result of this illness, which has both physical and mental effects, he found it increasingly difficult to remember his lines and this caused him great frustration. He disliked being given long passages of dialogue to learn and was frequently critical of scripts. Moreover, he came to feel – possibly with some justification – that he understood the Doctor's character far better than the writers did. In an interview with *The Daily Express* he said:

'I am fortunate to be given carte blanche with the role. This allows me tremendous range to improve and build on the original outline of *Doctor Who*.

'I think I represent a cross between the Wizard of Oz and Father Christmas. Yet I am always adding fragments to the part, always trying to expand on it.'

It would perhaps be more accurate to say that he demanded carte blanche. Although quite gentle at heart, Hartnell was an outspoken man of very forthright, prejudiced views, and was never one to suffer fools gladly. Having previously worked for some of the giants of the British film industry, he made no secret of the irritation he often felt at having to take instruction from inexperienced young TV directors.

With all these preoccupations, it is perhaps not surprising that during 1965 and 1966 Hartnell became progressively more ill-tempered and difficult to work with, something that has often been remarked upon by his colleagues of the time. Speaking to one journalist, he said '*Doctor Who* has given me a certain neurosis...I get a little agitated, and it makes me a little irritable with people.'

He was also something of a perfectionist,

The Doctor and Susan talk to Chenchu (Jimmy Gardner), a way station keeper, before setting out to investigate the Cave of Five Hundred Eyes. *Marco Polo*.

▲ *Private's Progress.*

**William Hartnell and ▶
Carole Ann Ford during
rehearsals for *Doctor Who*.**

The World Ten Times Over. ▲

The Ringer. ▲

demanding great professionalism both of himself and of other people, and when he lost his temper it was usually because some aspect of the production was failing to live up to his expectations.

Peter Purves, who played the Doctor's companion Steven Taylor, had great admiration for the skill with which Hartnell created the first Doctor's distinctive mannerisms: 'Television acting is really quite confined, and he would always hold his hands up in front of his chest, because if they were down by his sides and he was in close-up you wouldn't see them. If he made a gesture it wouldn't be a big one, because again that would take his hands out of shot. Instead, he used to make all those neat little gestures of his.'

In an early interview, speaking of the villainous characters he portrayed in films, Hartnell himself explained another important element of his acting style:

'Anyone can be horrific by gumming on lumps of hair and wax and by putting cotton wool up their nostrils to look like an ape, but I think the real shudder-creating villain is the one who looks the same as other men, except for the eyes. The eyes ought to reveal just how rotten to the core the heavy is, with subtle graduations such as "forced into crime by mental instability" or "gone to the bad through evil surroundings" or "not a bad chap at heart but just lacking in strength of character". It's a fascinating study.'

Hartnell used this technique of 'acting with the eyes' to great effect in his portrayal of the Doctor, giving him an extraordinary range of expression and helping to create a truly memorable character.

It was in 1966 that producer Innes Lloyd took the revolutionary decision to change *Doctor Who*'s lead actor. As he later recalled, he felt that this would be good both for the series and for Hartnell himself: 'I remember taking him home after a party at my flat on his last night, at about one in the morning. I told him "Bill, now you can have a rest," and he said "Yes, I'll be very pleased."'

In fact, Hartnell was deeply hurt and saddened to have to give up the role, and he later said that the events leading up to his departure were engraved on his heart. However, despite another nervous breakdown around 1967, he had no intention of retiring and the next few years saw him returning to TV in a number of one-off parts. He appeared in an episode of the Associated Rediffusion police series *No Hiding Place* (*The Game*, broadcast on 23 March 1967) and in one of the BBC's *Softly, Softly* stories (*Cause of Death*, transmitted on 4 January 1968). He also resumed his career in the theatre, taking on one of the title roles in the Bristol Old Vic's production of Robert Bolt's *Brother and Sister*, which began a four week run at the Theatre Royal, Bristol on 29 May 1968.

His health – both physical and mental – continued to decline, and by the early seventies, when he and his wife moved from Mayfield to the village of Marden in Kent, his arteriosclerosis had become so bad that it prevented him from working.

In 1972, he was contacted by the *Doctor Who* production office and invited to appear in the tenth anniversary story, *The Three Doctors*. Although he had rarely watched the series since his departure, finding it too emotionally upsetting, he still retained a great affection for the role of the Doctor and was delighted to accept. Like many people who suffer poor health, he did not realise just how ill he was, and still had hopes of making a recovery. However, Heather Hartnell knew that this was not to be. When she discovered what her husband had committed himself to, she quickly telephoned the production office and explained the situation. In the end, although Hartnell did appear in *The Three Doctors*, his part was cut down to a few pre-filmed inserts. Even these he found very difficult to make, and his memory had deteriorated to such an extent that he had to read all his lines from large cue cards placed just out of camera shot.

This was to be his last work as an actor. After suffering a number of strokes and spending a period in his local hospital, he died less than three years later, on 24 April 1975.

CHAPTER THREE

The First Doctor: Wanderer in the Fourth Dimension

I n some respects, the first Doctor was simply the latest in a long line of eccentric professor types that were virtually a stock ingredient of earlier science fiction serials for children. There were, however, a number of factors which immediately set him apart from the usual stereotype.

For one thing, there was his appearance: his formal, Edwardian-style clothes; his long white hair protruding from beneath an astrakhan hat; his small, wire-framed spectacles, all combined to create an impression somewhat different from the norm of paternal, lab-coated boffins. But this was nothing compared with the startling revelation that he was, in fact, an alien time traveller from an advanced civilisation. While it was hardly unexpected for a science-fiction series to involve extraterrestrial life forms, to have an alien as the central character was a very novel idea.

In the first episode, the Doctor explains his circumstances to the two school teachers, Ian and Barbara: 'Have you ever thought what it's like to be wanderers in the fourth dimension? Have you? To be exiles? Susan and I are cut off from our own planet, without friends or protection. But one day we shall get back. Yes, one day, one day.'

This is one of the few times the first Doctor ever mentions his home planet, and he never refers to it by name. However, we do learn just a little more about it from his grand-daughter Susan, in *The Sensorites*:

◀ **William Hartnell as the first Doctor, in a publicity shot taken prior to the recording of the first episode.**

ABSENTMINDEDNESS

One of the first Doctor's many endearing qualities was his absentmindedness, and this was something which William Hartnell deliberately emphasised in his performance. For example, as Russell Enoch (who played Ian Chesterton) confirms, it was Hartnell who came up with the idea that the Doctor would often get Ian's surname wrong: so instead of saying 'Chesterton' he would call him anything from 'Chesserman' (in **The Daleks***) to 'Chatterton' (when remembering him in* **The Massacre of St Bartholomew's Eve***). As Heather Hartnell recalled, 'I know Bill would have liked to have put more comedy into the part, and to a degree he did try with those exasperated little coughs and splutters.'*

No one knows where he came from. He is human in shape and speech and manner. He appears to be old and feeble and at the same time young and strong and active, as though the normal processes of ageing had passed him by.

Inclined to be absent-minded and forgetful, he is also very much subject to fits of impatience whenever his will is thwarted and whenever his ideas are doubted. He likes his own way all the time and can sulk like any baby when he doesn't get it. He is, after all, a citizen of all Space and Time and that must make a man feel there's nothing much he doesn't know.

He is mostly very gentle and kind-hearted and he has the utmost respect for life of any kind, small and feeble or monstrous and mighty. He has seen more specimens of living creatures than any other person in the history of all the worlds and his heart is big enough to respect every one of the countless forms life has taken in all the ages and all the worlds.

A planet in our galaxy would seem to have been his original home, but he has journeyed so many millions of miles and covered so many millions of years back into the Past and forward into the Future, that perhaps even the good doctor himself does not much remember his origins...
Extract from 'Who is Dr Who?', in The Dr Who Annual published 1965. Attributed to the series' first story editor, David Whitaker.

Marco Polo (Mark Eden) falsely accuses the Doctor of hoarding water in the Gobi Desert. *Marco Polo.*

'It's ages since we've seen our planet. It's quite like Earth, but at night the sky is a burnt orange, and the leaves on the trees are bright silver.'

At the start of the series, the Doctor and Susan have been living in twentieth-century England for five months, and Susan is distraught at the prospect of having to leave. The suggestion is that she and her grandfather have previously led a very unsettled, nomadic life to which she has little wish to return. This is confirmed in *Marco Polo* when she says, with obvious regret, 'I have had many homes in many places.' At the end of *The Sensorites*, she asks the Doctor when they will get back to their own world, and he replies, 'I don't know, child. This old ship of mine seems to be an aimless thing.'

During the course of the televised stories, we hear about a number of the TARDIS's earlier stopping-off points. Of the Doctor's personal background, however, we are given only the occasional snippet of information, and in this respect he remains a rather enigmatic figure. Since he has a grand-daughter he must presumably have other family as well, but he never speaks of them. In *100,000 BC* he does reveal that his title of doctor is not a medical qualification; and in *The Aztecs* he describes himself as 'a scientist, an engineer...a builder of things'. Later, in *The Chase*, he makes a comment which suggests that he might even have built the TARDIS, although this is a little uncertain. (Refer-

ring to an instrument called the Time Path Detector, he says 'It's been in the TARDIS ever since I constructed it' – which could mean that he constructed the TARDIS, or simply that he constructed the Time Path Detector.) At any rate, as he comments at the end of *The Daleks*, he was once a pioneer amongst his own people.

In physical terms, the Doctor does not appear to have any greater capabilities than a human being. He is rather frail, suffering all the aches and pains of old age, and he often carries a walking stick. Mentally, however, his powers are superior. He delights in his ability to outwit his opponents, as he does in *The Space Museum*, when the Morok Governor of the museum tries to interrogate him with a mind-reading device and he projects an extraordinary series of false images on to the screen. He can sometimes even sense when an evil presence is nearby, as he does in *The War Machines*; and we learn from *The Sensorites* that he has a certain degree of telepathic ability.

If his alien nature marks the Doctor as unique, so does his personality. When Ian and Barbara first encounter him while investigating the background of their mysterious pupil Susan, he appears very aloof and condescending, obviously evading their concerned questions about the girl's whereabouts. When they eventually force their way into the TARDIS, he refuses to let them go and at one point deliberately causes Ian

The Doctor visits a tailor's shop shortly after his arrival in Paris. *The Reign of Terror.*

▲ The many faces of William Hartnell as the first Doctor.

to receive an electric shock from the control console.

He may seem to be more an antihero than a hero, but this is essentially a false impression. From the Doctor's point of view, Ian and Barbara are strangers and trespassers, and he has no reason to trust them. His first concern is naturally for his own and Susan's continued safety on this alien world. Although he does eventually abduct the two teachers in the TARDIS, this is not a coldly calculated move; rather, it is a hasty act of last resort in an emotionally charged situation, as Susan has childishly threatened to leave the TARDIS and go off with the two strangers.

There is a scene in *100,000 BC* where the Doctor, worried that he and his fellow travellers are being delayed in their escape to the TARDIS, picks up a stone and holds it over the injured caveman Za, apparently intending to attack or even kill him. Ian suspects that he is up to no good. However the Doctor's explanation that he was simply going to ask Za to draw a map in the sand indicating the route back to the ship seems plausible; and his behaviour in the rest of the story does not suggest that he is capable of a cold-blooded murder. Indeed, in the fourth episode, he is visibly appalled by Za's brutal slaying of a rival tribesman, Kal.

Despite his initial distrust of Ian and Barbara, the Doctor is by no means hostile towards them even at this early stage. Only a short time after their arrival in the Palaeolithic era he saves Ian's life, intervening without hesitation as Za is on the point of killing him. A little later, when his party are held prisoner in the tribe's Cave of Skulls, he apologises profusely for having brought them into such a perilous situation; and Barbara later realises, rather to her surprise, that he is trying to help her through the ordeal.

The Doctor we see in these first few episodes is not an unsympathetic character, but he can certainly be selfish, as he demonstrates in the opening minutes of *The Daleks*. Here, he stages a malfunction of the TARDIS's systems when his companions veto his plan to stay and explore the alien city they have seen in the distance. He persuades them to visit the city on the pretext that he needs to find some mercury in order to repair the ship, and as a result their lives are placed in danger.

Plainly the Doctor likes to get his own way and his confidence in his own abilities is such that it occasionally borders on arrogance. 'The mind will always triumph,' he announces at one point during *The Daleks*. 'With me to lead them, the Thals are bound to succeed.' However, this attitude can sometimes be his undoing. A little later in the same story, he is so busy telling Susan how clever he has been that he fails to notice a group of Daleks arriving to take them both prisoner. His self-assurance serves only to highlight his vulnerability: it seems that he is alternately singing his own praises and apologising

▲ **The Doctor in Mavic Chen's Spar ship.** *The Daleks' Master Plan.*

for his mistakes. At the end of *100,000 BC*, Ian and Barbara are horrified to learn that he cannot even control the TARDIS properly. 'Of course I can't,' he admits. 'I'm not a miracle worker!' At times, he almost appears a charlatan.

Never is this more the case than in *Inside the Spaceship*, when he is completely at a loss to know what is causing a series of bizarre occurrences which he and his companions are witnessing inside an immobilised TARDIS. He resorts to making accusations and threats against Ian and Barbara, assuming that they must have sabotaged his ship in some way; later, when the root of the trouble is revealed to be nothing more than a jammed switch, he is forced once again to apologise for his earlier misjudgment.

This incident brings about a change in the Doctor's behaviour. While his early traits continue to be apparent, from now on they are very much tempered by a new-found spirit of trust and consideration and a greater receptiveness to other people's opinions. In *The Dalek Invasion of Earth*, for example, he initially baulks at the idea of taking advice from the young freedom fighter David Campbell but quickly sees the sense of it when Susan speaks up on her friend's behalf. Similarly, in *The Daleks' Master Plan*, he is quite happy to join forces with Space Security Service agent Bret Vyon once the young man has shown himself to be dependable.

As for Ian and Barbara, the Doctor comes to regard them as friends and allies, quickly adjusting to the new experience of travelling with human companions. Later, he welcomes other newcomers to the TARDIS much more readily. For instance, he is perfectly willing to accept Steven Taylor 'at face value' only shortly after meeting him, despite the fact that – like Ian and Barbara – the young astronaut has blundered into the ship completely uninvited. In the case of young women such as Vicki and Dodo, it seems that he is pleased to have someone whom he can take under his wing, perhaps helping to make up for Susan's absence after they part company at the end of *The Dalek Invasion of Earth*.

While his grand-daughter understandably holds a special place in his affections, the Doctor clearly cares deeply for all his companions. Indeed, he will go to great lengths to ensure their wellbeing, as he often demonstrates in rescuing them from dangerous situations. At one time or another they all have cause to thank him for saving their lives. He also acts as a wise and sympathetic counsellor to them, offering advice and encouragement and helping them to cope with the many unsettling experiences they face on their journeys through space and time.

If he sometimes loses his patience or even his temper, this can be excused in view of his age and his intellectual superiority. He is well aware

▲ **The first Doctor in action.**

The Doctor and the Celestial Toymaker (Michael Gough). *The Celestial Toymaker.*

of his own failings in this regard, as he acknowledges after one outburst in *Planet of Giants*: 'Oh my dear Barbara, was I rude to you just now? If so, I'm so sorry. I always forget the niceties under pressure. Please forgive me.' His occasional tetchiness can also be seen as cover for his deeper emotions, which he often seems afraid or embarrassed to reveal. For instance, when Ian and Barbara part company with him at the end of *The Chase*, he tries to mask his obvious sorrow with a show of bluster and annoyance.

Although clearly moved by the many distressing situations he encounters on his travels, and deeply affected by tragedies like the death of Katarina and Sara in *The Daleks' Master Plan*, the Doctor seems able to come to terms quite quickly with such incidents. His wisdom and experience give him the capacity to see things from a broader perspective. Moreover, as a 'wanderer in the fourth dimension' he realises the dangers of trying to tamper with the course of history. This is something his companions do not always appreciate, and disagreements sometimes result. One such clash occurs in the last episode of *The Massacre of St Bartholomew's Eve*, when Steven is incensed at the Doctor's apparently unfeeling decision to leave the young Huguenot girl Anne Chaplette in Paris at the time of the massacre, rather than taking her with them in the TARDIS: 'You just sent her back to her aunt's house, where the guards were waiting to

catch her. I tell you this much, Doctor: wherever this machine of yours lands next, I'm getting off. If your "researches" have so little regard for human life, then I want no part of them.'

When the TARDIS materialises, Steven pauses only to check the scanner before opening the doors and making ready to leave. The Doctor tries to reason with him: 'My dear Steven, history sometimes gives us a terrible shock, and that is because we don't quite fully understand. Why should we? After all, we're all too small to realise its final pattern. Therefore don't try and judge it from where you stand. I was right to do as I did. Yes, that I firmly believe.'

Unswayed by this argument, Steven walks out, although he later has second thoughts, and returns. For once, the Doctor is left alone in the ship and as he ponders on Steven's apparent departure we are given a rare insight into his private feelings:

'Even after all this time he cannot understand. I dare not change the course of history. Well, at least I taught him to take some precautions: he did remember to look at the scanner before he opened the doors. And now, they're all gone. All gone. None of them could understand. Not even my little Susan. Or Vicki. And as for Barbara and Chatterton...Chesterton, they were all too impatient to get back to their own time. And now,

A car-mounted camera films Dodo's first appearance, at the end of *The Massacre of St Bartholomew's Eve*.

The Tardis holds within itself many marvellous inventions which would be scientific miracles in many of the spheres Dr Who has visited. To him, they are commonplace tools and instruments, methods of doing what he wants to do.

Headlong he passes, in his Tardis, through all of Space and Time. Where is he going? What is his objective? What goal draws him on through the endless spheres, the millions of ages? No one knows. Perhaps he himself has long forgotten, so distant, in our years, is the time when he first set out on his odyssey. Are his voyages haphazard and merely satisfying the urge to travel everywhere and see everything, or is he seeking something definite? Again, no one knows.

Ceaselessly and restlessly he moves on, along the infinite strands of Energy that criss-cross all Space-Time. There is the deep and always unsatisfied curiosity of the scientist in him. There is the love of all life which fights against its surroundings.

Strange as his many adventures and experiences have been, how strange will be that time and place, no matter how far away or how distant in time, that point in Infinity-Eternity when, at long last, Dr Who will reach his final goal and find that for which he is searching.

Extract from 'Who is Dr Who?', in The Dr Who Annual *published 1965. Attributed to the series' first story editor, David Whitaker.*

The Doctor gets to know ▶ Kublai Khan (Martin Miller) while Marco Polo (Mark Eden) looks on. *Marco Polo.*

Steven. Perhaps I should go home. Back to my own planet. But I can't . . . I can't.'

The concern and tenderness which the Doctor shows towards his companions are merely a reflection of his basic approach to life. Wherever the TARDIS may take him, he always does what he can to help people. His benevolence is by no means confined to individuals, either; he also helps and advises entire groups of people – sometimes, in fact, whole civilisations.

In short, the first Doctor is a kindly, sentimental, compassionate character. True, he can at times be irritable, but scarcely more so than any of his later incarnations. He can be violent too – it is not unknown for him physically to tackle his adversaries, and in *The Romans* he even indulges quite gleefully in a bout of fisticuffs with the mute

The Doctor advises the ▶ Thal leader Alydon (John Lee) at the end of *The Daleks.*

assassin Ascaris – but such a tactic is never ill considered or unprovoked and, as he stresses in *The Dalek Invasion of Earth*, he never takes life unless his own is immediately threatened.

On the contrary, the Doctor is very humane, someone who clearly sees life in all its various forms as something to be valued and respected. Throughout his adventures he consistently sides with the wronged and the oppressed, setting himself against the forces of tyranny and evil. In doing so he relies almost entirely on his own intelligence and ingenuity. He generally eschews the use of any technological gadgetry and makes quite clear his aversion to weapons.

At times, it must be said, his successes appear to result more from luck than from good judgment. He tends to muddle his way through situations and often has a slightly bewildered air about him. If he seems a near-charlatan in some of the earlier stories, then in some of the later ones he could even be thought to be slightly senile, as Ian actually speculates in *The Rescue*. Indeed, there are aspects of his behaviour, such as his occasional bursts of almost hysterical laughter, which do appear manic.

The first Doctor can certainly be said to show a great passion for exploration and discovery. Whenever the TARDIS materialises in a new location, he is always eager to venture outside and find out what fresh mysteries and wonders lie in store – such is his excitement in *The Web Planet* that he runs outside – and although the TARDIS may have lost the ability to blend in with its surroundings, the Doctor does so with consummate ease. Whether he be on an alien planet like Marinus or Xeros or in some extraordinary period of Earth's history such as the French Revolution or the American Wild West, he invariably succeeds in assimilating the local customs and winning the acceptance of the population.

Even in his last story, *The Tenth Planet*, he has lost none of his restlessness and curiosity, ushering his companions out of the TARDIS to investigate even though he knows that they have arrived in Antarctica, 'the coldest place on Earth'. Nor has his moral courage diminished, as is evident from the outrage he expresses at the Cybermen's unfeeling nature: 'Love, pride, hate, fear! Have you no emotions, sir?' However, when he collapses partway through the story, apparently exhausted, and later speculates that his old body might be 'wearing a bit thin', it becomes clear that something very unusual is happening. This is confirmed in the closing moments of the final episode when he demonstrates perhaps his most remarkable and unexpected ability of all.

CHAPTER FOUR

Season One: The Journey Begins

The early part of *Doctor Who*'s first year was a time of nervousness, argument and uncertainty behind the scenes. Waris Hussein, the director of the opening story, remembers this well:

'I think one has to look at *Doctor Who* as a bridge between the old and the new. It was the first time that Sydney Newman's presence had really been felt. Subsequently of course *The Wednesday Play* happened, and all those other shows, but *Doctor Who* was a definite transition from the old to the new. I remember *Doctor Who* was so new then that whenever I told anyone what I was doing the reaction would be a kind of "What...?" People would say "Oh, you don't mean *Doctor No*?" – because at that time the first James Bond film had just been made – so there was a lot of confusion!

'It was actually a time of some anxiety. I don't regret having been through it now – in retrospect I think it was very good for me – but I can't say that I was a very happy person to start with. I felt that I was made for better things – and so did Verity, of course. In a funny way we made it happen out of a kind of resilience against the implicit criticism at the BBC. We had this sense of everybody wanting it to fail, and we were absolutely determined that it wouldn't.'

Story editor David Whitaker also recalled the trepidation he and Verity Lambert felt at the beginning:

'The first thing to remember about *Doctor Who* then was that we actually had a very reasonable budget for the time and were consequently feeling very vulnerable to failure; if it failed our careers would have been at least slightly tarnished. As it was Verity's first job as a producer, she had a lot to live up to and we were, to be mild about it, terribly, terribly nervous. We were also terribly, terribly excited in the faith we had been shown and about the series itself which, as an idea, got more interesting by degrees.'

Although its innovative nature was the main reason for the animosity with which many at the BBC viewed *Doctor Who*, there were other sources of resentment. The Children's Department were concerned that a programme aimed mainly at young people was being handled by Serials and not by them, and many producers were jealous of what they saw as the excessive amounts of money being lavished on it, not realising that the high cost of the science-based stories – and particularly the TARDIS interior set – was counterbalanced by savings made on the relatively cheap historical adventures for which many of the props and costumes were hired in or taken from stock rather than made from scratch. More fundamentally, science fiction as a genre has always been widely disliked within the BBC, where it tends to be regarded as low-brow and unworthy of serious attention.

Not surprisingly, *Doctor Who*'s strongest supporters amongst the BBC hierarchy were Sydney Newman and Donald Wilson, who frequently spoke up in its favour at departmental meetings. However, even they did not see eye to eye with the production team on every aspect; Newman

SEASON ONE

CODE	TITLE
A	100.000 BC
B	THE DALEKS
C	INSIDE THE SPACESHIP
D	MARCO POLO
E	THE KEYS OF MARINUS
F	THE AZTECS
G	THE SENSORITES
H	THE REIGN OF TERROR

RATINGS

Figures in millions

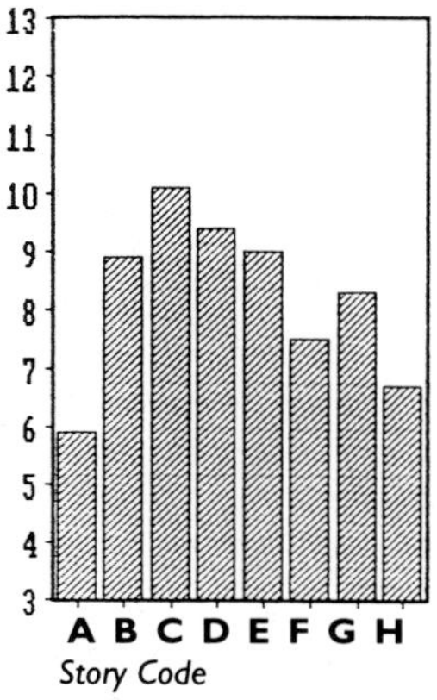

Story Code

Barbara and Ian watch from hiding as the Doctor opens the TARDIS door. *100,000 BC.*

Television history will be made on Saturday when the BBC launch the first programme of a year-long series, *Doctor Who*. Never before has a series been guaranteed such a long run.

Television planners usually work in batches of 13 weeks or less. *Emergency Ward Ten* was first designed as a six-week show.

Ask anybody at the BBC about *Doctor Who* and you will get an unhelpful reply. After one or two leaks from the cast, security was clamped down and mum's the official word.

But there's no doubt the programme chiefs will be disappointed if the show doesn't strike high into the ratings, dislodging many followers from ITV's serials for the young in heart.
**David Hunn From 'Titbits'
(23 November 1963)**

**One of the publicity ▶
photographs printed in *Radio
Times* to publicise *Doctor
Who*'s first episode.**

had originally disliked the theme music and the title sequence and wanted them changed, and both Newman and Wilson had disapproved of the Daleks.

Whatever doubts the BBC might have had, the series was duly covered by the corporation's own listings magazine, *Radio Times*. Staff photographer Don Smith had been assigned to take some publicity shots of the regular cast, for which a number of mock-up sets were specially constructed, and one of these – showing Ian, Barbara and Susan in a classroom – was printed the week before *An Unearthly Child* went out, to whet viewers' appetites. This was followed up in the week of transmission with two more photos – one of the Doctor and Susan and the other of the Doctor – and a short preview article, a privilege

subsequently accorded almost every other story in the sixties.

Unfortunately, because it was transmitted the day after President Kennedy's assassination, *An Unearthly Child* made less of an impact than it might have done. To compensate for this, it was given an unscheduled repeat the following week, immediately before the second instalment, when it picked up about a million and a half more viewers than the 4.4 million recorded in the BBC's official ratings for the original transmission.

From the outset *Doctor Who* was generally well received by public and critics alike and it therefore came as quite a shock to Verity Lambert when, only a few weeks into its run on TV, she heard rumblings that it might have to end after thirteen episodes. (At that time, programme planners generally worked in blocks of thirteen – and the first three *Doctor Who* stories were arranged to form one such block, as were the next two.)

The real turning point for *Doctor Who* came with the phenomenal success of the Daleks. Making their debut in the second story, Terry Nation's *The Mutants* (more usually referred to now as *The Daleks* to avoid confusion with the 1972 story *The Mutants*), they took Britain by storm – a fact which caught everyone at the BBC, not least the *Doctor Who* production team, completely by surprise. After *The Daleks*, Donald Wilson gave Verity Lambert virtually free reign with the programme, candidly admitting that she obviously understood it far better than he did; and

The tribesmen cut off the travellers' escape to the TARDIS. 100,000 BC.

WHAT'S IN A NAME?

*None of the first 25 **Doctor Who** stories was given an overall title on screen – instead, each individual episode had its own separate title. With one exception, the story titles used in this book are those which the series' production team used at the time of the stories' original transmission. These have been established by careful research through BBC scripts and other documentation, and in some cases do not correspond to the ones in common usage. (For example, the first story is generally called **The Tribe of Gum** or **An Unearthly Child**, but the title used here is the more accurate **100,000 BC**.) However, the second story was originally called **The Mutants**, but the more familiar title **The Daleks** has been adopted in order to avoid confusion with the 1972 **Doctor Who** story of the same name.*

Sydney Newman also came to accept that the Daleks were perhaps not such a bad idea after all.

However, this is not to say that all criticism of *Doctor Who* was silenced overnight. For one thing, the Daleks' popularity took time to build – or at least to sink in – and they themselves were also the cause of some concern, as Sydney Newman confirms:

'At the BBC, every Wednesday morning there was a meeting called the Weekly Programme Review, where all the departmental heads got together to talk about the previous week's programmes and decided what was wrong and what was right about them. Some of the departmental heads voiced criticism that the Daleks were too frightening. I didn't agree with them, so I protested. Huw Wheldon, who as Programme Controller was chairing the meeting, fortunately sided with me. "Nonsense," he roared out, "I've got two little kids and they put waste paper baskets on their heads and run around yelling 'Exterminate, exterminate!'" And of course that calmed everything down.'

Doubts about the level of violence in the series – which were to plague *Doctor Who* on and off throughout its history – were particularly acute at the beginning. They came to a head when in the third story, *Inside the Spaceship*, a mentally disorientated Susan was seen to wield a pair of scissors as a weapon, at one point frenziedly stabbing them into her bed. The Children's Department were up in arms at what they saw as the irrespon-

sible inclusion of a scene which could be easily copied by children with potentially dangerous results. For once, Verity Lambert had to admit that she had made an error of judgment. Apologising, she gave an assurance that nothing like this would happen again.

Gradually the initial controversy died down and the new programme came to be tolerated – albeit grudgingly – by the BBC establishment. Waris Hussein recalls that when he returned to direct the fourth story, *Marco Polo*, he found the working atmosphere much more relaxed than it had been at the beginning. By this time, all talk of early cancellation was forgotten. *Doctor Who* had already become a household name, with consistently respectable ratings, and the production team were basking in a sense of achievement.

◀ **A rehearsal shot taken on the TARDIS interior set. 100,000 BC..**

THE TARDIS CONTROL ROOM

The original TARDIS control room set, designed by Peter Brachacki, was particularly impressive, due both to its size – it sometimes took up almost half the studio – and to such extraordinary aspects as the large hexagonal unit suspended from the ceiling.

The control console was the dominant feature, with its six instrument panels and its transparent central column (which was intended to rise at the start of a journey, rotate during flight, then fall again on landing, although later it would usually just rise and fall continuously). Brachacki's reason for grouping all the controls together on one console was that the TARDIS was supposed to be capable of being operated by a single pilot. He had initially wanted to create special controls, moulded to the pilot's hands, but this proved too expensive so standard switches and dials were used instead.

Budgetary restrictions also ruled out some of Brachacki's other ideas, such as having translucent wall panels which would pulsate during flight. However, the set was still complex and expensive, and even during the course of season one was considerably scaled down and simplified.

One feature which did remain constant was the distinctive pattern of indented circles on the walls. Brachacki's intention in using a geometric shape was to create a timeless feel. However, the reason he chose circles rather than, say, hexagons was simply that the plastic from which he made his original model of the set happened to have circles on it!

The Daleks in their city on Skaro. *The Daleks.*

It has often been suggested that the success of the Daleks had a major impact on the type of stories featured in *Doctor Who*. While this is certainly true in the longer term, its short term significance has been somewhat exaggerated. The fact is that most of the early scripts had

The time travellers ▶ prepare to leave Skaro at the end of *The Daleks.*

already been commissioned before *The Daleks* was even transmitted, and the tight production schedule allowed little room for manoeuvre.

Having said this, at least two stories were dropped. Ironically, the first of these was by Terry Nation, the creator of the Daleks. On 24 September 1963 he had been commissioned to write a seven-part historical segment with the working title *The Red Fort*. Set during the Indian Mutiny, this would have seen the four time travellers become involved in events which took place on 11 May 1857 at the so-called Red Fort in Delhi. However, in the wake of the Daleks' enormous popularity Nation was asked to abandon this idea and write another science-based story instead. This late replacement, commissioned only about a month before it was due to go into the studio, was *The Keys of Marinus*, the fifth transmitted adventure.

The second story to be dropped was *The Hidden Planet* by Malcolm Hulke (co-writer of the *Pathfinders...* serials produced by Sydney Newman for ABC TV). This six-parter, of which episode one is thought to have been called *Beyond the Sun* – a title sometimes mistakenly used for *Inside the Spaceship* – and episode two was definitely called *Year of the Lame Dog*, had been commissioned on 2 December 1963 on the basis of a storyline received by David Whitaker on 2 September 1963. Interviewed in 1978, Hulke recalled these events:

'The story was about a planet which is the same size as the Earth but on the other side of the Sun, and therefore we have never seen it. The Doctor and his friends go to the planet and, for obvious reasons, they think they are on Earth. But then they find little things that are different. The TARDIS lands in a field and Susan notices a four-leaf clover, then they see that all the clovers have four leaves. Little things like that mysteriously happen. Birds fly backwards or have double wings, things of that sort.

'It was to have been the third or fourth story. What happened was that they asked me to write it, and they explained to me what *Doctor Who* was all about as they saw it at that time. I produced a storyline, they agreed to it, and then I went ahead and wrote it, and they paid me. But then, in the second story, the Daleks turned up and they gave a different view of how this new series was going to be. The script they had commissioned from me no longer fitted – but that's show business!'

Despite these developments, the package of scripts which David Whitaker put together for the 52-week series still reflected Sydney Newman's original idea that there should be a balance between the science-based and the historical.

Ian joins the Thals in a raid on the Dalek city. *The Daleks*.

PRODUCTION BASE

*Initially, **Doctor Who** story editor David Whitaker had to work in makeshift conditions in a shared caravan parked outside the BBC Television Centre in Wood Lane, London W12. Verity Lambert's first office, meanwhile, was on the fifth floor of Television Centre. During 1963, however, a permanent production office was established, nearby, in Threshold House, one of a number of BBC premises overlooking Shepherd's Bush Green.*

*Just around the corner from Shepherd's Bush Green, off the Uxbridge Road, is Lime Grove, where the BBC studios of the same name were situated. It was here that the great majority of the season one episodes were recorded – all in Studio D, except for the first four parts of **The Reign of Terror**, which were done in Studio G. In fact, there were only seven episodes not recorded at Lime Grove, of which four – episodes two and three of **The Aztecs** and episodes one and two of **The Sensorites** – were done in Studio TC3 ('TC' standing for Television Centre), and the other three – episode four of **The Sensorites** and episodes five and six of **The Reign of Terror** – in Studio TC4.*

During the early part of the season, rehearsals took place in a small drill hall at 239 Uxbridge Road, just a short walk away from Lime Grove. Later, the venue was changed to the London Transport training facility opposite Television Centre.

Only two season one stories do not fall easily into either category – *100,000 BC* and *Inside the Spaceship*.

As the introduction to the series and its four regular characters, *100,000 BC* was perhaps bound to be a little different from all the rest. The first episode, *An Unearthly Child*, takes place in contemporary London – a setting *Doctor Who* would not revisit for some time – and can almost be considered a separate story. It tells of how two ordinary school teachers, Ian Chesterton and Barbara Wright, become intrigued by the mysterious behaviour of one of their pupils, Susan Foreman, and decide to investigate her home background. 'Home' turns out to be a junkyard at 76 Totter's Lane, where they find both the incongruous form of a police box and a supercilious old man who appears to have locked Susan up inside it. Concerned for the girl's safety, they force their way into the box.

Nowadays, most people would be aware that this particular police box is not at all what it seems. In 1963, however, viewers shared the two teachers' stunned amazement at finding themselves inside a large, brightly lit control room dotted with scientific instruments, antique furniture and assorted *objets d'art*.

At an instruction from the old man, who is in fact her grandfather the Doctor, Susan operates a switch on the central control console, causing the huge double doors to swing closed behind them. At first, Ian and Barbara are unable to take in what has happened. They are incredulous as the Doctor and Susan reveal themselves to be time travellers from an alien civilisation and this 'police box' their ship, TARDIS. 'I was born in another time,' Susan insists, 'another world.' Gradually, Barbara comes to believe what she is being told, but Ian remains sceptical: 'I know that free movement in time and space is a scientific dream I don't expect to find solved in a junkyard!'

Although irritated by Ian's refusal to accept the facts, the Doctor's main concern is that if allowed to leave the ship, the two teachers will alert other people to what they have seen. He concludes that he and Susan will have to move on to a different time and place, to avoid becoming 'a public spectacle, a subject for news and idle gossip.' Susan, however, refuses to go, saying that she loves England in the twentieth century and would rather leave him and the TARDIS. Finally, in an act of frustration, the Doctor activates the controls, sending the ship careering on a journey through time and space... but to what destination?

This question is answered in the next three episodes when the four unwilling companions find themselves on a planet (presumably Earth, although this is never explicitly stated) in prehistoric times. Here, they become caught up in a fierce power struggle between two rivals for the leadership of a Stone Age tribe which has lost the

TERRY NATION
WRITER

*Terry Nation was originally a comedy writer, and when David Whitaker first asked him to contribute to **Doctor Who** on the basis of his three previous science fiction scripts for ABC TV's **Out of This World** he initially declined. Following his work on **Doctor Who**, he went on to write for and script-edit a whole string of popular shows, including **The Avengers**, **The Saint**, **The Baron** and **The Persuaders!** – and, of course, he contributed many more stories to **Doctor Who**. In the seventies, he also created the successful BBC telefantasy series **Survivors** and **Blake's 7**. He has since emigrated to America, where he now works in Hollywood.*

JOHN LUCAROTTI
WRITER

John Lucarotti was born in England and spent nine years in the Royal Navy during and after the Second World War. He then went to North America to work for Imperial Oil. It was here that he began writing. Later, he scripted an 18-part series about the life of Marco Polo for the Canadian Broadcasting Corporation, but at one point found himself earning more money as an encyclopedia salesman than as a writer and he decided instead to focus on the US market. By the late fifties he had taken Canadian citizenship, and then returned to England, where he became involved in TV work, including writing **City Beneath the Sea, Secret Beneath the Sea** *and* **Dimension of Fear,** *all for ABC TV. He had recently moved to Majorca when, at Sydney Newman's suggestion, David Whitaker approached him to write for* **Doctor Who.** *Remembering his CBC series, he chose Marco Polo as his subject. Throughout the sixties and seventies, Lucarotti continued a successful TV career. In 1974 he submitted a four part* **Doctor Who** *story which was not used, but was eventually re-worked into* **The Ark in Space.**

PETER R. NEWMAN
WRITER

Peter R. Newman was born in Essex in 1926 and educated at St Egbert's College, Chingford. During and after the War he served as a pilot and parachutist, and was later in the Intelligence Corps. His first experience of the entertainment business was directing and acting in repertory theatre and writing short stories for radio stations in Melbourne, Malaya and Hong Kong. In 1958, he wrote his first TV script for the BBC, a play entitled **Yesterday's Enemy,** *based on his wartime experiences in Burma. The following year, Hammer Films commissioned him to script a cinema version of* **Yesterday's Enemy,** *directed by Val Guest and starring Stanley Baker and Leo McKern. He also adapted the play as a book for Corgi and worked on two more Hammer film scripts,* **Inquisitor** *and* **Brutal Land. The Sensorites** *was Newman's next BBC credit, and was his last work for British television.*

secret of fire. Having shown the victorious leader, Za, how to kindle a flame, they narrowly manage to escape to the TARDIS.

Regardless of any reservations the production team might have had, this debut story was in many ways remarkable. The first episode in particular is now regarded as a classic, and a genuine milestone of television science fiction. Also worthy of note is the excellent characterisation of the four principals – something which was to continue throughout the season, probably reaching its peak in that other atypical story, *Inside the Spaceship.*

Set almost entirely within the TARDIS, *Inside the Spaceship* is a bizarre two-parter featuring just the four regular characters. Having been knocked unconscious by an explosion from the control console, they wake to find the ship silent and in semidarkness. As the story unfolds, the travellers suffer memory losses and blackouts, as if affected by some alien influence; the main doors open to reveal a white void, then close again with no apparent reason; control panels become electrified; the scanner screen displays a baffling sequence of images and every clock and watchface suddenly melts.

An intense psychodrama is played out as the four travellers grow increasingly suspicious of one another. In the heat of an argument the Doctor even threatens to throw Ian and Barbara off the ship, accusing them of sabotage. In the end, however, it is Barbara who saves the day, correctly identifying the TARDIS's defence mechanism as the cause of all the strange phenomena they have witnessed.

It transpires that a jammed switch on the control console has sent the ship plunging backwards in time, threatening it with imminent destruction, and it has been trying to warn them of this ever since. With the switch restored, the travellers continue their journey, but they are not unaffected by this traumatic incident. In the sort of character development rarely seen in later years, the Doctor realises his mistake in distrusting the two teachers, and his attitude towards them softens. 'As we learn about each other, so we learn about ourselves,' he tells Barbara. While there would still be disagreements in later stories, *Inside the Spaceship* saw the last of any serious hostility between the four travellers, leaving them not just companions but also friends.

Although *100,000 BC* and *Inside the Spaceship* both contained science-fiction elements, the first genuine science-based story was the one transmitted between, Terry Nation's *The Daleks.* When the TARDIS lands on the planet Skaro, a seemingly dead world, the travellers discover an imposing alien city made entirely of metal. Of course, the planet is not as dead as it at first

A rehearsal shot from *The Daleks* – note the identification numbers on the Daleks' domes, and the cardboard tube protecting the gun-stick of one of the props.

appears: lurking inside the city are the Daleks, once a noble race of scientists and philosophers, now the hideously mutated survivors of a nuclear war, confined to mobile life-support machines. Outside the city are the Thals, whose own mutation has come full circle, turning them from a race of warriors into Aryan visions of physical perfection.

As the story unfolds, the Doctor and his companions have to persuade the pacifist Thals to fight for their own survival as the Daleks prepare to wipe them out by releasing a further dose of radiation into the atmosphere. The Thals cannot understand why the Daleks should hate them, but Ian supplies the answer: 'A dislike for the unlike... They're afraid of you because you're different from them.' As Terry Nation once put it, the Daleks are the ultimate Nazis.

Aside from such allegorical references, *The Daleks* can be seen as a homage to the novel which formed part of Sydney Newman's original inspiration for *Doctor Who* – *The Time Machine* by H. G. Wells. The Daleks parallel Wells's carnivorous Morlocks and the naive, peace-loving Thals resemble the childlike Eloi. Even the story's cliffhanger ending, which leads into *Inside the Spaceship*, recalls events at the close of Wells's novel in which the Traveller inadvertently sends his machine hurtling thousands of years into the future. In *Inside the Spaceship* the TARDIS is also plummeting through time, although in the opposite direction.

Although H. G. Wells had perhaps the biggest literary influence on *The Daleks*, the plot also owes much to the Jules Verne school of writing, notably in the lengthy trek which Ian, Barbara and a group of Thals make through monster-infested swamps and labyrinthine caves to attack the Dalek city from the rear. In Verne's works, such as *A Journey to the Centre of the Earth* and *Around the World in Eighty Days*, the journey is typically more important than the destination, and forms the focus of the story.

This philosophy is even more apparent in *Doctor Who's* second science-based foray, *The Keys of Marinus*. In this case, the journey takes the form of a quest. When the TARDIS materialises on the planet Marinus, the time travellers are forced by a man named Arbitan to retrieve for him the four missing microcircuit keys to a justice machine known as the Conscience of Marinus. These were hidden in different locations around the planet to prevent them falling into the hands of the evil Yartek and his followers, the Voords, who planned to seize the machine and use its originally benevolent mind-influencing power for their own sinister purposes. Now the machine has been modified to overcome the Voords and can be reactivated, so the keys must be recovered.

The Doctor and Dyoni (Virginia Wetherell) study the Thal history records. *The Daleks*.

Ian encounters the Daleks. *The Daleks*.

William Hartnell, out of costume, rehearses with his co-stars. *The Daleks*.

PROBLEMS WITH THE DALEKS

*The pilot is not the only **Doctor Who** episode to have been recorded twice – it appears from BBC documentation that the same was also done in the case of **The Dead Planet**, the opening instalment of **The Daleks**. The reason for this is unknown, but it seems that having originally been recorded, as scheduled, on 15 November 1963, the episode was then remounted on 6 December 1963 and it was this version which was later transmitted. Consequently the fourth episode – which should have gone into the studio on that date – was put back a week, as were all subsequent episodes. Another oddity concerning **The Daleks** is that the fourth episode, **The Ambush**, was transmitted not from videotape but from a 35mm telecine recording. This was probably because an unusually large amount of editing work was required which was much easier and cheaper to do on film than on tape.*

COMMISSIONING SCRIPTS

In a number of places, this book makes reference to story editors commissioning scripts from writers. This is, in fact, a simplification of the BBC's procedures. Having asked a writer to write a storyline or a script, the story editor would then brief the Copyright Department formally to commission the work. Where commissioning dates are given in the text, these refer to the date when the story editor briefed the Copyright Department.

Altos (Robin Phillips). ▲
The Keys of Marinus.

TELESNAPS

'Telesnaps' was a service offered by photographer John Cura to the producers of sixties television programmes. For a fee, he would take a series of photographs off the television screen during transmission and subsequently offer copies for sale. Before the days of video recorders, this was the only way directors and cast could keep an accurate visual record of their work. Cura would normally take about sixty photographs from an individual half-hour episode and provide these as a contact sheet. Enlargements were then available. Contact sheets or stills are currently known to exist from a number of black and white **Doctor Who** stories, including **The Daleks, The Rescue, The Romans, The Savages, The War Machines, The Power of the Daleks, The Highlanders, The Moonbase** and **The Macra Terror.**

Carol (Ilona Rodgers) ▶
confronted by a Sensorite.
The Sensorites.

Barbara and Susan comfort
the deranged John (Stephen
Dartnell). *The Sensorites.* ▼

Ian and Barbara discover the true rulers of Morphoton. *The Keys of Marinus.*

In their quest, the travellers, transported from place to place by Arbitan's wristwatchlike travel dials, visit such exotic locations as the city of Morphoton, where they almost fall prey to the hypnotic influence of disembodied brains in bell

jars; a ruined citadel being overrun by rampaging plant life; a snowy wasteland where the dangers include wolves, an unscrupulous hunter and a group of fearsome Ice Soldiers; and Millenius, a city where Ian is falsely accused of murder and discovers that the legal rule is 'guilty until proven innocent'. Eventually, having found the four keys, they return to the island. In their absence, the Voords have murdered Arbitan and taken control, but Ian tricks Yartek and, as a result, the Conscience machine is destroyed – a fact the Doctor is not altogether unhappy about as he does not believe that man should be controlled by machine.

Verity Lambert's brief was to aim *Doctor Who* primarily at 8–14-year-olds, but she was keen that it should not talk down to its young audience, a conviction she had formed right at the outset after reading a report, sent to her by Sydney Newman, analysing children's reactions to episode seven of *Pathfinders to Venus.* Consequently, one notable aspect of all these early stories is that they maintained a fairly sophisticated level of dialogue and plotting and embraced some quite adult concepts such as the racism allegory of *The Daleks* and the hunter Vasor's attempted rape of Barbara in *The Keys of Marinus.*

The only season one story which arguably does show some signs of having being 'written down' is the final science-based one, Peter R. Newman's *The Sensorites,* in which the explanations are

▲ **A courtier of Kublai Khan's palace.** *Marco Polo.*

▲ **Ping Cho (Zienia Merton).** *Marco Polo.*

▲ **The travellers shelter from the cold of the Pamir Plateau.** *Marco Polo.*

JOHN SMITH DOES NOT EXIST!

The music heard playing on Susan's transistor radio during **An Unearthly Child** *was not by John Smith and the Common Men, as stated in the episode, but a 55-second excerpt from* **Three Guitars Mood 2** *by the Arthur Nelson Group, published by Berry Music Co. Ltd.*

◀ **Marco Polo (Mark Eden) refuses to return the Doctor's TARDIS to him.** *Marco Polo.*

Ian encounters Arbitan ▲
(George Coulouris). *The Keys
of Marinus.*

The Ice Soldiers. ▲
The Keys of Marinus.

UNSCHEDULED BREAK

*There was an unexpected break between parts two and three of **The Sensorites** as the BBC's sports programme **Grandstand** was extended on 4 July 1964 and that evening's episode was postponed. It was rescheduled for the following week.*

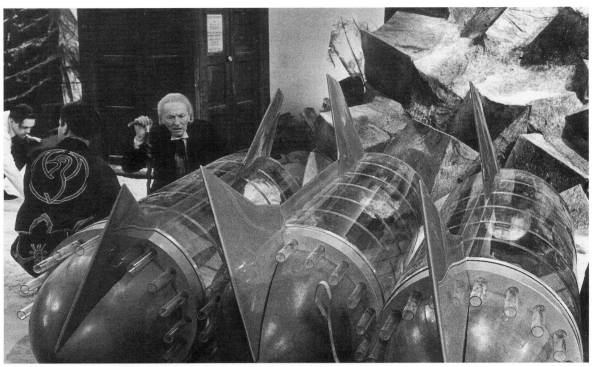

William Hartnell and William Russell rehearse a scene where the travellers discover Voord submarines on the glass beach of the island in *The Keys of Marinus.*

somewhat laboured. Even so, the plot – involving three human astronauts held captive in their own spaceship by the alien Sensorites – is interesting and well structured, highlighting the dangers of misplaced trust and unprincipled exploitation. The Sensorites themselves are fascinating creatures, on the one hand possessing extraordinary telepathic powers yet on the other afraid of the dark and unable to withstand loud noises. They are also dying of a mysterious plague, which the Doctor eventually manages to cure when he discovers it to be the result of deliberate poisoning by three deranged survivors of an earlier Earth expedition.

Doctor Who's first fully historical tale, John Lucarotti's ambitious seven-parter *Marco Polo*, is another story based around an epic journey. Arriving in Central Asia in 1289, the Doctor and his companions join the caravan of the famous Venetian explorer Marco Polo as it makes its way from the snowy heights of the Pamir Plateau, across the treacherous Gobi Desert and through the heart of imperial Cathay. Having witnessed many incredible sights and survived a variety of dangers, they eventually arrive at the mighty Kublai Khan's Summer Palace in Shang-Tu, where the Doctor strikes up an extraordinary friendship with the now aged ruler. In the final episode, as the action moves to the even more sumptuous Imperial Palace in Peking, the travellers manage to save the Khan from an assassination attempt by the Mongol warlord Tegana, supposedly on a peace mission, before departing once more in the TARDIS.

Later in the season, Dennis Spooner's *The Reign of Terror* gave viewers another opportunity to see some famous figures from Earth's history. This time the action centres around Paris in 1794, one of the bloodiest years of the French Revolution, where the travellers become involved with an escape chain rescuing prisoners from the guillotine and get caught up in the machinations of an English undercover spy. Twice the Doctor, posing as a civic dignitary, is brought before the great tyrant Robespierre and has to talk himself out of trouble. Meanwhile, Ian and Barbara have a close encounter with a future ruler of France, Napoleon Bonaparte. As events reach their climax, Robespierre is overthrown, shot in the jaw

Susan and the Doctor explore the Cave of Five Hundred Eyes. *Marco Polo.*

Camera 2 lines up on a scene in which Ian holds down the Perfect Victim (Andre Boulay) while Tlotoxl (John Ringham) prepares to carry out the sacrifice. *The Aztecs.*

▲ **William Hartnell rehearses out of costume for a scene with John Ringham and Jacqueline Hill.** *The Aztecs.*

and dragged off to prison, and the Doctor and his friends slip quietly away.

The other season one historical story, *The Aztecs*, although featuring no real-life characters, is none the less engrossing. Here, the focus is on the Aztec culture itself, and in particular on the contrast between its wonderful achievements, exemplified by its magnificent architecture and ornate gardens, and its barbaric practice of human sacrifice. As Susan observes in the first episode, 'It's incredible, isn't it? Beauty and horror developing hand in hand.' Mistaken for the divine reincarnation of the High Priest Yetaxa, Barbara tries to use her influence to put an end to the sacrifices, but as the Doctor warns her, the attempt is doomed to failure: 'You can't rewrite history – not one line!'

Of all the many themes explored in season one, perhaps the strongest is that of trying to find 'home'. According to the Writers' Guide, this was always one of the Doctor's main motivations in his travels; and certainly it becomes a prime concern after *100,000 BC* as with every new journey in the TARDIS he strives to return Ian and Barbara to the place from which he abducted them.

Within the individual stories, too, the action is invariably catalysed by the travellers being cut off from and attempting to return to the safety of their adopted home, the TARDIS. In some cases they are separated from it by virtue of imprisonment, as in *100,000 BC* and *The Reign of Terror*; in

others, such as when Marco Polo confiscates the Doctor's keys, when Arbitan places a force field around the ship and when the Sensorites steal the lock mechanism, they are deliberately denied access; and sometimes there is a physical barrier to be overcome, such as the tomb door in *The Aztecs*, or a vital component to be recovered – the fluid link in *The Daleks*. Some of the other principal characters encountered in the stories are also trying to reach their respective homes, most notably Marco Polo, who longs to return to Venice, and the three astronauts held prisoner in *The Sensorites*.

Good scripts are not the only prerequisite for successful TV drama: good production values are also called for.

The primary responsibility for bringing each *Doctor Who* story to the screen rested with its director. At this time, the BBC had a large pool of on-staff directors who would be allocated to particular productions according to their respective aptitudes and availability; but, as with most other aspects of *Doctor Who*'s early history, this was not as straightforward as it might seem. Although Rex Tucker was at one point scheduled to direct *The Daleks*, this task eventually fell to Christopher Barry and Richard Martin. Similarly, Paddy (Patricia) Russell, the director originally assigned to *Inside the Spaceship*, was superseded by Richard Martin and Frank Cox. Fortunately fewer complications arose as the series became better established.

MUSIC

Story	Composer
100,000 BC	Norman Kay and Stock (Three Guitars Mood 2 by The Arthur Nelson group)
The Daleks	Tristram Cary
Inside the Spaceship	Stock (Musique Electronique by Eric Siday, Musique Concrete by Desmond Leslie and Buxton Orr)
Marco Polo	Tristram Cary (played by Eddie Walker Ensemble)
The Keys of Marinus	Norman Kay
The Aztecs	Richard Rodney Bennett (Marcus Dods conducting)
The Sensorites	Norman Kay
The Reign of Terror	Stanley Myers

Barbara enjoys a drink ▲ with Leon Colbert (Edward Brayshaw). *The Reign of Terror.*

The Doctor presents ▲ forged credentials to Lemaitre (James Cairncross) while the jailer (Jack Cunningham) looks on. *The Reign of Terror.*

TRISTRAM CARY
COMPOSER

Tristram Cary was born in Oxford in 1925, the third son of the novelist Joyce Cary. He was educated in Oxford and London and started to produce electronic scores in the mid-fifties. He went on to work in the theatre, radio, film (including the scores for Hammer Films' **Quatermass and the Pit** *in 1967 and* **Blood from the Mummy's Tomb** *in 1971) and television (including* **Jane Eyre** *and* **The Ballad of Peckham Rye** *as well as* **Doctor Who***). His first involvement with* **Doctor Who** *came when Rex Tucker asked him to provide the incidentals for the first story and the opening title music. This fell through when Tucker left, but director Christopher Barry, whom Cary had worked with previously on the BBC series* **No Cloak, No Dagger***, had been impressed with his work and so asked him to compose the score for* **The Daleks***.*

Susan and Barbara are taken with another prisoner to the guillotine. *The Reign of Terror.*

One thing most of the early directors had in common was their inexperience, reflecting Sydney Newman's belief that *Doctor Who* should be a programme on which young people worked. In particular, he saw it as a good proving ground for directors fresh off the BBC training course who weren't yet ready to tackle major dramas but who needed to cut their teeth on something demanding. As Verity Lambert recalls, this meant that she was generally able to choose people whose short training films she had seen and liked, or who had previously directed only a few shows. However, mindful of the potential pitfalls of this approach, she also aimed to maintain a balance by including a few established stalwarts such as Christopher Barry and associate producer Mervyn Pinfield on whom she could rely to run a smooth production. On *The Daleks*, for example, she allowed the inexperienced Richard Martin to direct three episodes under Christopher Barry's wing and gave him an opportunity to find his feet.

Certainly *Doctor Who* was an unusually complex and exacting programme to direct. Indeed in one case these demands proved too much. According to Timothy Combe, who worked as production assistant on *The Reign of Terror*, Henric Hirsch, the young Hungarian director chosen to handle that story, found himself quite unable to cope with its punishing schedule. On the day episode three was recorded, Hirsch collapsed outside the studio control room and Verity Lam-

bert had to make hasty arrangements for a stand-in – John Gorrie, who had earlier been responsible for *The Keys of Marinus*. No director was credited on screen for that episode.

The director's job entailed liaising not only with the production team but also with the other BBC staff who would be heavily involved in making the programme – principally the designers and the technical crew. In later years, these key personnel would generally change from story to story; in the sixties, however, they tended to be

The Doctor and Cameca (Margot van der Burgh). *The Aztecs.*

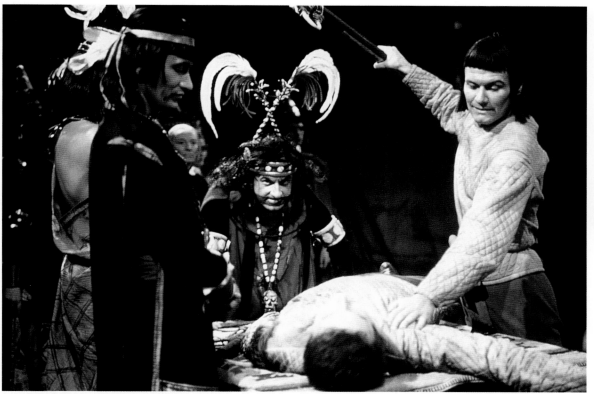

Ixta (Ian Cullen) prepares to kill Ian, while Tonila (Walter Randall), the Doctor and Tlotoxl (John Ringham) observe the contest. *The Aztecs.*

▲ **Barbara and Autloc (Keith Pyott).** *The Aztecs.*

▼ **Barry Newbery's original design sketch for the Aztec temple roof, and as the set appeared on screen.**

assigned to *Doctor Who* for longer periods of time. Costume designer Daphne Dare, for instance, worked on almost every story of the first four seasons. In an even longer stint, Brian Hodgson of the Radiophonic Workshop was responsible for providing the sound effects for virtually the whole of *Doctor Who*'s first decade.

At the beginning, a similar policy applied to the series' set designers. After the pilot episode, which was handled by Polish-born Peter Brachacki, the design work on the seven stories up to and including *The Sensorites* was split between just two people: Barry Newbery, who did all the historicals, and Raymond P. Cusick who took on the science-based ones. Barry Newbery suggests an explanation for this:

'I don't think it was anything to do with the logic of having a team of designers on the series who could get to know its particular requirements. It was simply a planning convenience. With two designers, their time could be blocked in for the whole year, turn and turn about, and that was one less thing for the planners to worry about.

'The reason other designers started to come in at the end of the first year was simply that Ray Cusick and I each had to go on leave at some point and this upset the routine. We continued to work on the series regularly for another year or so after that but never quite got back into the pattern

whereby I had been doing the historical stories and he the science fiction ones.'

As David Whitaker observed, *Doctor Who*'s budget – averaging around £2,500 per episode – was quite reasonable for the time. Nevertheless, in view of the ambitious nature of many of the stories, particularly the science-based ones, it was

Barbara and Susan with ▲ John (Stephen Dartnell). *The Sensorites.*

The Doctor, Ian and ▲ Susan in the Sensorite city. *The Sensorites.*

RICHARD MARTIN
DIRECTOR

*Richard Martin started his career as an actor in the theatre and then joined the BBC, where he trained to be a director. Assigned to the newly-established Serials Department, he worked on one thriller, **Medusa and the Salesman**, before becoming involved with **Doctor Who**. This was in early 1963, when he and the series' temporary producer, Rex Tucker, were asked to attend a feasibility meeting with Sydney Newman in which the format was explained to them. When production got underway, Martin worked as back-up director to Christopher Barry on **The Daleks** and handled the first episode of **Inside the Spaceship**, Frank Cox taking charge of the second. Then, in season two, he was given the responsibility of directing all three six-part stories, **The Dalek Invasion of Earth, The Web Planet** and **The Chase**. This was to be his last work on **Doctor Who**, a fact which did not disappoint him as he detested the series. Subsequently, he directed a number of other productions for the BBC before returning to freelance work, mainly in the theatre, both as a director and as an actor. He has also taught drama and television direction.*

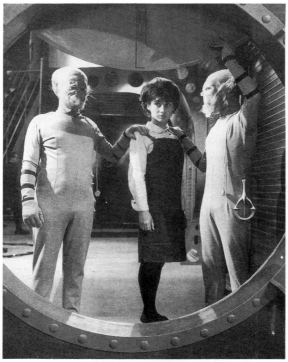

Susan with two of the Sensorites (Ken Tyllson and Joe Greig). *The Sensorites.*

still spread very thinly and in Whitaker's words, the designers had to create 'absolute miracles out of cellophane paper and battery bulbs!' Their task was more onerous than it might have been as they also had to take responsibility for almost all the series' visual effects work. As Barry Newbery recalls, this was simply because the BBC's Visual Effects Department did not have sufficient resources to cope with the new programme:

'Verity Lambert had approached them at quite an early stage to see if they wanted to handle the series' effects work – of which there was obviously going to be quite a lot – but they'd said that they couldn't do it unless they had four more staff and an extra four thousand square feet of space. The powers that be weren't prepared to go along with that so it was declared that the set designers would have to be their own visual effects designers. The only exception was where fire or explosives were concerned.'

A considerable amount of work was required to prepare each story for recording. At an early stage, the director would call a meeting of all the main parties involved in the project to discuss the script, which at that point might be in first draft form only, and in particular to decide how the budget should be divided up between their different departments. This division would vary, depending upon the story's precise requirements. Following this, he would have further discussions with each of the designers and technical supervisors as they carried out their respective tasks to ensure everything was proceeding satisfactorily.

This whole process leading up to the recording of the story's first episode would generally take around six to eight weeks, during which time it might also be necessary to shoot any film inserts required. For most of those concerned, this would be just one of a number of projects with which they were involved, each at a different stage of development; and for the director, there would be still further work to do in auditioning and choosing the guest cast.

In later years, it would become standard practice for *Doctor Who* stories to be recorded out of script sequence, the individual episodes then being edited together, patchworklike, in lengthy post-production sessions, a trend all television drama would follow as it enables more efficient use to be made of studio time and staff resources. At the outset, however, recording was invariably approached on an episode-by-episode basis, and although there were a few exceptions even in season one, scenes were generally shot in strict story order. Not only was this the natural and accepted way of working in an era when many programmes were still transmitted live, it was also preferable because of technical limitations.

Electronic post-production was still a thing of the future, so the only way a video recording could be edited was by physically cutting the tape with a blade and splicing it together again in the desired order. Quite apart from the fact that this was a difficult and time-consuming process, it meant that the tape could not be re-used – something to be avoided at a time when tapes were still very expensive. If a programme was to be kept for possible repeat or overseas sales purposes, as in *Doctor Who*'s case, it would be preserved in the less costly and more durable form of a telerecording – a 16mm or 35mm film negative shot from a specially adapted TV monitor screen. Therefore the aim would be to record continuously as much material as possible, as if for a live transmission. The occasional pause or break in recording was unavoidable on such a complex production, whether it was for the movement of actors or cameras from one part of the studio to another, for the repositioning of scenery, for the execution of a special-effects sequence or for some other reason. However, such instances had to be kept to an absolute minimum. Certainly during *Doctor Who*'s first year it was unusual for there to be more than two or three planned breaks in an episode and in some cases – notably episodes two to five of *The Sensorites* – there were none at all. The general rule at the BBC was that only five breaks were allowed per programme. Not only did this have implications for the way in which the scripts were structured, but on a more practical level it also meant that retakes during recording were very much a luxury. If something went wrong, it was often considered preferable to re-record a whole

Ian and the Doctor examine a piece of glass from the island beach. *The Keys of Marinus.*

▲ The set of the aqueduct on the Sense Sphere. *The Sensorites.*

DENNIS SPOONER
STORY EDITOR

Dennis Spooner was born on 1 December 1932 in Tottenham, North London. The Second World War broke out on the day he was due to start school, and so he had no formal education. His interest in the entertainment business was kindled by some shows in which he appeared while a boy scout and during his national service in Egypt, when he was involved with the Forces Broadcasting Service. After the War he worked unsuccessfully as a stand-up comic and later turned to writing. His first TV scripts were for half-hour comedy shows, and he went on to have an enormously prolific career in the industry. Amongst the many programmes he wrote for were **Hancock, The Avengers, No Hiding Place, Fireball XL5, Stingray, Thunderbirds, The Baron, Doomwatch, The New Avengers, The Professionals** *and* **Bergerac.** *He also created or co-created a number of popular series, such as* **Man in a Suitcase, The Champions, Department S** *and* **Randall and Hopkirk (Deceased).** *His final work for* **Doctor Who** *was a four-part storyline entitled* **Nightmare Planet** *in 1975 which proved unsuitable. He died on 20 September 1986 of a heart attack.*

section of the episode, starting from the last scheduled break, than to do a short retake and thereby incur extra editing work. In the case of the pilot episode, for example, everything after the one and only recording break which was necessary to allow Jacqueline Hill, William Russell and William Hartnell to move from the junkyard set to the TARDIS interior set was done twice, with a brief 'false start' before the second take.

With so little room for error, everything had to be thoroughly rehearsed. Episodes were made on a strict weekly turnaround to keep pace with the weekly transmission schedule and a great deal had to be achieved in a relatively short time.

Preparations would begin each week on a Monday morning, when the full cast would assemble at the rehearsal hall for an initial round-table read-through of the next episode's script. This would be in the presence of the director, who would supervise the whole rehearsal process, David Whitaker and, usually, the writer. Verity Lambert and Mervyn Pinfield might also be on hand to offer advice and guidance. The main purpose of this session was to iron out any unforeseen problems the script might present. A rough timing would be made to ensure that it was about the right length, and the cast would have an opportunity to raise any points of dialogue with which they were unhappy. Either David Whitaker or the writer would then make any necessary amendments.

Following this, the main rehearsal work would

take place between the Monday afternoon and the Thursday afternoon of each week. (The standard working day was from ten until five, or sometimes ten-thirty to five-thirty). The director's production assistant would earlier have marked out the floor, usually with strips of tape, corresponding to the designer's plans for the layout of the studio sets, and thus the cast would be able to prepare their moves quite accurately, gradually refining their performances under the director's instruction while the director himself decided on his camera positions and angles. As for most studio-made TV programmes, a multicamera technique was used so that a variety of different angles could be obtained on just a single recording of a scene.

Also during this stage, time would have to be found for other essential preparations such as costume fittings and make-up tests, and the regular cast might even be called away to work on film inserts for the next story under a different director's supervision – usually, for ease of planning, the inserts for a whole story would be shot in a single block during one episode's rehearsal period. The added complication of location filming did not arise during season one as at this stage the programme's production was almost entirely studio-bound. The only exception was *The Reign of Terror* which featured one short location sequence of the Doctor walking down a poplar-lined track, supposedly en route for Paris. The filming was actually done near Denham in Buckinghamshire, with actor Brian Proudfoot doubling for William Hartnell.

Susan and the Doctor ▲ with Altos (Robin Phillips) in Morphoton. *The Keys of Marinus.*

The Doctor addresses ▲ the court in the city of Millenius. *The Keys of Marinus.*

CHRISTOPHER BARRY
DIRECTOR

*Christopher Barry joined the BBC in 1955, having previously worked for Ealing Films on several productions, including **The Ship that Died of Shame**. He first directed on the soap opera **Starr and Company** in 1958. Other early directing credits were gained on the series **Private Investigator**, **The Net** and **No Cloak – No Dagger**. His Doctor Who debut came in 1963 on the second story, **The Daleks**, which he co-directed with Richard Martin, and he went on to direct many more stories for the series. Amongst the numerous other BBC productions he worked on were **Nicholas Nickleby**, **Out of the Unknown**, **Poldark**, **All Creatures Great and Small** and **The Tripods**. In the late seventies he left the Corporation and went freelance. He also taught courses in TV direction. Since the mid-eighties he has been in semi-retirement.*

On Fridays the production would finally move into the television studio. The sets would already have been erected and the studio lights positioned overnight, leaving only the finishing touches to be put to them. This would be done between eight-thirty and ten-thirty in the morning. The director would then lead the cast and crew through a full camera rehearsal lasting until seven in the evening. Unlike the cast, the cameramen and the studio technicians would have had little or no opportunity to study the script beforehand. There would be frequent pauses for adjustments to be made to camera moves, lighting arrangements, microphone positions and so on, and for last-minute repairs and modifications to be made to the scenery. In addition, careful planning would be required to synchronise the playback of incidental music, sound effects and film inserts to the relevant parts of the action, which would all be added during recording, to save on later editing work.

Activity would be quite intensive, with just an hour's break for lunch at one and a half-hour's tea break at around a quarter to four; and the main cast might have to stay in the studio for part of this latter break, as this was often the best opportunity for publicity photographs to be taken, usually by Joan Williams of BBC Pictorial Publicity or Don Smith from *Radio Times*, or both.

Towards the end of the camera rehearsal, at around half-past five, there would usually be a final trial run-through of the whole episode, from opening titles to closing credits. Work would stop for dinner from seven until eight, then all concerned would return to the studio for the actual recording. The first half-hour would be set aside for 'line-up' purposes: that is, for final technical adjustments to be made, for finishing touches to be put to costumes and make-up and for everyone to take up their starting positions. Recording would then be scheduled to take place between eight-thirty and a quarter to ten.

Once all recording had been completed, the director would call a 'wrap', bringing the day's work to a close. The night scenery staff would then move in to strike (dismantle) the sets, which would be destroyed if no longer required or else put into storage. The cast, meanwhile, would remove their costumes and make-up and head for home, perhaps calling in at the bar for a drink on the way. For guest cast members, this might be their last involvement with the production; if, however, they were to appear in the next episode as well, they, like the four regulars, would have to return to the rehearsal hall the following Monday morning to start the whole process over again.

The master videotape would be sent to the BBC Television Centre where, in a three-hour session on the Monday evening of that following week, it would be edited into its final form. All planned recording breaks would be removed, retakes substituted for flawed original sequences and any pre- or post-recorded inserts added. Some general tidying up and trimming of scenes might also be required, either to improve the flow of the action or for timing reasons. The tape would then be put into storage until its transmission date some three or four weeks later.

This was the basic production routine followed for each of the first year's stories, but things did not always go according to plan. Indeed, actress Carole Ann Ford recalls that frequently the cast would arrive for rehearsals only to find that the script had still to be completed: 'We literally used to sit there round a big table waiting for the scripts to come in.' Perhaps as a result of comments like this, it has often been suggested that David Whitaker wrote *Inside the Spaceship* as a last-minute stopgap when a crisis arose, and Whitaker himself has been quoted as saying that he completed the scripts in 'about two days and most of two nights'. However BBC documentation from the period seems to disprove this – the story is included in a listing dated as early as 1 November 1963.

Fortunately, despite the pressures under which the programme was being made, *Doctor Who* thrived; and in 1964 as its popularity continued to grow, the production team were given the go-ahead to make a follow-up season. It was decided that the last ten episodes to be recorded as part of the first year's block – the stories *Planet of Giants* and *The Dalek Invasion of Earth* – would not be transmitted in their intended slots but would instead be held back for a few weeks to launch the new run. Consequently season one lasted a total of 42 weeks, not 52 as originally planned, and ended with the last episode of *The Reign of Terror*. To mark this fact, a short closing scene was written into the script in which the four companions, recovering in the TARDIS after their latest ordeal, reflect on their inability to change established history. To Ian and Barbara this is a source of frustration; however, as the TARDIS's scanner focuses on a spectacular starscape, the Doctor tells them that they are belittling things:

DOCTOR: Our lives are important, at least to us. But as we see, so we learn.

IAN: And what are we going to see and learn next, Doctor?

DOCTOR: Well, unlike the old adage, my boy, our destiny is in the stars. So let's go and search for it.

CHAPTER FIVE

Season Two: Growing Success

A gap of just seven weeks separated the transmission of *Doctor Who*'s second season from its first, so for many members of the viewing public it must have seemed like the series had never been away. Despite this, its return – at 5:15 p.m. on Saturday 31 October 1964 – was still thought sufficiently noteworthy to merit a well-illustrated full-page feature in *Radio Times*.

The season, an unbroken run of 39 episodes, all in the usual Saturday teatime slot, began with the two stories held over from the initial production block: *Planet of Giants* and *The Dalek Invasion of Earth*. The first of these (originally to have been called *The Miniscules*) told of the dangers encountered by the Doctor and his companions when a malfunctioning TARDIS reduces them all to just an inch in height – an idea which had been mooted ever since the earliest stages of the series' development and which could be traced back to Swift's famous novel *Gulliver's Travels* and to movies such as the 1957 Universal–International production *The Incredible Shrinking Man*.

SEASON TWO

CODE	TITLE
J	PLANET OF GIANTS
K	THE DALEK INVASION OF EARTH
L	THE RESCUE
M	THE ROMANS
N	THE WEB PLANET
P	THE CRUSADE
Q	THE SPACE MUSEUM
R	THE CHASE
S	THE TIME MEDDLER

RATINGS

Figures in millions

Richard the Lionheart (Julian Glover) and the Doctor. *The Crusade.*

The laboratory bench set ▲ from *Planet of Giants*.

Barbara and the Doctor ▲ discover a giant earthworm. *Planet of Giants*.

KOQUILLION

For the 'whodunit' aspect of **The Rescue** *to succeed, it was vital that the TV audience should be just as unaware as the Doctor and his companions that Koquillion and Bennett were actually one and the same person. To have had actor Ray Barrett credited for both roles at the end of the first episode or in* **Radio Times** *would obviously have given the game away, so instead it was stated that Koquillion was played by 'Sydney Wilson' – a pseudonym made up by the production team from Sydney Newman's forename and Donald Wilson's surname!*

SEASON TWO:
EVENTS OF 31 OCTOBER 1964 – 24 JULY 1965

Winston Churchill dies aged 90.

US Marines land in Vietnam.

The first American walks in space.

The death penalty is abolished in the UK.

The millionth Mini motor car is built.

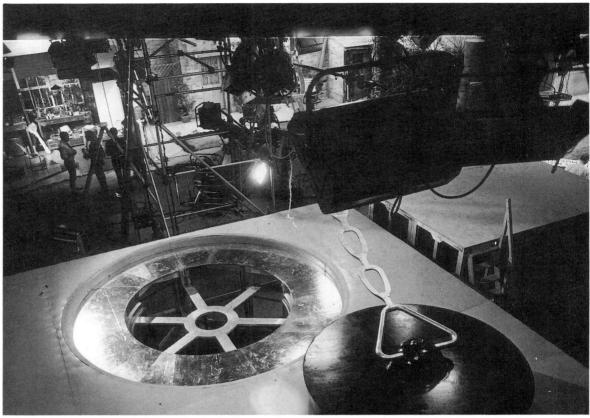

The studio sets for *Planet of Giants*. In the background can be seen Smithers' laboratory and the garden.

In their miniaturised state, the four travellers arrive in contemporary England and stumble across a plot by a ruthless businessman, Forester, and his misguided scientist colleague, Smithers, to launch a new insecticide, DN6 – a product so destructive that it would kill not only those insects harmful to agriculture but also those vital to it. Forester is even willing to commit murder to ensure the success of his business, as civil servant Arnold Farrow discovers to his cost. The criminals are eventually brought to justice when the Doctor and his friends, hampered by the fact that Barbara has herself been made ill by the insecticide, tamper with the telephone in Smithers's laboratory, thus fuelling the suspicions of Hilda Rowse the local exchange operator, who sends her police constable husband, Bert, to investigate.

Planet of Giants was a highly impressive production. Of particular note were the detailed and convincing giant-sized sets designed by Raymond P. Cusick. Also of interest is the fact that this was the first *Doctor Who* story to deal with an ecological issue, writer Louis Marks having been inspired by *Silent Spring*, by environmentalist Rachel Carson. However, the story does seem somewhat dated, even by 1964 standards.

It was because of the rather undramatic nature of the plot that between recording and transmission of the story, Verity Lambert had the last two instalments – *Crisis* and *The Urge to Live* – cut

down and edited together to form a single, standard-length episode. The original fourth episode of *Planet of Giants* also marked the official directorial debut of Douglas Camfield, who would go on to become one of *Doctor Who*'s longest-serving directors.

For the following story, *The Dalek Invasion of Earth* (originally titled *The Return of the Daleks*), *Radio Times* again gave *Doctor Who* some good publicity, this time going as far as to make the first episode the subject of its front cover, a privilege granted the series only once before, when *Marco Polo* began. By this time, the Daleks were a household name throughout Britain and, as story editor David Whitaker explained, it was this which had prompted their return: 'We did not intend to bring the Daleks back. I felt very strongly that we should search constantly for new ideas. As it turned out, the huge popularity of the Daleks in fact blackmailed us into commissioning a sequel.'

The story was actually commissioned as early as March 1964, at which point writer Terry Nation was still working on his scripts for *The Keys of Marinus*. Having failed to anticipate what an enormous hit the Daleks would be, Nation had effectively killed them off at the end of their first serial: 'Nobody has ever killed off their brainchild as thoroughly as I annihilated mine – with the possible exception of Sir Arthur Conan Doyle trying to rid himself of Sherlock Holmes. Fortu-

The Daleks invade Trafalgar Square. *The Dalek Invasion of Earth.*

nately, though, the trusty TARDIS came to my rescue – I was able to bring the Daleks back in a time era before the date they were exterminated!' In fact, this rationalisation does not stand up to very close scrutiny, as it is virtually inconceivable that the Daleks as seen in their debut story could once have been the space-travelling conquerors of the sequel. However, in 1964 no one was too worried about such technicalities – it was enough that the Daleks were back.

Successful as season one had been, it was *The Dalek Invasion of Earth* which really established *Doctor Who* as one of the nation's premier shows. It won average ratings of 11.9 million viewers per episode, an increase of over a third on the 8.6 million average gained by *Planet of Giants*, and propelled the series into the weekly top ten chart for the first time – an achievement which the next few stories would consolidate and build upon. *The Rescue* and *The Web Planet* both earned phenomenal average ratings of 12.5 million viewers per episode, with *The Romans* not far behind at 11.6 million, and during this period *Doctor Who* was rarely out of the top fifteen weekly programmes, reaching a peak of number seven with the debut episodes of *The Romans* and *The Web Planet*. Later in the season, when the Daleks made their third appearance in *The Chase*, the series climbed back into the top ten, again reaching number seven with the story's final instalment. Judged in purely statistical terms, season two could be considered the most popular period of the series' entire history.

The Dalek Invasion of Earth was the first of many *Doctor Who* stories dealing with an alien attack on our own planet, although this was, of course, a tried and trusted theme in science

MONSTER SUCCESS?

*Following the enormous success of the Daleks, there were high hopes at the BBC of making a similar impact with other **Doctor Who** monsters. Consequently, every time a new species was introduced, a photocall was set up and a few tantalising snippets of advance information released to the press. Sure enough, the following day, most of the popular papers would run a small story about 'the next Daleks'. In season two, the monsters given most publicity – after the Daleks themselves – were the Zarbi from **The Web Planet** and the Mechanoids from **The Chase**. Sadly, however, the public never really took to them, demonstrating just how difficult it is to come up with a winning formula. Story editor Dennis Spooner had another, far more practical, explanation for the relative lack of success of the Zarbi and the Mechanoids: they were simply too unwieldy and took up too much space in the studio which meant that all the other actors had to be very precise in their movements – something which annoyed William Hartnell in particular as he liked to be given a lot of leeway in this respect. Consequently neither ever made a return appearance.*

GUEST CAST

*To start with, when **Doctor Who** was still something of an unknown quantity, many actors, not wanting to be associated with a science fiction series – and, what's more, one aimed mainly at children – were rather reluctant to appear in it. All this changed during season two, and especially when director Douglas Camfield persuaded a very distinguished performer to take a role in **The Crusade**: 'People used to turn down parts in the early days because there was a sort of snobbish attitude towards it. I think that from the time I used Julian Glover as Richard the Lionheart the tide was turned. It slowly became more "fashionable" and "in" to appear in the programme.'*

◀ **Dortmun (Alan Judd).** *The Dalek Invasion of Earth.*

PRODUCTION ROUTINE

Season two followed basically the same production routine as season one, with episodes still made on a strict weekly turnaround. The main change was that Lime Grove Studios were no longer used for recording of the programme. **Planet of Giants,** **The Space Museum** *and* **The Time Meddler** *were taped at Television Centre (all in TC4 except* **The Time Meddler** *episode two, which was taped in TC3), and the rest of the season in Studio 1 at the BBC's Riverside Studios in Hammersmith, London W6.*

RECORDING

During season two, recording was still done continuously wherever possible, although a little more flexibility was allowed than in season one. Only one episode – **The Space Museum** *part three – had no planned recording breaks, and one –* **The Crusade** *part four – had as many as seven and an additional recording pause. There were also further isolated instances of out-of-sequence recording. Additional flexibility was apparent in the fact that slight adjustments were sometimes made to the studio day's standard timetable in order to meet a particular production requirement. Episode one of* **The Space Museum,** *which included a number of trick photographic effects, was accorded the unusual luxury of a second editing session – the first was from 7:00 until 10:00 on the evening of Monday 5 April 1965 (three days after recording of the episode) and the second from 8:00 until 10:00 on the evening of 8 April.*

THE FUNGOIDS

After arriving on the planet Mechanus in **The Chase,** *the Doctor and his companions encounter some Fungoid creatures shaped rather like giant mushrooms. Three Fungoid costumes were made for the scenes in question, and to avoid confusion during rehearsals they were each given a pet name – 'Fungoid Fred', 'Toadstool Taffy' and 'Mushroom Malone'. The three central pillars of the Mechanus forest set were also referred to rather oddly in the script as 'Gubbage Cones'.*

fiction. What is unusual in this case is that by the time the Doctor and his companions arrive, sometime after the year 2164, the invasion has already taken place and the aliens are firmly in control, aided by humans subjugated both surgically, as zombie-like Robomen, and physically, as slave workers. This was a clever piece of writing on Terry Nation's part as it enabled him to return to the source – the Nazis – which had been a large part of his original inspiration for the Daleks, and to make the story an allegorical study of what might have happened had the Allies lost the Second World War. So we see shots of the Daleks parading around well-known London landmarks, sucker arms outstretched in Nazi-like salutes, and chanting of their 'final solution' – total extermination of the humans – while the four time travellers team up with an underground resistance organisation.

The Daleks' scheme – to extract the Earth's core and replace it with a propulsion unit enabling them to pilot the planet around the galaxy – is pure B-movie material, but the quality of writing and production transcends such limitations. In particular, the inclusion for the first time in *Doctor Who* of a significant amount of location filming adds considerably to the overall impact. The images of a shattered London under Dalek rule are stark and chilling, while those of the huge mining area the invaders have established in Bedfordshire are no less impressive.

Characterisation is another of the story's strong points, the human resistance workers being an

Susan, Tyler (Bernard Kay) and Barbara seek refuge underground. *The Dalek Invasion of Earth.*

interesting and believable group; and the climax of the action, as the Daleks and their mine are consumed in a huge explosion leading to the extraordinary phenomenon of a volcanic eruption in England, is suitably awe-inspiring.

Something else which makes this story a particularly important one in *Doctor Who's* development is the fact that its conclusion marked the first change in the regular cast of characters, the Doctor leaving Susan behind on Earth to start a new life with freedom fighter David Campbell. Actress Carole Ann Ford had been keen to leave the series for some time, feeling frustrated at what she saw as a failure on the writers' part to develop Susan's character, and the expiry of her contract at this point – the last episode of the first production block, recorded on 23 October 1964 – enabled her to make the break.

The following story, *The Rescue*, was written

The Doctor, Thatcher (Tony Caunter) and Ben Daheer (Reg Pritchard) at Daheer's shop. *The Crusade.*

Saphadin (Roger Avon), Saladin (Bernard Kay), Barbara and the English knight Sir William des Preaux (John Flint) at Saladin's encampment. *The Crusade.*

specifically to introduce a replacement character, and as the original line-up had worked so well from a dramatic point of view, it was decided that the newcomer should be superficially similar to Susan – a young girl whom the Doctor could 'adopt'. A number of possible names were considered for the character – 'Valerie' and 'Tanni' both appear in rehearsal scripts – but the final choice was 'Vicki'.

The actress selected to portray Vicki was Maureen O'Brien, one of whose former teachers at the Central School of Speech and Drama, now working for the BBC, had gained her an audition with producer Verity Lambert. It was her first television role and she made her debut on 4 December 1964 with the recording of the opening instalment of *The Rescue*.

Although well made and highly entertaining, *The Rescue* was a fairly simple story only two episodes long. Arriving on the planet Dido in the twenty-fifth century, the time travellers come upon a crashed spaceship from Earth. Its two occupants, an apparently paralysed man named Bennett and a young girl, Vicki, are living in fear of the imposing figure of Koquillion, a native whose people have supposedly killed the other members of the human expedition. However, it does not take the Doctor long to work out that Koquillion is in fact Bennett in disguise and that he had killed the others in order to conceal an earlier murder he had committed on the ship. Confronted by two of the humanoid Didonians

whom he thought he had completely wiped out, Bennett falls from a high rock ledge to his death.

The discovery that Vicki's father was amongst the murdered crewmen and that she is now an orphan gives the Doctor the excuse to offer her a place aboard the TARDIS.

The start of the new production block brought changes not only in front of the cameras but also behind them. Although he would still receive on-screen credits for the first two stories, *The Rescue* and *The Romans*, associate producer Mervyn Pinfield had effectively bowed out with *The Dalek Invasion of Earth*. By this time, Verity Lambert was well able to cope with the full demands of the producer's job without the benefit of the advice Pinfield had previously provided. Of far greater significance was the departure, also at the close of production on *The Dalek Invasion of Earth*, of original story editor David Whitaker who, having completed his year's assignment on *Doctor Who*, handed over the reins to writer Dennis Spooner.

Spooner had been appointed to the production team around the end of September 1964, partway through recording of *The Dalek Invasion of Earth*, so that he would have a few weeks in which to learn the ropes before Whitaker left. Whitaker had already commissioned several new scripts, which were now in various stages of preparation, and he would continue to take a friendly interest in the series for some weeks to come. Also, it had been decided that Whitaker should himself write the

LOUIS MARKS
WRITER

Having gained a PhD from Oxford University, Louis Marks made the perhaps surprising career move of becoming a TV scriptwriter. He broke into the business in 1959, and the following year contributed three scripts to the last season of Sapphire Films' **The Adventures of Robin Hood**. *This led on to a longer stint as script editor and writer on the Associated Rediffusion crime drama* **No Hiding Place**. *In 1970, he joined the BBC as a script editor, and amongst the many memorable programmes he was responsible for commissioning were Nigel Kneale's cult classic* **The Stone Tape** *and a series of six supernatural dramas entitled* **Dead Of Night**, *all produced by Innes Lloyd. He also contributed three more stories to* **Doctor Who** *in the seventies. More recently, Marks has produced drama for the BBC, his credits including* **The Lost Boys, The Crucible, A Month in the Country** *and* **Precious Bane**.

BILL STRUTTON
WRITER

Born in 1918 in the derelict copper-mining town of Moonta in South Australia, Bill Strutton started his working life as a clerk after spending two years at university in Adelaide. When the Second World War broke out he joined the Australian army, serving in the Middle East and in Greece before being captured by the Germans in Crete. His next four or five years were spent as a prisoner of war, until he was liberated by the Allied forces. After being demobbed, he made England his home, working as a journalist, novelist and scriptwriter. Amongst the many TV series he contributed to were **Ivanhoe, No Hiding Place** *and* **The Saint**. *It was in late 1964 that he wrote* **The Web Planet** *for* **Doctor Who**, *subsequently novelising the story for publishers Frederick Muller. Some six years later, he was commissioned to write another story for the series, but this one – entitled* **The Mega** *– fell through before production. In the late seventies Strutton was forced to give up writing due to ill health and retired to his home in Surrey.*

The crashed spaceship on ▲ Dido. *The Rescue.*

Vicki and Koquillion (Ray ▲ Barrett). *The Rescue.*

Vicki, the Doctor and the ▶ Centurian (Dennis Edwards). *The Romans.*

Delos (Peter Diamond) ▶ and Ian are held as slaves on a galley ship. *The Romans.*

first story of the new block, partly to help smooth the transition. However, it turned out that Spooner had to do quite a bit of work on *The Rescue*, as he has since mentioned:

'*The Rescue* was already written when I came into the job as script editor, but then I had to do a big rewrite as it was vastly overwritten. I mean, it was so long, we'd have had to make each episode two hours long to film it!'

Spooner's approach to the series was rather different from Whitaker's. For one thing, his early writing experience had been in comedy and he had always been keen on the use of humour to add interest and variety to dramatic stories – as can be seen in some light-hearted moments and serio-comic characters in his season one contribution, *The Reign of Terror*. On the whole, season two would feature rather more humour than had season one. More importantly, whereas David Whitaker had initially approached *Doctor Who* as a one-off project, Spooner knew that it had now become an ongoing one and that this second season would be crucial in setting the ground rules for its future development.

'What had happened by then,' Spooner later recalled, 'was that we had realised the show was now destined to run for a long time. And in television you have to learn very quickly what you are going to get away with, because once a series becomes at all established you cannot change it.

'With the second series of *Doctor Who* we knew that whatever we could establish would mark the boundaries for a long time to come. *The Romans* was done for comedy, while in *The Web Planet*, which followed it, we wanted to see how far we could go being weird.'

The Romans placed quite a heavy burden on Spooner, as script editor and author – he had been commissioned to write it at the end of August 1964, about a month before he joined the production team. Having agreed with Verity Lambert that it should be a comedic story, he drew part of his inspiration from one of the popular *Carry On* films: 'At that time I lived virtually next door to the actor Jim Dale, who was making the film *Carry on Cleo* when I was writing *The Romans*. I went down to Pinewood and watched them filming.'

Set in AD 64, *The Romans* opens with the four principals enjoying a rare holiday from their travels at a villa not far from Rome. However, the Doctor soon becomes restless and sets off to visit the city, taking Vicki with him. In their absence, Ian and Barbara are kidnapped by slave traders. So begins an action-packed and amusing adventure incorporating, like *Carry on Cleo*, many of the standard clichés of cinematic Roman epics – a slave auction, a gladiatorial contest, an assassination plot, an early Christian agent, and so on.

Having been mistaken for the famous lyre player Maximus Pettulian and asked to perform at the court of the Emperor Nero, the Doctor has to devise ever more elaborate schemes to avoid revealing that he cannot actually play the instrument. The story eventually reaches its climax when, by accidentally setting light to the Emperor's plans for the rebuilding of Rome, he inadvertently gives him the idea of having the city razed to the ground. Hence, in the ultimate cliché, Nero fiddles (or, more accurately, plays the lyre) while Rome burns.

Although most of the overt humour in *The Romans* was confined to the third episode, the whole tone of the production was considerably jokier than viewers had come to expect from *Doctor Who*. Nero was portrayed as being like a spoiled brat, forever having temper tantrums and childish sulks. It was performed with great relish by comic actor Derek Francis, who had been offered the part because he was a friend of Jacqueline Hill's husband, Alvin Rakoff.

Looking back, Spooner later judged that the experiment with comedy had not been a success. When broadcast, however, *The Romans* attained high ratings and appreciation figures, and the feeling then was somewhat more positive. As its director, Christopher Barry, has said, 'Some people have criticised *The Romans* as not being *Doctor Who* material but, at the time, we thought it worked as *Doctor Who*... I think that ever since the show started, there's always been an element of humour in it. To write an out-and-out comedy was a bit daring, but you have to break new ground and the only way to do that is to try it.'

Certainly humour was not completely abandoned at this point: it was also an important element of Dennis Spooner's other season two story, *The Time Meddler*.

On this occasion, the TARDIS brings the Doctor and his companions to the Northumbrian coastline in the year 1066. Here, they meet a group of Saxon villagers and come into conflict with a party of marauding Vikings on a reconnaissance mission for their king, Harald Hardrada, prior to a planned invasion of England. What sets the story apart from earlier historicals, however, is the fact that the main adversary with whom the travellers have to contend is not one of the human characters but an alien – and a member of the Doctor's own race.

The Monk is a mischievous rogue who travels from place to place in his TARDIS attempting to 'improve' things – for example, enabling the ancient Britons to build Stonehenge with the aid of his antigravitational lift. He is now engaged in

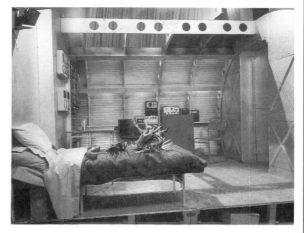

◀ **Bennett's room in the crashed spaceship. Note Koquillion's ray-tool, gloves and mask on the bed. *The Rescue*.**

his master plan, trying to engineer events so as to reverse the outcome of the Battle of Hastings. Appalled at such frivolous interference with the course of history, the Doctor determines to put a stop to it and eventually succeeds by removing the dimensional controller from the Monk's TARDIS, reducing its interior to miniature proportions.

In season one there had been an even balance between historical and science-based stories, but in season two the balance shifted in favour of the latter. This was simply because, following the success of the Daleks, press and public alike now perceived *Doctor Who* primarily as a conventional science-fiction series. What the great majority of viewers wanted to see were not historic

GLYN JONES
WRITER

*Glyn Jones was born in Durban, South Africa, and attended stage school in his native country before moving to England at 22. In between acting jobs he had a stint working as a junior copy-chaser on the **Sunday Times,** at which point he also wrote his first play. He later worked as an actor and writer. His first work on **Doctor Who** came in late 1964 when he was commissioned to write **The Space Museum**. In 1970 he submitted a further story, but this was rejected by the then script editor Terrance Dicks. At around this time, Jones became a script editor himself, on the children's series **Here Come The Double Deckers!**, before returning to freelance writing and acting. In 1974, he made one further contribution to **Doctor Who** – this time in front of the cameras, playing the part of Krans in **The Sontaran Experiment**. More recently he has been lecturing and directing his own plays at various American universities.*

Some of the lifeforms of Vortis: a venom gun, a Menoptra and a Zarbi. *The Web Planet*.

A Mechanoid. *The Chase.*▲

LOCATIONS

The Dalek Invasion of Earth
Westminster Bridge,
London; Trafalgar Square,
London; Westminster
South Bank, London;
Albert Memorial and
Memorial Hall, London;
Hammersmith Bridge,
London; Whitehall,
London; exterior of
Riverside Studios, London;
Queen Caroline Street,
London; unknown quarry

The Chase
Camber Sands, East
Sussex, White City
Underground Station,
London

MUSIC

Story	Composer
Planet of Giants	Dudley Simpson
The Dalek Invasion of Earth	Francis Chagrin
The Rescue	Tristram Cary (re-use of music composed for The Daleks)
The Romans	Raymond Jones
The Web Planet	Stock (Les Structures Sonores)
The Crusade	Dudley Simpson
The Space Museum	Stock (various tracks and composers)
The Chase	Dudley Simpson
The Time Meddler	Stock (various tracks and composers) Charles Botterill (Drums)

King Richard (Julian Glover), Princess Joanna (Jean Marsh) and (right) the Earl of Leicester (John Bay). *The Crusade.*

events in Earth's past but strange alien worlds and, more importantly, the monsters which inhabited them. The use of humour in *The Romans* and the introduction of the Monk – played by well-known comic actor Peter Butterworth – in *The Time Meddler* can be seen as attempts on the production team's part to broaden the appeal of the historical stories. That they were justified in taking this approach is arguably demonstrated by the fact that the season's other foray into Earth's past, *The Crusade*, which was in the more serious vein of earlier productions like *Marco Polo* and *The Aztecs*, coincided with a very noticeable dip in the series' viewing figures.

Of course, ratings are often a poor indicator of a programme's quality, and such was the case with *The Crusade*. Director Douglas Camfield, for one, was highly impressed by David Whitaker's story:

'It was the best *Doctor Who* script I ever worked on. Beautifully written, meticulously researched, and I don't remember having to alter a line. David Whitaker, at his best, is great! I enjoyed working on a costume piece because of the research involved and the challenge of trying to recreate another world in another time.'

The Crusade was set in twelfth-century Palestine, then caught in the grip of the Holy War between King Richard the Lionheart and the Saracen ruler, Saladin. Having got caught up in a Saracen ambush during which Barbara is abducted by the attackers, the Doctor, Ian and Vicki are welcomed at King Richard's palace in the city of Jaffa. Ian is granted permission to ride off in search of Barbara as an official emissary, the King knighting him Sir Ian of Jaffa to fit him for the role, while the Doctor and Vicki stay behind and try to avoid getting involved in court intrigue.

King Richard is secretly planning a marriage between his sister, Joanna, and Saladin's brother, Saphadin, in the hope of ending the war, but when Joanna finds out about it she refuses point blank. The Doctor and his young ward flee the palace as the King is convinced that they have revealed his plan to Joanna. When they eventually reach the wood where the TARDIS materialised, Ian is already waiting there with Barbara, having rescued her from the savage clutches of the Saracen Emir El Akir; however, the travellers' escape is almost thwarted when the Doctor is seized by a party of English soldiers. Fortunately, they manage to regain the safety of the ship by means of a ruse, the soldiers believing that the brave Sir Ian has been spirited away by sorcerers!

David Whitaker's scripts for *The Crusade* (an alternative title for which was *The Saracen Hordes*) were complemented by Douglas Camfield's assured direction and some uniformly high production values, of which designer Barry Newbery's sets are an example. As usual, Newbery relished carrying out his detailed research: 'I discovered that a lot of the buildings in Jaffa were built by Christian masons who were there for the Crusades. Previously these masons had used semi-circular Norman arches in their work but while they were in the Middle East they learnt how to cut the centre section out of the semicircle and move the two end pieces together to make a pointed shape, now known as a Gothic arch, which was much stronger and capable of taking more weight. Of course, when they returned from the Crusades they brought these principles back with them, so I looked at a lot of English Gothic architecture when I was researching the interior of King Richard's palace.

'For some of the other interiors I referred to a book called *Behind the Veil of Arabia*. This was written by a Dutchman who had actually gone into Arabia in the 1950s disguised as an Arab (complete with contact lenses to change the colour of his irises from blue to brown). He had come back with a lot of photographs and stories of things he had seen on his travels, some of them quite horrific. For example, he had witnessed one man having his hand cut off for stealing and another being whipped for adultery, while the woman was buried up to her neck so that the other villagers could come and stone her head! He had also seen some harems which were supposed to be illegal then. Although the book was obviously about contemporary Arabia I still got a lot of useful information from it – particularly visual. There are parts of the world where styles of architecture and decoration don't change very much over the centuries.' Regardless of the story, this attention to detail was important on *Doctor Who*.

The most ambitious story in season two was *The Web Planet*. The story begins with the TARDIS being seized by a mysterious force and dragged down to Vortis, a craggy, forbidding world where the dangers include pools of lethal acid. Here, the Doctor, Ian, Barbara and Vicki get involved in the struggles of the moth-like Menoptra to reclaim the planet from an alien parasite, the Animus, which has invaded it and taken control of the once-docile, ant-like Zarbi, turning them into vicious drones. Eventually, with the time travellers' help, a group of Menoptra manage to infiltrate the Animus's web-city, the Carsenome, and confront the creature directly, destroying it with a weapon, the Isop-tope, devised by their scientists.

The writer of *The Web Planet* was Bill Strutton, who had been given the commission on 28 September 1964 after discussing his basic ideas with producer Verity Lambert. His original inspiration for the Zarbi came from an incident in his childhood when he had naively tried to separate two fighting bull ants and been badly bitten by them – an experience of which he had recently

▲ Preparing for an abortive attempt to film the scene of a Dalek emerging from the sands of Aridius at the end of part one of *The Chase* – a scene eventually achieved with model work.

◄ A Dalek on Aridius. *The Chase.*

▼ John Wood's original design sketch for a Zarbi, and the creatures as they appeared on screen.

been reminded by the sight of his two unruly stepsons brawling. One of the most unusual aspects of the serial was that apart from the four regulars, it featured no humanoid characters.

The need to create so many different creatures put a considerable strain on the programme's resources. The production was in many respects an extremely imaginative one, but Dennis Spooner was left with mixed feelings about it:

'It worked insofar as it was virtually the butterflies versus the ants, with the butterflies being

DUDLEY SIMPSON
COMPOSER

Born in Australia in 1922, Dudley Simpson was introduced to music at the age of four by his mother and went on to win an award as the top amateur musician in Australia in 1936. Following the War, he studied at Melbourne University and eventually came to England to conduct at the Royal Opera House in Covent Garden. He started composing music for television in 1963 on a series called **Moonstrike** *which led to Mervyn Pinfield asking him to compose for* **Doctor Who**. *Simpson continued to work on* **Doctor Who**, *as well as* **Thirty Minute Theatre**, **Target**, *several* **Wednesday Plays** *and* **Blake's 7** *and others, up until 1980. In 1988 he returned to Australia where he works as a freelance composer.*

DONALD TOSH
STORY EDITOR/ WRITER

Donald Tosh began his career in the theatre but then joined Granada TV where, amongst many other projects, he discovered the format for **Coronation Street.** *After six years he moved to the BBC, and, despite suggestions that he would be assigned to the classic serials, found himself working as story editor on* **Compact**. *After eighteen months he was offered the chance to transfer either to another bi-weekly serial or to* **Doctor Who**, *and chose the latter. John Wiles has fond memories of working with Tosh: 'He was so out of the BBC mould. He really played up being something of an eccentric. He was the first person, for example, to start wearing the Beatle caps and the flowered shirts which came into fashion about then – and he loved to have people talking about him. But he was wonderfully mercurial in mind and very erudite.' Tosh left the TV industry in the mid-seventies and is currently working as the caretaker of a castle in Cornwall.*

A rehearsal shot from *The Chase*. Note actor John Scott-Martin in the Dalek base on the left. The Daleks' time machine is in the background. In the centre of the picture another Dalek is being attacked by Frankenstein's monster (John Maxim). The Grey Lady (Roslyn de Winter) watches from the balcony.

"free enterprise", if you like, and the ants being the "communists". That serial was written on a lot of different levels, if you really looked at it. But I think we went too far. I wouldn't have gone that far, in fact, and I know that Verity got a bit upset. I think everybody got a bit carried away on *The Web Planet*. Everybody got inspired, and in TV inspiration costs money.

'The Costume Department, for example, suddenly said, "No, we're not going to skimp on this one"; and so did all the others. It all got out of hand, because nobody would backtrack. On that serial, more than any other, there were sort of private wars; not wars where no one would talk to each other, but where department began to go against department. Usually in *Doctor Who* if you

The Doctor meets ▶ Frankenstein's monster and Dracula (Malcolm Rogers) on the haunted house set. ***The Chase.***

said to Costume, "You're overspending", they'd apologise and rectify it. On *The Web Planet* if you said "Save a thousand pounds", they'd say "Why can't Make-up save it?" They had their ideas, you see, and wanted them to be carried through... The story lost out as a result. It's hard to explain the atmosphere on that one.'

Partly because of overspending on *The Web Planet*, savings had to be made later in the season. The production which seemed to suffer most in this respect was *The Space Museum*, which had a rather sparse, drab look to it. Unfortunately, the characters it featured were also rather unexceptional. It did, however, have a very thought-provoking script. Whereas previous stories had tended to use the TARDIS simply as a device to get the Doctor and his companions from one place to another, this one dealt head-on with some of the complex issues raised by the concept of time travel.

Having apparently reached a new destination – a space museum on the barren planet Xeros – the four travellers discover that the TARDIS has in fact 'jumped a time track', giving them a glimpse into a future in which they end up as static exhibits in museum display cases. The rest of the adventure sees them trying to avert this possible outcome by altering events in the present, never quite knowing whether the steps they are taking will lead to their demise or their salvation. Fortunately they win through in the end, helping a

Saxons Wulnoth (Michael Miller), Edith (Alethea Charlton) and Eldred (Peter Russell). *The Time Meddler.*

▲ The Monk (Peter Butterworth). *The Time Meddler.*

▲ Gunnar the Giant (Ronald Rich) attacks Edith. *The Time Meddler.*

group of youthful Xeron rebels to overthrow the warlike Morok invaders who have established the museum as a monument to their galactic conquests.

The Space Museum was another of the stories commissioned by David Whitaker before Dennis Spooner joined the production team, as its author Glyn Jones confirms:

'I went to dinner with Trevor Bannister (later famous for appearing in *Are You Being Served?*), who was in a play of mine at the time. The script editor, David Whitaker, was there and suggested I write him a storyline, which I did. He liked it, so he commissioned it, and that's how I came to do the story.'

The scripts were actually written during the period when David Whitaker was handing over to Dennis Spooner and, as it turned out, Jones was not too happy with the way Spooner edited them. In his original version of the story, as he recalls, he had included much more humour, which he felt added an extra dimension to the Doctor's character; Spooner, however, disliked it and so cut it out.

This tends to confirm that there remained some doubt in the production team's minds as to the appropriate level of humour in the series. Only one science-based season two story featured a significant amount of humour: Terry Nation's

third Dalek tale, *The Chase* (working title: *The Pursuers*). This was written between mid-December 1964 and February 1965 as a replacement for another (possibly non-Dalek) story which Spooner had commissioned from Nation in early October 1964 but which had subsequently fallen through.

The less than serious aspects of *The Chase* included many lines of jokey dialogue; a comical encounter between a Dalek and an American sightseer, Morton Dill, on the observation platform of New York's Empire State Building; and even a dimwitted Dalek struggling to understand its orders. Although Dennis Spooner has since said that Nation's scripts needed fewer changes made to them than any of the others he worked on, his own comic touch certainly influenced some of these scenes.

In plot terms, *The Chase* bears a slight similarity to one of Nation's earlier stories, *The Keys of Marinus*, in that it sees the four principals visiting a number of completely different locations during the course of the action. However, while their journey in *The Keys of Marinus* takes the form of a quest, here they are fleeing from a group of Dalek executioners equipped with their own time machine, referred to in the scripts, though not on screen, as a DARDIS.

The chase begins on the desert planet Aridius and takes in such unlikely stopping-off points as the nineteenth-century sailing ship *Mary Celeste*,

DOUGLAS CAMFIELD
DIRECTOR

Douglas Camfield started out as an army reserve and might have become an SAS officer had he not been prone to heart flutter. In 1955 he joined the BBC as a trainee assistant film editor and by 1963 had risen to the post of production assistant and had also written some episodes of the **Garry Halliday** *series. His first* **Doctor Who** *work was as PA on* **100,000 BC** *and* **Marco Polo**, *for which he also directed most of the film inserts. His official directorial debut came on part four of season two's* **Planet of Giants** – *the first of many* **Doctor Who**s *he would handle over the next twelve years. Camfield later left the BBC and became a freelance director. Amongst the many productions he worked on were* **Van der Valk**, **Public Eye**, **The Onedin Line**, **Target**, **Danger UXB**, **The Sweeney**, **Shoestring**, **The Nightmare Man**, **Ivanhoe** *(a three-hour TV film, co-produced by Columbia Pictures) and* **Beau Geste**. *He died from a heart attack on 27 January 1984.*

A HOLIDAY FOR THE DOCTOR

As **Doctor Who** was made virtually year-round during the sixties, members of the regular cast would occasionally be allowed a short holiday during production. This would entail them being written out of that week's episode or appearing only in film insert sequences shot in advance. In season two, for instance, William Hartnell was absent from the third part of **The Space Museum** and the second of **The Time Meddler**, in each case being seen only in the reprise from the previous episode. Similarly, Jacqueline Hill did not appear in part three of **The Web Planet** and William Russell was not present for recording of part three of **The Crusade**. However, William Hartnell's absence from episode four of **The Dalek Invasion of Earth** was for a different reason: he was being carried down a ramp from the Dalek spaceship on a stretcher, at great speed, when the ramp supports collapsed (this was during rehearsal for episode three). Hartnell landed awkwardly on his spine and for a while was paralysed and couldn't move. X-rays showed that no drastic damage had been done but he was given the following week off to recover fully. (Actor Edmund Warwick has said that he was called in at the last moment to double for Hartnell in a short scene, shot from behind, where the Doctor collapses due to the after-effects of an anaesthetic – a plot device to justify his non-appearance in the rest of the episode.)

Images of the Doctor ▲ and Steven from the special end sequence marking the close of season two. **The Time Meddler.**

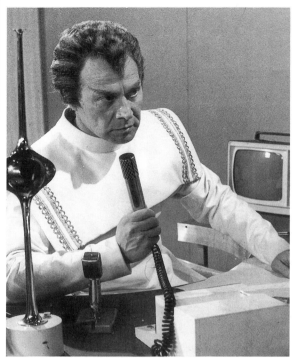

The Morok leader Lobos (Richard Shaw). **The Space Museum.**

where the Daleks' appearance causes all the crew and passengers to jump overboard, and a spooky haunted house which, although the Doctor and his friends do not realise it, is actually a futuristic funfair attraction. Eventually the action moves to the planet Mechanus, where the travellers are taken prisoner by the Mechanoids, a group of robots sent some fifty years earlier to prepare landing sites for human colonists who, in the event, never arrived. At the story's climax, the Daleks and the Mechanoids engage in a fierce battle which ultimately results in their mutual destruction, the Doctor's party seizing this opportunity to escape.

Just as the start of season two had seen changes taking place both in front of and behind the cameras, so did the end. After some eighteen months of playing Ian and Barbara, William Russell and Jacqueline Hill both decided that it was time to move on to other projects. As Russell now puts it, 'I wanted to leave *Doctor Who* because I was getting into the nine-to-five mentality of it. I needed a change.' In plot terms the pair were written out quite simply at the conclusion of *The Chase*, the Doctor using the Daleks' abandoned time machine to send them back to twentieth-century England, although to a point over a year later than when they had left.

In place of Ian and Barbara, Verity Lambert decided to introduce just one new character, so reducing the series' regular complement from four to three. The character in question was Steven Taylor (referred to in early rehearsal scripts as 'Michael'), an Earth astronaut from the future

whom the Doctor first meets as a fellow prisoner of the Mechanoids in the closing instalment of *The Chase*. Fleeing from the climactic conflagration which engulfs both Daleks and Mechanoids, Steven comes upon the TARDIS. He has just enough strength to stumble inside before passing out, as he tells the Doctor and Vicki at the start of the next story, *The Time Meddler*, and the ship gains a new passenger.

No auditions were held for the role of Steven; instead, Verity Lambert invited young actor Peter Purves to play the part. She and Dennis Spooner, along with William Hartnell and Maureen O'Brien, had been impressed by his performance as Morton Dill in an earlier episode of *The Chase*.

Having served some eight months as the series' story editor, Spooner himself bowed out around the end of May 1965 to assist Terry Nation as script supervisor on *The Baron*. As his stint had been a relatively short one, there were only three broadcast stories – *The Crusade*, *The Chase* and *Galaxy 4* (the latter made during the second production block but held over until the start of season three on transmission) – for which he could claim full responsibility for having commissioned and developed. A number of others had, however, been under active consideration or reached at least the storyline stage, although for one reason or another they never made it to the screen. These included two (a resubmitted *The Hidden Planet* and a historical idea called *Britain 408 AD*) from Malcolm Hulke and one, entitled *The Dark Planet*, from Brian Hayles.

Spooner's replacement was Donald Tosh, a BBC staffer who had just completed an eighteen-month assignment as story editor on *Compact*. Although he was present during production of *The Chase*, Tosh's first credit was for *The Time Meddler*.

Perhaps the most important development was the fact that producer Verity Lambert was preparing to leave *Doctor Who* at the end of its second production block to go on to launch another BBC series, *The Newcomers*. After some eighteen months she felt that both she and the series would benefit from a change. The man chosen to succeed her was John Wiles, a BBC staff producer.

'I trailed Verity for about six months,' recalled Wiles in 1983, 'sitting in on all her conferences and getting to know people like Dennis Spooner and of course Bill Hartnell and Terry Nation. Gradually I began taking over more and more executive responsibility, especially for those shows I was slated to produce.'

It was a new production team that would take *Doctor Who* into its third year.

CHAPTER SIX

Season Three: A Time of Change

The last episode of *Doctor Who*'s highly successful second season had been transmitted on 24 July 1965; just seven weeks later, on 11 September 1965, the series was back again in its Saturday teatime slot for the start of a third batch of adventures.

The opening story of season three, William Emms's *Galaxy 4*, was actually made directly after *The Time Meddler*, but held back to launch this new run. Although credited as its producer, Verity Lambert was now nearing the end of her involvement with the series and her successor John Wiles had by this time taken over much of her responsibilities. Similarly, although the scripts had been commissioned by Dennis Spooner after Emms had submitted the idea unsolicited, Donald Tosh was now firmly installed as the new story editor and was given the on-screen credit. Derek Martinus was brought in to direct the story – his first TV assignment – quite late in the day, as its original director, Mervyn Pinfield, had to pull out due to illness. By the time Martinus took over, Pinfield had already completed the main casting and begun pre-filming at Ealing.

The Doctor, Vicki and Steven arrive on an arid planet in Galaxy 4, where they meet the occupants of two crashed spaceships: the beautiful Drahvins and the hideous Rills. Confounding audience expectations, the latter prove to be friendly, compassionate explorers while the former are a group of mindless cloned soldiers terrorised by a warlike matriarch, Maaga. Both ships were damaged when the Drahvins forced a confrontation in space, but while the Rills' ship is almost ready to take off again (having been repaired by their robot drones, which Vicki names Chumblies), the Drahvins' is irreparable. When the planet is discovered to be on the point of disintegration, Maaga tries to force the time travellers to help her steal the Rills' ship. Instead, the Doctor allows the Rills to draw power from the TARDIS in order to refuel and escape, leaving the Drahvins to their fate.

A guest cast of beautiful young women helped to secure *Galaxy 4* some good publicity in the popular press. The story seemed to go down well with the public, too, as it averaged 9.9 million viewers per episode – the highest ratings of the whole season – and a respectable appreciation figure of 55 percent. The lead actors, however, were not so happy with it: William Emms recalls that William Hartnell and Maureen O'Brien both

The Drahvins with one of the Chumblies. *Galaxy 4*.

SEASON THREE	
CODE	TITLE
T	GALAXY 4
T/A	MISSION TO THE UNKNOWN
U	THE MYTH MAKERS
V	THE DALEKS' MASTER PLAN
W	THE MASSACRE OF ST BARTHOLOMEW'S EVE
X	THE ARK
Y	THE CELESTIAL TOYMAKER
Z	THE GUNFIGHTERS
AA	THE SAVAGES
BB	THE WAR MACHINES

RATINGS

Figures in millions

Story Code: T, T/A, U, V, W, X, Y, Z, AA, BB

A Rill. *Galaxy 4.* ▲

PRODUCTION ROUTINE

*Riverside Studio 1 was the main venue used for recording of **Doctor Who** during season three. All episodes of **The Myth Makers, The Massacre of St Bartholomew's Eve, The Ark, The Celestial Toymaker, The Savages** and **The War Machines** were made there, as were parts two to four of **The Gunfighters**. All the rest were recorded in Television Centre Studio 3 except episodes one to three of **Galaxy 4**, episodes five and six of **The Daleks' Master Plan** and episode one of **The Gunfighters**, which were in Television Centre Studio 4.*

SEASON THREE:
EVENTS OF 11 SEPTEMBER 1965 – 16 JULY 1966

Mary Whitehouse forms the National Viewers' and Listeners' Association.

The Beatles are awarded the MBE.

Leonid Brezhnev becomes the General Secretary of the Soviet Union.

The 1966 World Cup begins in England, and is eventually won by the home team.

Steven, Vicki and the Doctor are menaced by a Chumbley. *Galaxy 4.*

argued with him about their respective parts, and Peter Purves has said that as the script was originally written with Ian and Barbara in mind, he was inappropriately given a lot of Barbara's dialogue and action – including being overpowered by Maaga in a fight. What Purves did not perhaps realise was that the Drahvins had originally been written as male characters and were changed to women at the casting stage without apparent change to the script.

The first story to be planned for *Doctor Who's* third production block was a new six-part Dalek adventure, which had been under discussion with writer Terry Nation as early as February 1965, before either John Wiles or Donald Tosh had joined the programme. By the time the first episode went into the studio on 22 October, this had become the epic twelve-parter *The Daleks'*

Original director Mervyn Pinfield supervises a scene at Ealing, while his replacement Derek Martinus looks on. *Galaxy 4.*

Master Plan. It was not the production team's choice to extend the story in this way: the decision was imposed on them from above by BBC Programme Controller Huw Wheldon, reputedly because his mother was a fan of the Daleks! Consequently, around May 1965, Dennis Spooner as story editor had to ask Terry Nation to rethink his ideas.

Preceding *The Daleks' Master Plan* by five weeks on transmission would be a single episode trailer known as *Dalek Cutaway*, featuring none of the regular cast. As Donald Tosh later recalled, this unique situation came about because the programme had been allocated an extra episode at the end of its second production block and the regulars could not appear in it as this would have encroached upon their already brief holiday period. However, it was known quite early on that this one-off episode would be required, so it was always discussed in tandem with *The Daleks' Master Plan*, even when the latter was still thought of as a six-parter.

The *Dalek Cutaway* episode was actually the first to be commissioned, on 25 February 1965. Terry Nation delivered his script, entitled *Mission to the Unknown*, in mid-May and it was recorded on Friday 6 August when, for the sake of convenience, it was handled by the same team, led by Derek Martinus, who had made *Galaxy 4*. Thus *Doctor Who's* second production block – and with it Verity Lambert's tenure as producer – was brought to a close.

When it came to *The Daleks' Master Plan* itself, it was decided that while Terry Nation would be

The Daleks and their alien delegates plan an attack on the solar system. *Mission to the Unknown.*

▲ **A Dalek succumbs to the effects of the time destructor.** *The Daleks' Master Plan.*

▲ **Douglas Camfield, Viktors Ritelis, William Hartnell and Peter Purves during rehearsals for** *The Daleks' Master Plan.*

responsible for the basic story ideas, the writing of the scripts should be shared between him and Dennis Spooner. Although no longer officially the story editor, Spooner commissioned Nation's six scripts on 16 July 1965, eleven days after his own six had been commissioned by his successor, Donald Tosh, this arrangement being adopted so as to circumvent BBC restrictions on story editors commissioning their own work. In the end, episodes one to five and seven were written by Nation and the others, following very brief discussions with Nation over general storylines, by Spooner.

Set on the planet Kembel, *Mission to the Unknown* tells of the secret mission of Space Security Service agent Marc Cory to investigate a recent sighting of a Dalek spaceship. Cory's suspicion that the creatures may have established a base on Kembel proves to be well founded. His two companions, Jeff Garvey and Gordon Lowery, both fall victim to the poisonous thorns of Varga plants – which come from the Daleks' home world, Skaro – and he has no choice but to shoot them before they are themselves transformed into Vargas. Having overheard the Daleks and their alien allies agreeing on a plan to invade the galaxy, Cory then records a warning message and prepares to send it into orbit with a rocket launcher. Before he can do so, however, he is discovered and exterminated.

Leading on from this, *The Daleks' Master Plan* sees the TARDIS materialising on Kembel, where the Doctor and his friends meet another Space Security Service agent, Bret Vyon, who has been sent in search of Cory. Learning of the Daleks' scheme to use the fearsome time destructor weapon, they determine to warn the authorities on Earth; this proves problematic as the human

leader, Mavic Chen, Guardian of the Solar System, is in league with the Daleks. Fortunately, the Doctor has managed to make off with the taranium core of the time destructor, thus disrupting the Daleks' plans.

In one of a number of attempts to regain the taranium, Mavic Chen dispatches Space Security Service agent Sara Kingdom (Jean Marsh) to track down the Doctor's party. Unaware of Chen's treachery, Sara has already killed Bret – her own brother – before the time travellers can convince her of the truth. She then joins forces with them and, after a brush with their old adversary the Meddling Monk, they all arrive back on Kembel. There, the Doctor contrives to steal the time destructor and turn it against the Daleks. Sadly, Sara has ignored his instruction to return to the TARDIS, and she too is killed.

Part seven of *The Daleks' Master Plan, The Feast of Steven,* is the only *Doctor Who* episode

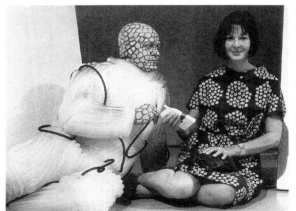

Verity Lambert at a photocall to mark her departure from *Doctor Who.* **The monster is Malpha (Robert Cartland) from** *Mission to the Unknown.*

RECORDING

Apart from the landmark first use of full out-of-scene-order recording in the final episode of **The Ark***, which was nevertheless still organised so as to require few actual breaks in recording, there were only two other examples of scenes being done out of sequence in season three: the opening of the gates of Troy, a particularly difficult sequence, was recorded as a video insert between 11:30 and 12:00 on the morning of the recording day for part four of* **The Myth Makers***; and the first eight scenes of episode four of* **The Savages** *were recorded directly after episode three, to be edited on to the following week's recording, as they involved the use of large quantities of dry ice in the studio.*

Sara Kingdom (played in ▲ this scene by May Warden) ages to death. *The Daleks' Master Plan.*

LOCATIONS

The Myth Makers
 Frensham Ponds, Surrey

The Massacre of St Bartholomew's Eve
 Wimbledon Common, South London

The Savages
 Gravel Pit near Chalfont St Peter, Buckinghamshire; Oxshott Sandpit, Oxshott, Surrey

The War Machines
 Fitzroy Square, London; Old Covent Garden, London; Battersea Power Station, London; Cornwall Gardens, London

The Egyptians attack the Daleks. *The Daleks' Master Plan.*

ever to have been transmitted on Christmas Day. It took the form of a humorous diversion from the main events of the story – the feeling being that viewers would not want to watch anything too serious on the holiday – and sees the travellers getting involved in a number of bizarre situations. At one point, they narrowly avoid arrest at a Liverpool police station – it had been hoped that the *Z Cars* cast would appear in these scenes, but this was vetoed by their production team – and later they even take part in a slapstick chase at a silent-era Hollywood film studio. The episode ends with the Doctor turning to camera and wishing a merry Christmas to everyone at home!

There was also a humorous slant to a few scenes of the following instalment, *Volcano*, broadcast on New Year's Day 1966. In one of these, the TARDIS materialises in the middle of the Oval cricket ground during a test match – an occurrence which the commentators take completely in their stride! But with the exception of these lighter moments, viewers remember *The Daleks' Master Plan* as a tense and gripping drama which kept them in suspense right up until its shocking conclusion.

The mammoth task of directing the story fell to Douglas Camfield, who saw it as a great challenge: 'If I could cope with this, I could cope with anything!' By all accounts, problems abounded during the course of the three months it took to record, not least because the scripts came in behind schedule and were generally too short. As Camfield later attested, he had to do a considerable amount of rewriting himself to ensure that

they were ready for the studio. Certainly John Wiles and Donald Tosh had no great affection for the story, as Wiles has since confirmed:

'It was an enormous rock in the middle of a sea, and one on which any boat we were going to run would be submerged. It was immovable and right in the middle of this period, handed to me by Verity and Dennis. Donald and I virtually washed our hands of it and it went on more or less without us in the hands of Dennis Spooner – who did most of the writing – and Dougie Camfield.'

This is a slight exaggeration, as Wiles was certainly in charge of the story's production and Tosh did do quite a lot of work on the scripts.

Wiles got on well with Tosh from the outset, and found that they had quite similar views on the direction in which they wanted to take the series:

'We were trying not so much to break the format as to develop it. I know that sounds very pompous, but with my experience as a writer I felt we could do it... Primarily we wanted to develop the programme and get it out of the somewhat childish rut we felt it was in. It was the boundaries I think we wanted to extend the most – to push it, if you like, a little bit more towards adult science fiction; probably less specified than it had been, so we could touch subjects that Verity and Dennis hadn't wanted to touch.'

A good example of the more sophisticated type of drama Wiles and Tosh had in mind is an idea which Wiles thought up for a story entitled *The*

A rehearsal shot of the Dalek time machine interior, designed by Barry Newbery. *The Daleks' Master Plan.*

▲ The interior of the Egyptian pyramid. *The Daleks' Master Plan.*

▲ Mavic Chen's Spar ship touches down on Kembel. *The Daleks' Master Plan.*

The Doctor studies the taranium core, watched by Bret Vyon (Nicholas Courtney), Katarina and Steven. *The Daleks' Master Plan.*

Face of God: 'Imagine being in a spaceship and you see yourself right up against this gigantic face – the very face of God. There is so much wonder of the miraculous in the Universe that is never exploited.'

Because of concern over viewers' religious sensibilities, this idea never got past the discussion stage. However, Donald Cotton's *The Myth Makers* – which, as the opening story of the third production block, was the first for which Wiles and Tosh were fully responsible as a team – is another good example of the approach they were aiming for. Cotton, an established playwright, had accepted Tosh's invitation to contribute to the series on condition that he could choose the subject matter and bring with him some of the distinguished artistes with whom he had been working on a string of intellectual dramas for BBC Radio's Third Programme. The story came to be centred around the fall of Troy – Greek myths were a special interest of Cotton's and had formed the basis of many of his radio plays – and to feature such accomplished players as Max Adrian,

Barrie Ingham and Frances White in major roles (as King Priam, Paris and Cassandra) and incidental music by the eminent composer Humphrey Searle.

When the TARDIS arrives on the plains of Asia Minor, not far from the besieged city of Troy, the Doctor is hailed by Achilles as the mighty god Zeus and taken to the Greek camp where he meets Agamemnon and Odysseus. Forced to admit that he is a mere mortal, albeit a traveller in space and time, he is given just two days to devise a scheme to capture Troy. Steven and Vicki, meanwhile, have been taken prisoner by the Trojans, and Vicki, believed to possess supernatural powers, is given two days to banish the Greeks and prove that she is not a spy. Having initially dismissed the famous wooden horse as a fiction of Homer's, the Doctor eventually resorts to 'inventing' it himself, thereby giving the Greeks the means to defeat the Trojans.

Stylistically, *The Myth Makers* was distinctly tongue in cheek, continuing the recent trend towards light-hearted historical stories, although the humour here was rather more intellectual than in season two's *The Romans* and *The Time Meddler* – indeed, the BBC's own promotional literature described it rather grandly as a 'high comedy'. On the other hand, it certainly had its more serious aspects – it ended with Steven being wounded by a sword-thrust to his shoulder and Vicki, having adopted the guise of Cressida, electing to remain behind on Earth with the Trojan prince Troilus, faced with a highly uncertain future in this war-ravaged land.

Although Maureen O'Brien disliked playing Vicki and was by no means sorry to be leaving *Doctor Who*, her departure had not been dis-

▲ The model of the Trojan horse used in *The Myth Makers.*

WHO'S THAT GIRL?

When Terry Nation started work on his scripts for **The Daleks' Master Plan** it was still thought that the female companion would be Vicki, and he had reached episode three before he was told otherwise. By the time he came to write episode four he had been briefed to kill off the new character; however, he still did not know what she was to be called, so for the sake of convenience he continued to refer to her as Vicki. Following her death scene, he indicated that the Doctor was to give a soliloquy: 'A speech here to cover the character of the girl. I'll leave this to you as the speech depends on what you have previously established.'

Before the story reached the screen, a number of changes were also made to its episode titles, including the following:

Original title	Title on transmission
Counter-Plot	
	Coronas of the Sun
There's Something Just Behind You	Counter-Plot
Land of the Pharaohs	
	Golden Death
Return to Varga*	
	Escape Switch
The Mutation of Time/A Switch in Time	
	The Destruction of Time

In the draft scripts, Kembel was called Varga.

JOHN WILES
PRODUCER

John Wiles was born in South Africa and came to England in 1949. He joined the BBC in the early fifties as a staff writer and adapter after his play **The Dancing Bear** (co-written with Richard Wade) was accepted by them. Later he became a story editor, working first on long-running series such as **Compact** and then, in 1964, on thriller serials for the recently started BBC2. At the same time he developed a parallel career as a director in the theatre. Having been promoted to producer by Head of Serials Donald Wilson, he was asked to take over from Verity Lambert on **Doctor Who**. He resigned from the BBC after only a short time as producer – a job in which he was never very comfortable – and returned to freelance writing and directing, mainly for the theatre.

The Trojan horse on the Ealing model stage for *The Myth Makers.*

cussed with her in advance and she was therefore rather taken aback to discover on her return from holiday that she was to be written out in the very next story.

In place of Vicki, there came a series of relatively short-term female companions. The first of these was Katarina (Adrienne Hill), handmaiden to the Trojan prophetess Cassandra, who boards the TARDIS after helping to carry the wounded Steven back there at the end of *The Myth Makers.*

Katarina is completely unlike any of the earlier regulars in that she can scarcely begin to understand most of the things she witnesses in her brief period of time and space travel. She refers to the Doctor as 'lord' and regards the TARDIS as his 'temple': in fact, as Cassandra has prophesied her death, she initially believes that she is being transported to dwell amongst the gods in the 'place of perfection'.

Introduced as a late addition to the closing episode of *The Myth Makers*, Katarina had a run of only five weeks in the series, making her last appearance in the fourth part of *The Daleks' Master Plan*. Held hostage in a spaceship airlock by a psychopathic criminal, Kirksen, who threatens to deliver her friends into the Daleks' clutches, she uses what little knowledge she has gained to open the outer door, consigning herself and her captor to the inky depths of space, an act of self-sacrifice which leads the Doctor to hope that she has finally found her place of perfection.

The production team had originally thought that Katarina might be a more lasting addition to the series, but had very quickly changed their minds when they realised the problems this would cause with story development and audience identification. Equally short-lived was the next companion, Sara Kingdom, first seen in

King Priam (Max Adrian) and Vicki outside the TARDIS in the Trojan courtyard. *The Myth Makers.*

Marshall Gaspard de Saux-Tavannes (Andre Morell) and Catherine de Medici (Joan Young). *The Massacre of St Bartholomew's Eve.*

Katarina's last episode and written out – aged to death by the Daleks' time destructor – just eight weeks later at the conclusion of *The Daleks' Master Plan.* (Sara's death scene was in fact shot on the same day as Katarina's, during the block of filming done at Ealing before recording of the story began – at which point director Douglas Camfield was virtually having to make up the action as he went along, as the scripts for the later episodes had still not been completed.) The Doctor and Steven travelled on alone to their next adventure, John Lucarotti's *The Massacre of St Bartholomew's Eve.*

When the TARDIS materialises in Paris, 1572, the Doctor decides to visit the famous apothecary Charles Preslin. Steven, meanwhile, is befriended by a group of Huguenots from the household of the Protestant Admiral de Coligny. Having rescued a young serving wench, Anne Chaplette, from some pursuing guards, the Huguenots gain their first inkling of a plan by the Catholic Queen Mother, Catherine de Medici, to have all French Protestants massacred. A further shock is in store for Steven when it appears that the hated Catholic

The Doctor visits Preslin's home. *The Massacre of St Bartholomew's Eve.*

dignitary the Abbot of Amboise is actually the Doctor in disguise.

Held responsible for the failure of a plot to assassinate de Coligny, the Abbot is subsequently executed by the Catholic authorities and his dead body left lying in the gutter. However, to Steven's relief, it transpires that the Abbot was not the Doctor after all, but merely his physical double. The two time travellers meet up again at Preslin's shop, where Steven has gone in search of the TARDIS key, and regain the safety of the ship just as the massacre begins.

Rehearsals on the Ark's kitchen set. *The Ark.*

Jackie Lane (Dodo) poses with a Monoid. *The Ark.*

MUSIC	
Story	**Composer**
Galaxy 4	Stock (by Les Structures Sonores)
Mission to the Unknown	Stock (Syncro-Stings by Trevor Duncan)
The Myth Makers	Humphrey Searle
The Daleks' Master Plan	Tristram Cary (Eric Walker ensemble) (including partial re-use of music originally composed for The Daleks)
The Massacre	Stock (Illustrations No. 4 by Pierre Arvey)
The Ark	Tristram Cary (re-use of music originally composed for The Daleks) also Stock (Drumdramatics No. 11 by Robert Farnon)
The Celestial Toyroom	Dudley Simpson
The Gunfighters	Tristram Cary (Ballad played by Tom McCall and Winifred Taylor)
The Savages	Raymond Jones
The War Machines	Stock (Musique Electronique by Eric Siday, and The Mood Modern by Johnny Hawksworth)

▼ The travellers encounter an elephant in the artificial jungle. *The Ark.*

The Queen of Hearts ▲
(Carmen Silvera). *The
Celestial Toymaker.*

The Joker (Reg Lever). ▲
The Celestial Toymaker.

WILLIAM EMMS
WRITER

Before contributing **Galaxy 4** *to
Doctor Who, William Emms had
written numerous one-off plays as
well as some adaptations and the
occasional series episode. He had
turned to writing after teaching
English in London's East End and
never really looked back. Brought up
on H. G. Wells, he was a fan of
science fiction and had watched*
Doctor Who *regularly before he
submitted his first script outline.
Following* **Galaxy 4**, *Emms
submitted several further ideas to the*
Doctor Who *office, including* **The
Imps**, *which fell through at the
scripting stage, but which was used
by Emms as the basis for his 1986
book* **Doctor Who: Mission to
Venus** *in Severn House's 'Make your
own adventure' series. Following*
Doctor Who, *Emms wrote for* **Z-
Cars, Ace of Wands, Crown
Court** *and* **Callan** *amongst others.*

Michael Gough as *The Celestial Toymaker*.

Although he had certainly approved of the
theme chosen for *The Myth Makers*, being very
interested himself in the myths of the Trojan War,
John Wiles had been less keen on the 'jokiness' of
it. This may be one reason why *The Massacre of
St Bartholomew's Eve* was in the more serious
mould of the season one historicals, two of which
had also been written by John Lucarotti.

It was not Lucarotti's idea to focus on the
massacre of the French Huguenots – he had
originally proposed a story about Eric the Red's
discovery of Newfoundland – but he was persuaded to do so by the production team. As it was,
his scripts were largely reworked by Donald
Tosh, and he was dissatisfied with the end result.
He particularly disliked the fact that the Doctor
played no part in the main events of the story,
appearing only in episodes one and four. To
Tosh, however, this was essential, not only to
preserve the mystery surrounding the identity of
the Abbot of Amboise but also to avoid William
Hartnell having to undergo a lot of time-consuming and technically difficult costume and make-up
changes in playing the dual role.

Tosh was in fact given joint credit with Lucarotti
for writing the fourth and final episode of the
story; by this time, he was no longer officially a
member of the production team, having given
over the story editor's job to Gerry Davis, who had
asked to be transferred to *Doctor Who* after a stint
on the BBC's football team soap opera *United!*.

The Massacre of St Bartholomew's Eve also

introduced another new female companion.
Originally, Anne Chaplette (Annette Robertson)
was to have joined the TARDIS team, but this
idea was eventually dropped as John Wiles and
Donald Tosh were concerned that the Doctor
should not be seen to interfere too much with
the course of Earth's history – another reason
why they had wanted him to remain on the
sidelines for most of the story. Instead, Tosh
added a short closing scene in which the TARDIS
materialises on Wimbledon Common in 1966
and a young woman, Dorothea 'Dodo' Chaplet
(Jackie Lane), runs inside believing it to be a real
police box. An attempt was made in the dialogue
to suggest that Dodo might be one of Anne's
descendants, thus indicating that the French girl
had survived the massacre, but this did not come
across as well as it might have done on screen as
William Hartnell inadvertently omitted some of
the explanation.

Dodo's first full story was *The Ark*, set some ten
million years in the future at a time when the Earth
is about to plunge into the Sun. The TARDIS
materialises on a huge spaceship carrying all the
world's plant, animal and human life, much of it
miniaturised and in suspended animation, on a
seven-hundred-year voyage to colonise the planet
Refusis II. Dodo is suffering from a cold and, as the
human Guardians of the ship and their servant
race, the Monoids, have no resistance to this
ancient virus, a plague breaks out. Fortunately,
the Doctor finds a cure and, as episode two draws
to a close, he and his companions leave in the
TARDIS.

This seems to be the end of the story. However,
a surprise is in store as the TARDIS immediately
rematerialises in what appears to be exactly the
same place. The travellers discover that they have
in fact returned to the ship – which Dodo has
nicknamed the Ark – at the end of its voyage.
Partly as a result of the earlier plague, the Monoids
have now grown strong and enslaved the humans. However, with the help of the invisible
Refusians, the Doctor is able to persuade both
races to live together in peace on Refusis II.

It was John Wiles who first thought of setting
a story on board a giant spaceship, and this idea
was then given to writers Paul Erickson and Lesley
Scott to develop. Erickson has since said that
Scott, his wife at the time, did not in fact contribute
to the writing of the scripts, and this seems to be
borne out by BBC documentation.

The Ark was something of a landmark in
production terms as, under Michael Imison's
direction, its final instalment was the first *Doctor
Who* episode to be recorded totally out of scene
order. Instead, shooting took place largely on a
set-by-set basis. The closing TARDIS scene, for

Steven and Dodo meet Cyril (Peter Stephens). *The Celestial Toymaker.*

▲ **The King of Hearts (Campbell Singer).** *The Celestial Toymaker.*

▲ **Cyril.** *The Celestial Toymaker.*

example, was the first to be completed, followed by a sequence taking place on the main bridge of the Ark, then all the scenes set in the Refusians' castle, and so on. It was only at the editing stage that everything was put together in the correct order.

In addition, this story was the last to be produced by John Wiles; he had resigned in early January 1966, about six or seven weeks before it went into the studio. Never entirely happy working as a producer, and feeling more at home as a writer and a director, he had decided to give up the job as his whole approach to the series was strongly opposed by William Hartnell. Moreover, as he later explained, both he and Donald Tosh had found the star extremely difficult to work with:

'He wasn't as old as he thought he was. When he was with me he treated himself almost as a seventy-five-year-old. It may well have been that he was physically not in the best of health and so could not learn lines. Consequently, studio days could be absolute purgatory for everybody. If Bill was in an unhappy mood then it put everyone into a terrible state.

'Eventually my directors devised a code for me. They would turn to their production assistant and say, "You had better phone the designer," which meant "Get John down here quick," so that Bill wouldn't know I'd been summoned.'

When a serious disagreement arose, Hartnell was quite prepared to take it to the Head of Serials, Gerald Savory, who he knew would support him.

'The feeling from above,' recalls Wiles, 'was that the show worked as it was and would continue to run as long as Bill Hartnell played the Doctor. So perhaps I was mad for wanting to change it. But our audience research had shown that many adults watched the show and so I felt we could do better than we were doing.

'I am still proud of all the things we tried to do on *Doctor Who* at that time... but I was heading very rapidly for a nervous breakdown and I decided that if I was going to have a breakdown it might as well be over something for which I had respect, rather than this programme which, at that stage, I did not like.'

BRIAN HAYLES
WRITER

Born on 7 March 1930 in Portsmouth, Brian Hayles set out to be a sculptor and taught art in Canada. Returning to England, he continued to teach while writing in his spare time and eventually turned to writing full time. His work included shows as diverse as radio's **The Archers** *and television's* **United!**, **Out of the Unknown**, **Doomwatch** *and* **The Regiment**. *His last TV work was* **The Moon Stallion** *which he also novelised. His film work included the adventure movie* **Warlords of Atlantis** *which was followed by* **Arabian Adventure**. *It was while working on the latter that he died on 30 October 1978.*

◄ **Sergeant Rugg (Campbell Singer) attempts to organise Steven and Dodo.** *The Celestial Toymaker.*

The Doctor confronts the ▲ Toymaker. *The Celestial Toymaker.*

DONALD COTTON
WRITER

Donald Cotton became interested in writing and acting after joining the drama society at Nottingham University, where he had studied zoology before transferring to English and philosophy. During the fifties he wrote for and appeared in numerous stage revues. His first TV work – a musical adaptation of **A Christmas Carol** *– was in 1955, for ITV. His BBC debut was in 1958, as a contributor to a late-night revue show,* **Better Late!***. This was followed by a period of radio work as a writer for the BBC's Third Programme. After* **The Myth Makers** *and* **The Gunfighters***, he submitted a further* Doctor Who *story idea,* **The Herdsmen of Aquarius** *which he has also referred to as* **The Herdsmen of Venus** *– revealing the Loch Ness Monster to be the cattle of Aquarian (or Venusian) farmers - but this was rejected by Gerry Davis. Having helped to develop the BBC series* **Adam Adamant Lives!***; he grew disillusioned with TV and concentrated instead on the theatre, where he had continued success as a playwright and actor throughout the sixties and seventies. He retired from acting in 1981, but continued his writing career into the eighties.*

It was because of Wiles's resignation that Donald Tosh had decided to give up the story editor's post – an act of loyalty which Wiles thought unnecessary.

The man chosen by Sydney Newman to take over as producer was Innes Lloyd, who accepted the job with some reluctance. By no means a fan of science fiction – although he did develop an interest in it while working on *Doctor Who* – he determined to concentrate on strong, realistic, 'gutsy' stories. It was, however, some time before he and Gerry Davis could really make their mark as the next few serials had already been planned by John Wiles and Donald Tosh.

The first of these was *The Celestial Toymaker*, in which the travellers arrive in a strange domain presided over by the eponymous character, an enigmatic, immortal entity who forces them to undergo a series of tests, failure at which will render them his playthings. The Doctor has to solve the complex trilogic game while Steven and Dodo are faced with defeating a succession of apparently child-like but potentially lethal animated toys in contests such as blind man's buff, musical chairs and 'hunt the key'. The Doctor finally overcomes the Toymaker by imitating his voice in order to complete the trilogic game from within the TARDIS, which then dematerialises as his foe's universe is destroyed.

Three of the chairs from the musical chairs game, with the Knave of Hearts doll seated on one of them. *The Celestial Toymaker.*

The original scripts for *The Celestial Toymaker* (then entitled simply *The Toymaker*) were written by Brian Hayles at the request of John Wiles, with whom he had previously worked on a BBC2 serial. They were still being finalised during the period when Tosh and Wiles were handing over to Davis and Lloyd. By this time, Tosh had already performed some major rewrites, removing a number of impractical effects sequences – including scenes set in a maze – and substituting two new games of his own, one of which was the trilogic game. It was also at this point that Tosh rejected two new Hayles storylines, *The White Witch* and *The Hands of Aten*, explaining that they

The Toymaker (Michael Gough) at his mobile desk, which was designed to spark at the back as it moved, like a friction-drive toy. On the right, in front of the giant dolls' house, is the trilogic game. *The Celestial Toymaker.*

Ike Clanton (William Hurndell), the Doctor and Kate Fisher (Sheena Marshe, daughter of director Rex Tucker) in the bar of the Last Chance Saloon in a scene from *The Gunfighters*.

were not in line with the style favoured by Lloyd and Davis, who would however be pleased to receive further ideas from Hayles. Additional changes to episodes three and four were then made by Wiles while Tosh was away on holiday, just before his eventual departure.

This should have been the final version of the story but shortly before it went into the studio an unexpected problem arose which necessitated a further rethink. In preparing the scripts, Donald Tosh had decided that it would be an amusing in-joke to incorporate the two title characters of a pre-War West End play, *George and Margaret*, which had been a big success for its writer Gerald Savory, now the BBC's Head of Serials. The gimmick of this play was that all the action led up to the arrival of George and Margaret, who were never actually seen. Although Savory had originally given his permission for this, he changed his mind after reading the scripts and thus Gerry Davis was left with little option but to do another major rewrite on *The Celestial Toymaker*, at a rate of about an episode a day. He also took the opportunity to tone down some of its more macabre elements, giving it a somewhat lighter feel.

When John Wiles saw the final scripts for the story, which he had always regarded as a model example of what he had been trying to achieve on *Doctor Who*, he strongly disapproved of the changes made by Davis. On 25 February 1966, shortly after leaving the series, he wrote a memo to Gerald Savory to put on record his views, pointing out that he might otherwise be open to criticism for wasting money on Hayles's original scripts which had been completely rewritten. He stressed that the story was supposed to have been one of great menace – although arising from a battle of wills between the Doctor and the Toymaker, rather than from ray-guns and monsters – and that this was what had given it its

Billy Clanton (David Cole), Seth Harper (Shane Rimmer) and Ike Clanton in the Last Chance Saloon. *The Gunfighters.*

▲ Top to bottom; Doc Holliday (Anthony Jacobs), Billy Clanton, Phineas Clanton (Maurice Good), Johnny Ringo (Laurence Payne) and Ike Clanton.

KIT PEDLER
ADVISER/WRITER

Christopher Magnus Howard Pedler was born in 1928 and trained in medicine, gaining a PhD for his work on the causes of retinal disease. His interest in vision and the eye led to his creation of the University of London's electron microscopy department and later to an early computer simulation of nerve cells. His first TV work was for **Horizon** *in 1966 and he was brought on to* **Doctor Who** *by Innes Lloyd and Gerry Davis who wanted a sounder scientific basis for the stories. He went on with Davis to create* **Doomwatch** *in 1969 and, following that, wrote five radio series about scientific concepts, two plays,* **Trial by Logic** *and* **Sunday Lunch,** *and co-wrote three novels with Davis:* **Mutant 59: The Plastic Eater, Brianrack** *and* **The Dynostar Menace.** *His last work for TV was the Thames production* **Mind over Matter** *which he co-presented and for which he wrote an accompanying book. Kit Pedler died on 27 May 1981 at the age of 53.*

PAUL ERICKSON
WRITER

Born in Cardiff on 22 November 1920, Paul Erickson spent most of his childhood and adolescence in San Diego, California, returning to England at the age of eighteen. After service in the RAF, he started out as an actor and worked fairly regularly in supporting roles on stage as well as in films and occasionally on TV. During the fifties he turned to administrative work in the theatre and spent about seven years with the Katharine Dunham and Jose Greco dance company, travelling widely. It was also in the fifties that his writing career began, and over the next two decades he contributed scripts to a wide variety of TV shows including **The Saint, Crossroads, Emergency Ward 10, Out of the Unknown, Paul Temple, Freewheelers** *and* **The Rivals of Sherlock Holmes.** *His last published work was the novelisation of his* **Doctor Who** *adventure,* **The Ark,** *in 1986. He died suddenly on 27 October 1991, following a stroke.*

The Western street set at Ealing Studios. *The Gunfighters.*

relevance to *Doctor Who*. In his opinion, this had now been lost as the Toymaker had been reduced virtually to a bystander and his conflict with the Doctor downplayed. He ended by expressing his regret that the story has gone ahead at all after the producer and story editor who commissioned it had both left.

Donald Cotton's *The Gunfighters* (originally called *The Gunslingers*) was another story initiated by Donald Tosh and John Wiles before their

Barry Newbery's realistic Western set at Ealing. *The Gunfighters.*

departure. A spoof of the Western genre, it tells of events leading up to the famous gunfight at the OK Corral in Tombstone, 1881. The Doctor, suffering from toothache, seeks out the local dentist, who turns out to be none other than the notorious Doc Holliday, currently engaged in a feud with the Clanton family. Lawmen Wyatt Earp and Bat Masterson are meanwhile doing their best to keep the peace. For once, the Doctor is unable to help and, in the climactic shoot-out, the young Clanton brothers and their gunman ally Johnny Ringo are all killed by Holliday, Earp and Earp's brother Virgil.

Although somewhat more serious than *The Myth Makers*, *The Gunfighters* is still a light-hearted adventure, and much of the humour centres around the Doctor himself as he struggles to come to terms with the Western lifestyle – he is horrified, for example, that people keep giving him guns!

One of the most unusual aspects of the story is that it is punctuated by snatches of a pastiche Western song, 'The Ballad of the Last Chance Saloon', which serves as an ongoing commentary on the action. The music for this was written by Tristram Cary and most of the lyrics by Donald Cotton (although additional verses were later added by director Rex Tucker). Pre-taped (apart from a sequence in episode two where Winifred Taylor accompanies Peter Purves), to be played in on cue by the grams operator during the making of the programme, it was performed by resident

Camera 3 focuses on Jackie Lane as Dodo, during rehearsals for a scene in *The Savages*.

▲ Steven and Dodo escape from two attacking Savages. *The Savages.*

▲ The crew prepare for the filming of a scene on location. *The Savages.*

▲ Exorse (Geoffrey Frederick) blasts Nanina (Clare Jenkins) with a light gun. *The Savages.*

BBC pianist Tom McCall with vocals by Lynda Baron. Baron in fact found the melody extremely difficult to master, with the result that numerous takes were required and the recording session went on far longer than anticipated. (It had originally been intended that Rex Tucker's daughter Sheena Marshe, who played Doc Holliday's girlfriend Kate Fisher in the story, would sing the song, but her voice was considered too young and fresh.)

Ian Stuart Black's *The Savages* (which had had the working title *The White Savages*) was the last of the commissions left over from Donald Tosh's time as story editor, although in this case Gerry Davis fully oversaw the development of the scripts. Black, a highly accomplished TV writer, had asked to contribute to the series as his children were fans of it. 'They didn't believe I was really a writer, because I hadn't done a *Doctor Who*,' he now jokes.

Having arrived on a far-distant and seemingly idyllic world, the Doctor, Steven and Dodo discover that it hides a terrible secret: the apparently civilised Elders maintain their advanced society by draining off and transferring to themselves the life force of a group of defenceless Savages. Outraged at this exploitation, the Doctor is seemingly helpless to prevent it when some of his own life force is tapped by the Elders' leader, Jano. However, in the process, Jano acquires some of the Doctor's attitudes and conscience and, turning against his own people, he enlists the help of the

Savages to destroy the Elders' transference laboratory, a task with which the time travellers gladly assist.

A dramatic allegory of man's inhumanity to man, *The Savages* – the first story to have an

Chal (Ewen Solon), leader of *The Savages*.

A War Machine near the ▲ Post Office Tower. *The War Machines.*

Ben (Michael Craze) and ▲ Polly (Anneke Wills).

IAN STUART BLACK
WRITER

*Born in 1915, Ian Stuart Black began writing at an early age. After national service, he worked for the Rank Organisation for three years, developing film ideas. His TV debut came in 1954 on the BBC's **Fabian of the Yard**. This was followed by writing and editing work on a number of other series, mainly for ITV, including **The Adventures of William Tell** and **H.G. Wells' The Invisible Man** (1958/9). He also wrote several novels and cinema films and in 1960 assisted in devising the series **Danger Man**. After his three transmitted stories he wrote an idea for a further six-part **Doctor Who** tale entitled **The Furies**, but this was not taken forward. Subsequently he continued a prolific TV career on series such as **Adam Adamant Lives!**, **The Champions**, **Star Maidens** and **Elephant Boy**. Since the mid-seventies he has concentrated on writing books, including the supernatural thrillers **Creatures of A Dream** and **Cry Wolf**.*

Sir Charles Summer (William Mervyn) and the Doctor study a War Machine captured in Cornwall Gardens. *The War Machines.*

overall title on screen, rather than individual episode titles – was further distinguished by Christopher Barry's direction and the luxury of a small number of location scenes. It was also the final story to feature Steven Taylor, who decides to stay behind on the planet after being asked by the Elders and the Savages to become their new leader. Peter Purves had been dissatisfied for some time with what he regarded as a lack of development of Steven's character, and this, he feels, was why he was written out: 'The producer got a bit fed up with me moaning – and quite rightly so. If I was a producer, I'd get fed up with an artist who was always complaining. But at the time I thought it was justified and so, in the end, they decided to sort it out in their own way.' Another important factor was that the new production team were simply not keen on the character of Steven, and felt that a change was called for.

Further cast changes were in store in the next serial, *The War Machines* – which, unusually, was commissioned from the same writer, Ian Stuart Black.

When the TARDIS arrives in London, 1966, the Doctor visits the Post Office Tower, having sensed evil emanations from the building. There he meets Professor Brett, who demonstrates his revolutionary new computer, WOTAN – Will Operating Thought Analogue. Designed as a universal problem-solver, this machine can actually think for itself. Moreover, it is shortly to be linked up to other major computers around the world – a project overseen by civil servant Sir Charles Summer. However, WOTAN has decided that humans are inferior to machines and should therefore be ruled by them. Exerting a powerful hypnotic influence, it initiates the construction of War Machines – heavily armed, self-contained mobile computers – with which to effect its plan of world domination. The War Machines prove more than a match for troops, but by establishing a magnetic force field the Doctor is able to capture

one of them and then reprograms it to destroy WOTAN.

Now back in her own time, Dodo decides to leave the Doctor at this point (her final appearance being in the second episode). The Doctor soon finds himself with two new companions – Brett's secretary Polly (Anneke Wills) and her merchant seaman friend Ben Jackson (Michael Craze) when they come aboard the TARDIS just as it is about to dematerialise.

Polly and Ben were very contemporary characters, straight out of swinging sixties London. Like the hard-edged style and present-day setting of *The War Machines* – featuring some of the most extensive location filming yet seen in *Doctor Who* – this was a good indication of the new, more realistic approach favoured by Innes Lloyd and Gerry Davis. Although the scripts for *The War Machines* were written entirely by Ian Stuart Black, the basic idea for a story involving computers and the Post Office Tower had actually come from the production office. To achieve greater believability, Lloyd and Davis had decided that they needed a scientific adviser and as Davis later recalled, a number of potential candidates – including such well-known figures as Patrick Moore and Dr Alex Comfort – were considered:

'I was trying to get someone who might provide ideas and vet programmes, hardening up the science. Then one of Innes Lloyd's former colleagues in the BBC's Outside Broadcast Unit recommended Kit Pedler. I invited him round and tried him out.

'I was sitting in the office, from where you can see the Post Office Tower, which had just been built. I used to bounce this off people: "What would happen if the Post Office Tower took over?" From most people nothing really came back, nothing original anyway. But Kit Pedler was a real science-fiction fan and he gave me a few ideas, which were more science fiction than *Doctor Who*. We then suggested ideas to each other, and before we knew it we were into a really good creative session. I think that during that first session we pretty well mapped out the storyline that became *The War Machines*.'

Pat Dunlop, an ex-BBC staff writer, also did some work in developing the idea for *The War Machines* (then under its original title *The Computers*), for which on 29 March 1966 he was paid a small copyright release fee. It was then handed over to Ian Stuart Black to produce the final scripts.

The last part of *The War Machines* was transmitted on 16 July 1966, bringing to a close the unbroken 46 episode run of *Doctor Who's* third season – the longest run the series' had had so far.

CHAPTER SEVEN

Regeneration: An End and a New Beginning

The life span of a television programme which revolves around a central character is generally limited to the length of time the lead actor or actress wishes or is able to carry on in the role; and while audiences in later decades would come to accept major cast changes in already established and ongoing series, in the sixties this was almost unheard of. *Doctor Who*'s longevity owes much to its unique solution to the problem of changing its star.

In August of 1966 it was announced in the press that William Hartnell would shortly be leaving. It has often been suggested that Hartnell's declining health was the main reason for his departure, and no doubt it was a contributory factor. Of much greater significance, however, were his continuing artistic differences with the production team. While talk of behind-the-scenes arguments may have been exaggerated, it is certainly true that by 1966 the working atmosphere on the series had become very strained.

Therefore, when Hartnell's contract expired, producer Innes Lloyd took the revolutionary step of recasting the lead role. Tired and frail though he was, Hartnell was not at all happy to be leaving the series, as director Derek Martinus recalls:

'Bill was under the impression that *Doctor Who* would not exist without him. He had created the character... and he was being given the star treatment all around the country. But, you know, he'd had a hard struggle. He'd been up and down in his career... he lived life to the full, and in later life one must say he was a little difficult, a little cantankerous. Also, he used to like to have an input on scripts, which wasn't always to their advantage. So it was decided, I think, that a change was necessary. And he didn't see how this could ever be done.

'I was given the task of handling the transformation from one Doctor to another, and of course that was a little tricky because it was not a transformation that Bill Hartnell was terribly interested in, as you can imagine.'

INNES LLOYD
PRODUCER

Innes Lloyd's interest in drama stemmed from appearing in a school play. Having served in the Royal Navy during the War he trained at the Central School of Speech and Drama and became an actor in repertory theatre. Some five years later, in 1953, he joined BBC Radio as a studio manager, and quickly moved sideways into TV. After spells in the Presentation Department and Outside Broadcasts – where he handled projects as diverse as state occasions, the Wimbledon tennis tournament and the **Eurovision Song Contest** *– he transferred to Drama, directing episodes of serials such as* **United!** *and* **The Newcomers***. He was then persuaded, somewhat against his wishes, to become producer of* **Doctor Who***. He continued to produce dramas for the BBC right up until his death on 23 August 1991. These included* **The Stone Tape, The Snow Goose, Across the Lake, Reith, Bomber Harris,** *as well as many written by playwright Alan Bennett, including* **An Englishman Abroad** *and* **Talking Heads.***

◄ **William Hartnell as the Doctor in** *The Web Planet.*

GERRY DAVIS
STORY EDITOR/
WRITER

Gerry Davis became a BBC story editor in 1965 at the invitation of Head of Serials Donald Wilson, who had been impressed by a course he had written on TV scriptwriting. He had previously been a newspaper reporter, a merchant seaman and a writer for the Canadian Broadcasting Corporation, and had studied opera and worked as a cinema translator in Italy. His first BBC assignments were on **199 Park Lane** *and* **United!**, *and he was then given the chance to take over from Donald Tosh on* **Doctor Who**. *Although he never saw entirely eye to eye with producer Innes Lloyd, he remained in this post for over a year before moving on to edit another show,* **First Lady**. *He later returned to freelance writing, his greatest success coming in the early seventies with the BBC's ecological drama series* **Doomwatch**, *which he co-created with Kit Pedler. From the mid-seventies he spent most of his time in Hollywood, writing for American films and TV series and teaching screenwriting courses at the UCLA Film School. He died on 31 August 1991, aged 64.*

The Doctor regenerates ▲ for the first time. *The Tenth Planet.*

William Hartnell in his final year as the Doctor. *The Celestial Toymaker.*

When asked in later years about his decision to change the Doctor, Innes Lloyd gave a tactful reply:

'Bill had been in the role for a long time. He was getting on and he was getting tired. I thought that the tiredness and the irascibility were not going to be good for the show, or for him, and I would always have advised him to leave.'

Although a number of other possibilities were considered, including Sir Michael Hordern, the actor eventually chosen as Hartnell's replacement was Patrick Troughton. As Lloyd later recounted, this was a suggestion which was approved of by Hartnell himself:

'I recall him saying to me – though I don't know if he said it to anyone else – "There's only one man in England who can take over, and that's Patrick Troughton."'

Lloyd regarded Troughton as 'an absolutely ideal choice. He had versatility going for him – he was a distinguished character actor with a great many varied roles behind him. He was always in demand. He was a popular actor with a great following. Most important of all, I think, was that he had a leading actor's temperament. He was a father figure to the whole company and hence could embrace it and sweep it along with him.'

Although he felt that *Doctor Who* had perhaps been 'done to death', Troughton was eventually persuaded to accept the role, knowing that the regular income would help to pay for his sons' education.

What still remained for the production team to solve was the problem of explaining away in story terms the change of lead actor. How could it be done without confusing or alienating the pro-

gramme's loyal followers? The answer they came up with was the concept which later in *Doctor Who*'s history would become known as 'regeneration'. Since the Doctor was an alien, they reasoned, he might well possess some extraordinary and hitherto unsuspected powers – including the ability, when his old body wore out, to rejuvenate himself. In other words, he might undergo a process of physical renewal in which his appearance, and even his personality, would be bound to change drastically.

When asked who had thought up this premise, story editor Gerry Davis recalled that Innes Lloyd had turned out a few pages of ideas and that writer Dennis Spooner had also been involved, but that in the end it had been a committee decision. Another person who may well have contributed was Dr Kit Pedler, the programme's scientific adviser, with whom Davis was working on the scripts for the first Doctor's final story, *The Tenth Planet.*

Other matters to which the production team had to turn their attention included both the look and the characterisation of the new Doctor. Troughton still harboured some doubts as to whether or not the audience would accept him in the role, but it was agreed at an early stage that he should not even attempt to copy the style of Hartnell's performance but should instead endeavour to create a completely new persona. The big question was: what should that persona be?

The scripts for the new Doctor's debut adventure had already been written by David Whitaker. However, they were a source of some concern to Patrick Troughton and Sydney Newman, as Troughton explained in a 1985 convention interview:

'We had script conferences and there was a first script which was sort of written for Billy but in a way it was written for, it struck me reading it, a very verbose, autocratic Sherlock Holmes type – who never stopped talking! I thought, "That's not going to do for me over three years every week," so I said that I didn't see my Doctor quite like that: I saw him really as a listener. I thought that this Doctor listened to everyone and totted it all up and then made his own decision about things. Then in comes Sydney Newman and he starts talking about a "cosmic hobo", who obviously wouldn't talk like an intellectual, autocratic Sherlock Holmes type at all. So I leapt at it: I said "What a good idea!. . . A man like that'd be more of a listener, wouldn't he?". . . I was very keen on the idea of doing it as a cosmic hobo.'

As Head of Drama, with overall responsibility for hundreds of programmes each year, Newman would not normally concern himself with the day-to-day production of a single series. However, he

The Doctor (Patrick Troughton) suffers the after effects of his transformation. *The Power of the Daleks.*

DEREK MARTINUS
DIRECTOR

*Born in April 1931, Derek Martinus started as an amateur actor but, thinking that would be too difficult as a career, turned to directing instead. He studied at the University of Oklahoma in America before moving to Yale drama school and finally to Canada where he wrote TV commercials. Returning to England, he continued acting in theatre until he joined the BBC. The first thing he directed for the BBC was **Doctor Who – Galaxy 4** – which was followed by many other productions, including the Sunday Classic **The Black Tulip**, episodes of **The Doctors** and **United!** and Henry James' **What Maisie Knew**. In the mid-seventies he left the BBC to go freelance, his credits including Southern TV's **The House in Regent Place**, Tyne Tees' **The Paper Lads**, and for the BBC, **A Legacy**, **In the Labyrinth** and **Blake's 7**. In 1977 and 1980 he directed for Southern TV's army series **Spearhead** and in the eighties he directed Susan Howatch's **Penmarric** for the BBC. The early nineties saw Derek directing theatre in Sweden: Harold Pinter's **The Homecoming**, Ben Jonson's **Volpone** and two Shakespeare productions, **Shakespeare in Love** (a compilation play) and **Twelfth Night**.*

did keep a watchful eye on *Doctor Who* and he would always have to be consulted about important developments such as major format or cast changes. Hence his involvement in the initial discussions concerning Troughton's portrayal of the Doctor.

Gerry Davis later described how the detailed characterisation had been arrived at:

'We spent a whole day – producer, Head of Serials, Patrick Troughton, myself and some others – at a meeting. As the morning went on it became chaotic. Everyone was giving ideas, but there was no real cohesion. I could see that Troughton was getting very irritated. He was very uneasy about taking the job anyway, thinking that he might be typecast. At the end of the morning I realised we were getting nowhere, so I ejected everyone else from the meeting and just Patrick Troughton and I worked out the character. Really it came mostly out of Troughton's own personality. In an odd sort of way he was playing himself. He was hard to pin down, shifting, always eluding the issue. This was very different from the positive, dogmatic character of Hartnell. So at the end of the day we went back and I said I thought we had it.

'I thought it would be very interesting to have a character who never quite says what he means, who, really, uses the intelligence of the people he is with. He knows the answer all the time; if he suggests something he knows the outcome. He is watching, he's really directing, but he doesn't want to show he's directing like the old Doctor.'

Davis was inspired in part by the character, Destry, portrayed by film star James Stewart in the Western *Destry Rides Again*: someone who when asked a question would always reply by way of a parable rather than giving a straight answer.

As the changes to Whitaker's scripts had to be made at the last minute, and as Whitaker did not have the time to take on the job himself, Gerry Davis contacted Dennis Spooner to do a rewrite over the weekend of the 8–9 October 1966. The start of rehearsals for the first episode was postponed until 17 October as a result. Whitaker agreed to the rewrite on condition that neither his fee nor his overseas rights were affected, that the characterisation of the Daleks was not changed and that he still received sole writer's credit.

When it came to choosing the costume and make-up that Troughton would wear, a number of colourful suggestions were considered. It was thought, for example, that he might black up and put on curly-toed slippers and a turban; or perhaps adopt the guise of a sea captain in full Victorian-style naval uniform. A number of ideas were actually tried out in costume tests; and each time Troughton was kitted out in a new look, Sydney Newman would be fetched to pass judgment. Newman's reaction was invariably negative and, as Troughton later said, he eventually asked: 'But whatever happened to the cosmic hobo?'

Troughton's eventual costume, designed by Sandra Reid, was a tramp-like, Chaplinesque parody of Hartnell's, with stove pipe hat, spotted bow tie, disreputable old frock coat and enormously baggy checked trousers.

▲ **The Doctor with his diary and recorder.** *The Power of the Daleks.*

Ben holds up a mirror for ▲ the Doctor to see his new face, but instead his old face is reflected. *The Power of the Daleks.*

After three years of *Dr Who* Mr. William Hartnell will be leaving the programme to return to stage and film work, the BBC said last night. His last appearance will be on October 29. The BBC quoted him as saying: 'I think three years in one part is a good innings and it is time for a change.'

The BBC is now searching for a new Dr. Who.

From 'New Dr. Who Sought' The Times (6 August 1966)

The time travelling doctor is back as usual on BBC 1 this afternoon – and advance reports say that his return will be an explosive event to woo the kids away from Guy Fawkes bonfires.

But something is very much out of the ordinary – instead of being played by William Hartnell, the doctor is spooky character actor Patrick Troughton.

When veteran Bill Hartnell decided to drop out it could have meant the end of *Dr. Who*.

Scriptwriters have been turning mental somersaults to explain why a new hero is appearing, without warning, to young fans. Full details of his debut are being kept a secret, until today, though you can see what he looks like in our picture.

But one thing is certain – millions of people will be glad to share his shudders – and tune in again next week.

Shaun Usher
From 'We Just Love to be Scared Out of Our Minds' The Daily Sketch (5 November 1966)

It was on 29 October 1966 at the conclusion of *The Tenth Planet*, that the series' viewers were given their first brief glimpse of the new Doctor.

Set in the TARDIS interior, the transformation scene opens with the Doctor standing at the console operating the controls. The doors are closed, the ship is pulsating with sound and the wall roundels are throbbing with an intense radiance. A succession of rapidly mixed shots is seen, including images of the Doctor's hand on the controls, the console lights flashing, and the Doctor's ashen face. The doors open and the Doctor collapses to the floor as Polly and Ben enter and the TARDIS takes off. The two companions cross to the Doctor's side as the TARDIS controls operate by themselves. As they gently move his cloak away from his face, the picture cuts to a close-up of the Doctor. His features start to flare and glow and then, as the glow fades, the new Doctor is revealed.

In technical terms, the transformation was essentially a simple mix from one camera shooting a close-up of Hartnell to another taking an identically composed shot of Troughton. What really made the sequence, however, was the strange flaring, glowing effect, devised on the day of recording by vision mixer Shirley Coward, in discussion with director Derek Martinus and other members of the team. At that time, the BBC's mixing desks had two banks of faders – Bank A and Bank B – one of which could be used as a back-up to the other. In Riverside Studio 1 where the episode was made, Bank B was faulty and was not supposed to be used. However, Shirley Coward decided that this was just what was needed to create the desired effect. The sequence started with the close-up of Hartnell on Bank A, which was then mixed to the identical shot on Bank B. Because of the technical fault, the picture started to flare and break up as required. It was then mixed to the close-up of Troughton – still on Bank B – and finally to the same shot of Troughton, back on Bank A. The whole scene took a considerable amount of time to rehearse and line up, but was eventually completed in about two takes.

After the episode was transmitted, the audience had to wait for the first instalment of David Whitaker's story, originally called *The Destiny of Doctor Who* and now retitled *The Power of the Daleks*, to discover just how different this new Doctor was.

In the aftermath of the transformation, the Doctor suffers blurred vision and loud whining and drumming noises in his head. He soon recovers, however, and in response to persistent questioning by an incredulous Polly and Ben is eventually persuaded to give an oblique explanation of the change he has undergone:

BEN: (*Picking up the Doctor's ring*) The Doctor always wore this. If you are him it should fit. (*He tries the ring on the Doctor's finger, but it doesn't fit*) That settles it.

DOCTOR: I'd like to see a butterfly fit into a chrysalis case after it spreads its wings.

POLLY: Then you did change.

DOCTOR: Life depends on change, and renewal.

BEN: (*Sceptical*) Oh, that's it, you've been renewed have you?

DOCTOR: (*Half to himself*) Renewed? Have I? That's it, I've been renewed. It's part of the TARDIS. Without it I couldn't survive.

The Power of the Daleks was directed by *Doctor Who* stalwart Christopher Barry. He was a good friend of Troughton's and had worked with him at a number of stages throughout his career and he was delighted to be handling his first story as the Doctor. However, as he now admits, there was still some uncertainty at this stage as to how Troughton should approach the part:

'I don't think Sydney Newman was entirely happy with Patrick's first appearance during rehearsals. I think we had to tone it down a little, and try to incorporate more of Troughton's youth and humour.'

At one point during the rehearsal process Troughton reportedly was even going to play the part wearing a frizzy, Harpo Marx-type wig. In the end, however, his own hair was simply cut into a Beatle-style mop.

Anneke Wills also recalls this period of doubt:

'Everybody was a bit worried, because there was no knowing whether or not the public would accept the transformation. Later, of course, it became an accepted feature of *Doctor Who*, but that was the first time it had been done, and the production team were very concerned about it. They weren't sure if the series would have as much support from everybody as it had had before. But of course it did, because Pat Troughton was just incredible!'

The gamble had paid off. Having come in as producer midway through season three, Innes Lloyd had succeeded in his aim of remodelling the series to ensure its continued success. With the help of story editor Gerry Davis, he had made the stories more realistic and contemporary; he had phased out the two companions remaining from his predecessor's time and introduced two new ones; and now he had even transformed the Doctor.

Not only had the good Doctor been regenerated, but so had *Doctor Who*.

CHAPTER EIGHT

Who Was Patrick Troughton

Patrick Troughton was born on 25 March 1920 and grew up in North London, where he was educated at Mill Hill Public School. In his teens he attended the Embassy School of Acting at Swiss Cottage, under Eileen Thorndike. From there he won a scholarship to the Leighton Rallius Studios at the John Drew Memorial Theatre on Long Island in New York, USA.

When the Second World War broke out, he returned to Britain on a Belgian ship. Just in sight of the coast it hit a mine and sank, but Troughton was fortunate enough to escape in a life boat. In 1939 he joined the Tonbridge Repertory Company before joining the Royal Navy in 1940, rising through the ranks to attain the captaincy of a motor gunboat on duty in the North Sea. When he was demobbed in 1945 he returned to the theatre, working with the Amersham Repertory Company, the Bristol Old Vic Company and the Pilgrim Players at the Mercury Theatre in Nottingham.

He first broke into television – always to remain his favourite medium – in 1947, not long after it restarted after the war. Notable early work included parts in *Robin Hood* (BBC 1953, title role), *The Adventures of Robin Hood* (ITC 1957, 1959), *Paul of Tarsus* (BBC 1960, title role), *Dr Finlay's Casebook* (BBC 1962, semiregular) and, perhaps best remembered of all, *The Old Curiosity Shop* (BBC 1962, as Quilp).

His cinema debut came in 1948, with small roles in *Hamlet* and the TCF production *Escape* (one of the stars of which was William Hartnell). He had frequent film roles during the fifties and early sixties, often in character parts and hidden beneath elaborate costume and make-up.

So highly regarded was Troughton that he seemed never to be out of work, whether for television, films or the theatre, and as he later recalled in Peter Haining's book *The Doctor Who File*, he was away on a film location when he was offered the part for which he is now best remembered:

'My association with *Doctor Who* began in Ireland. I was there in 1966 filming *The Viking Queen* with Nicola Pagett when the phone started ringing. It was the BBC production office and they were looking for a replacement for Billy Hartnell, who was then a very sick man. "Come and play Doctor Who," the voice on the phone

THE FILMS OF PATRICK TROUGHTON

Hamlet (1948); Escape (1948); Chance Of A Lifetime (1950); Treasure Island (1950)*; The Woman With No Name (US title: Her Panelled Door) (1950); The Franchise Affair (1951); White Corridors (1951); The Black Knight (1954)*; Richard III (1955)*; The Curse Of Frankenstein (1957)*; The Moonraker (1958)*; The Phantom Of The Opera (1962)*; Jason And The Argonauts (1963)*; The Black Torment (1964)*; The Gorgon (1964)*; The Viking Queen (1967)*; The Scars Of Dracula (1970)*; Frankenstein And The Monster From Hell (1974)*; Tendre Dracula (1974)*; The Omen (1976)*; Sinbad And The Eye Of The Tiger (1977)*; A Hitch In Time (1978)*.
* = colour film.

◄ **Patrick Troughton as Tristram in *The Viking Queen* filmed in 1966.**

A VERY (UN) CONVENTIONAL APPEARANCE

Those who witnessed Patrick Troughton's appearance at the **Doctor Who** *Appreciation Society's 1985 convention surely felt a little in awe of this friendly and unassuming man, who so clearly loved his time as the Doctor and who was more than willing to talk about and relive many happy memories of working on the programme. When he appeared at the back of the hall and made his way to the stage amidst a deafening barrage of applause and a light show of flash-bulbs he was no longer Troughton but the second Doctor himself – complete with checked trousers, jacket and bow tie. He had actually taken the trouble to bring a costume with him so that he could slip back into the character. Few fans who attended that event will ever forget seeing and hearing the second Doctor in the flesh.*

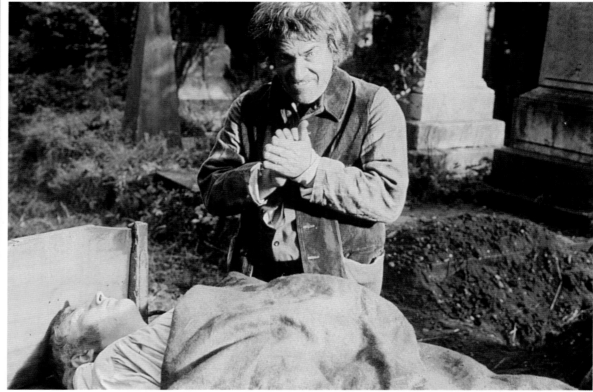

Patrick Troughton as the bodysnatcher from *The Curse of Frankenstein* (1957).

Klove, *The Scars of ▲ Dracula* (1970).

said. "No, no," I said equally emphatically, "I don't want to play Doctor Who." Anyway, the phone kept on ringing and I kept on saying, "No, I really don't want to play it. It wouldn't last more than six weeks with me!" But they kept on phoning and pushing the money up, so that in the end I began to have serious doubts... After about a week of these calls, I decided I must be crazy to keep refusing. It was ridiculous. Even if it only lasted six weeks it was still worth doing.'

Troughton rarely gave interviews during his tenure as the Doctor, seeing himself very much as a jobbing actor who put the characters he played away when he left the studio. However, *Reveille's* Margaret Pride and Gillian Mills did speak to him during recording of *The Highlanders* at the end of 1966, shortly after he joined the series:

'You're Press,' he accused. 'I heard you were coming. It's no good. I never give interviews. Never.'

Patrick smiled a wicked smile and said: 'Just tell them that I am that mystery man of television, Dr Who.'

It was not enough. Eventually, he relented a little and told me about himself and the reasons for his not co-operating.

'You see, I think acting is magic. If I tell you all about myself it will spoil it.

'People talk about television being in the sitting room and becoming an everyday thing. But it is not true, especially for the children. It is still magic, and I hope it always stays that way.

'Dr Who? I like him. The whole thing is a jolly romp.'

...I asked him where he had learned to play the flute. He roared with laughter. 'Learned? You must be crazy. Do you think I could play as badly as this if I had had lessons? No, I just jiggle my fingers around on it.'

...He began to play his flute again. 'This calms me down, but nobody else.'

'Want to dance?' he giggled, then became serious. 'I'm on now. Got to rush. That's all, anyway. This is the first time I've been interviewed. It is probably the last.'

He looked at me impishly. 'I've only talked to you because you're a girl. And I like girls.'

I do not think Patrick Troughton is Dr Who at all. I still think he is a leprechaun in disguise.

Fortunately, in later years, the actor became a little more open about his work. Interviewed in 1985, he explained how he had at first played the Doctor in a rather extravagant manner but then mellowed his performance:

Melanthius the Sage. *Sinbad and the Eye of the Tiger* (1977).

▲ The bodysnatcher *The Curse of Frankenstein* (1957).

'It worked very well when I first took it on because one was saying to everybody, "This is the way we're going to do it. It's going to be different. If you don't like it, you can lump it." So we were exaggerating it a bit, and afterwards we toned it down as we got more confident in what we were doing. It became more subtle and the scriptwriters began to get on our wavelength, which made a hell of a difference. They began to write for you rather than you having to change the script to fit what you wanted to do. Fortunately, that happened very quickly.

'As for the hat I wore at the beginning, well, I think it was dear old Campbell Logan, or it might have been Andy Osborne, who said to me in the BBC Club one evening, after the first episodes had been transmitted, "Oh splendid. It'll go on for another three years. Have to get rid of the hat though." So the hat went!'

Another justification for the rather outlandish outfit of the early episodes and the even more bizarre suggestions considered in the planning stages was that Troughton wanted to disguise himself and thereby lessen the danger of being typecast. This was a worry which was to remain with him throughout his time on *Doctor Who*, but he was soon persuaded to wear a more conservative version of the costume – it was arranged for his baggy trousers to be taken in an inch at a time as the weeks went by, so that he would not notice!

In developing his characterisation, Troughton

was given a relatively free hand: 'They left me to it. Oh yes. I think they cast me because I'd done about twenty years of character acting and so could cope working with something like that. We had talks to get ideas, with scriptwriters and the producer, so it was a communal affair in a way. We knew from day one that we wanted it to be vaguely Chaplinesque, which is not to say that I

▲ Klove. *The Scars of Dracula* (1970).

◄ Dracula (Christopher Lee) punishes his manservant Klove *The Scars of Dracula* (1970).

Patrick Troughton in the ▲
twentieth anniversary story
The Five Doctors.

Patrick Troughton ▶
interviewed for BBC Wales
during location filming for
The Abominable Snowmen.

Patrick Troughton and ▲
Frazer Hines on location for
Fury from the Deep.

approach his ability, but that was the idea.'

Despite his reservations about typecasting, Troughton loved playing the Doctor and found the character's heroic nature not at all limiting:

'I don't think he was a goody. He was a bit naughty, wasn't he? Of course, you've got to be

Inspector Kanof and the policeman (Michael Peake).
The Gorgon (1964).

on the right side when there's a villain about, but he was naughty all the same. If you're going to be totally moral it's boring, so you have to colour it a bit. Let's face it, it's a smashing part!'

Troughton had an excellent working relationship with all his co-stars in the series and acquired a reputation as something of a practical joker.

'Ah, yes, he loved practical jokes,' recalls Anneke Wills, 'except when they were played on him! I remember one time during rehearsals Michael Craze and I came out wearing T-shirts printed with the words "Bring Back Bill Hartnell", but the joke rebounded on us because he was really upset! Then on another occasion – it may have been his birthday – we bought him a pair of socks as a present, but only gave him one of them (at least, I think that's what we did!). We couldn't have teased him like that if we hadn't loved him – we were a very, very close team – but he got quite upset. We then had to go to him and say "Look, we're terribly sorry, you know this was just a joke!" That was all part of his intense sensitivity, which also made him such a brilliant actor.'

Wills is just one of many colleagues to have paid tribute to Troughton's consummate professional skills. However, with typical self-effacement, Troughton himself was always sceptical of suggestions that there was any creativity involved in acting in a series like *Doctor Who*: 'Creative? I don't like that word at all. We're not creative, we just do it.'

Towards the end of his second year in the series, Troughton was very undecided whether or not to sign a contract for a third. Barry Letts, who directed *The Enemy of the World*, remembers discussing it with him at the time and advising him to request a reduction in the number of episodes to be recorded, as Troughton was finding the current schedule wearing. Although no such reduction was made, Troughton stayed on anyway.

Throughout his tenure as the Doctor, Troughton tended to shun publicity, making only the occasional promotional appearance such as when he judged the *Blue Peter* 'Design a Monster to Beat the Daleks' competition in 1967. Peter Bryant, story editor and producer on many of Troughton's serials, believes that this was due more to the intensity of the schedule than to any reticence on the actor's part:

'I wouldn't have said he was particularly shy, Patrick. It's quite an onerous role, you know, this Doctor Who part; you carry the whole bloody show really. It takes it out of you. I think Patrick wasn't keen on any side bits of publicity that would come up. He'd want just to do the job and

Israel Hands in John Lucarotti's dramatisation of *Treasure Island* (1977).

The Doctor in *Fury from the Deep*.

▲ **The Doctor and Lemuel Gulliver (Bernard Horsfall) in *The Mind Robber*.**

go home to his wife and kids. He really wasn't interested in it.'

Towards the end of his third year, Troughton made it known that he did not want to continue for a fourth. By this time, the strain of making the series was beginning to take its toll.

'We were aware that Pat wanted to leave, of course,' says Derrick Sherwin, one of the producers of his last season. 'He had had a hard slog – don't forget, we were doing about forty episodes a year in those days – and he was very, very tired. He had been consistently getting pretty shoddy scripts, too, and he was a perfectionist, he really wouldn't say poor dialogue. Consequently he was becoming very edgy towards the end, and there were a few rows. Eventually he decided that he had had enough. The Doctor had changed before, so we knew that we could change him again, and that's what we did.'

Director Paddy Russell also recalls the reputation that Troughton acquired for being rather difficult to work with:

'It was interesting because I talked to Pat about *Doctor Who* much later when he was doing a classic serial for me. Having found him a superb actor to work with, I found it extraordinary when I heard that he had begun to give himself a very bad reputation on *Doctor Who*. We were chatting away one day and I said I couldn't believe these stories and he said, "Well, I couldn't believe what I was doing. That's in the end why I left. The part

overwhelmed me and it almost gave me schizophrenia."'

Frazer Hines, who played the Doctor's companion Jamie, has commented that Troughton's wife at the time was opposed to him continuing as the Doctor, and that this contributed to his decision to give up the role.

When he left *Doctor Who* in June 1969, Troughton quickly got back into the swing of his career as a jobbing character actor. His return to films came in *The Scars of Dracula* (Hammer/EMI 1970), and this was followed by several other cinema roles, most notably as Father Brennan in *The Omen* (TCF 1976). As before, however, his main work was in television. Amongst his most memorable appearances were in *The Six Wives of Henry VIII* (BBC 1970, as the Duke of Norfolk), *Coronation Street* (Granada 1971, semiregular), *A Family at War* (Granada 1971, semiregular), *The Glories of Christmas* (Yorkshire 1973, reprising

▲ **Israel Hands and O'Brien (Tim Condren) in *Treasure Island* (1977).**

◄ **Patrick Troughton as Gerald, with Pat Heyward as Joan *Long Term Memory* (1985).**

A selection of telesnaps ▲ from Troughton's first story as the Doctor, *The Power of the Daleks.*

Kay Harker (Devin Stanfield) and Cole Hawlings in *Box of Delights* (1984).

his success as Quilp), *Jennie – Lady Randolph Churchill* (Thames 1975, as Disraeli), *Play for Today – Love Letters on Blue Paper* (BBC 1976) and *The Feathered Serpent* (Thames 1976, 1978, as Nasca the High Priest). He also made three return visits to *Doctor Who* in special reunion stories, *The Three Doctors* (1972/73), *The Five Doctors* (1983) and *The Two Doctors* (1985). It is a real tribute to Troughton's skill that even some sixteen years after his last regular appearance in *Doctor Who* he was still able to recapture his familiar characterisation of the second Doctor.

In April 1983, shortly after *The Five Doctors* was recorded, a huge BBC Enterprises-organised convention was held at Longleat House, Warminster, Wiltshire, to celebrate *Doctor Who*'s twentieth anniversary. Much to the delight of the thousands of fans in attendance, Troughton was for once persuaded to appear, and in many ways this experience changed his outlook on such events. Following a further appearance in October 1983 at 'Doctor Who – The Developing Art', a weekend of screenings and interviews organised by the National Film Theatre in London, he became a regular guest on the US convention circuit. His participation in British events remained rare, however. 'I don't like going to conventions in this country,' he explained in 1985, 'because I don't want to become too associated with *Who* again. In the States that doesn't matter.' In fact, he made only one appearance at a fan-organised British conven-

tion, the *Doctor Who* Appreciation Society's annual PanoptiCon, in Brighton in 1985.

Troughton's last film work came in 1978 on the Children's Film Foundation production *A Hitch in Time* in which he played a time travelling inventor named Professor Wagstaffe, a character with a certain similarity to the Doctor. However, he continued to take on numerous TV roles right up until the end of his life. Some of his most acclaimed work of this period was in *The Box of Delights* (BBC 1984, starring role), *Swallows and Amazons* (BBC 1984), *Long Term Memory* (BBC 1985, starring role), *The Two of Us* (LWT 1986, semiregular), *Yesterday's Dream* (Central 1987, semiregular) and *Knights of God* (TVS 1987, semiregular).

Patrick Troughton died on 28 March 1987, just three days after his 67th birthday, having suffered a heart attack in his hotel room during a convention in Columbus, Georgia, USA, at which he was a guest. 'One of the last things he said to me,' remembers actor Anthony Ainley, who also attended, 'was "Do you think these *Star Trek* actors will mind if I ask them for their autographs for one of my grandchildren?" which was rather sweet. His death was a terrible shock. I had dined with him on the Thursday night and the Friday night, and on the Saturday morning at breakfast I was told he was dead. We had two days to go at the convention. People were visibly moved and some were weeping. It was a big shock.'

CHAPTER NINE

The Second Doctor: A New Broom

Who is the Doctor? This question has been asked many, many times, sometimes on screen by way of making the pun 'Doctor who?', sometimes more seriously by researchers and fans probing the programme's depths. But never was it more pertinent than when the Doctor regenerated for the first time.

One of the most important aspects of the regeneration is that it reinforced and heightened the mystery surrounding the Doctor. The person whom we thought we knew and whose actions we thought we could predict became a stranger with new mannerisms and uncertain lineage. We now had proof positive that he wasn't human.

The Power of the Daleks introduced us to someone we were not even sure was the Doctor, even though we, together with his companions Ben and Polly, had witnessed the dramatic change in his appearance.

Following the regeneration, Ben and Polly find slumped on the TARDIS floor an unfamiliar figure wearing the Doctor's cloak. Underneath the cloak, he wears different clothes; he is smaller in stature and the Doctor's large, blue-stoned ring no longer fits his finger. Although Polly is prepared reluctantly to accept that this is the Doctor in a different body, Ben remains highly sceptical, suspecting that an imposter has infiltrated the ship. Their dilemma is made no easier by the Doctor himself:

DOCTOR (*rummaging through a trunk*): The Doctor was a great collector, wasn't he?

POLLY: But you're the Doctor!

DOCTOR: Oh, I don't look like him.

BEN: Who are we?

DOCTOR: Don't you know?

And later:

DOCTOR: The Doctor kept a diary, didn't he?

POLLY: Yes...

DOCTOR: Thought so. I wonder where... I wonder where...

◀ **The second Doctor with his 500-year diary.** *The Power of the Daleks.*

RECORDER TUNES

Although the second Doctor is famed for his blue-and-white striped recorder, he actually plays only three recognisable tunes on it during his first story. The recorder is fished out of a large trunk by the Doctor in episode one of **The Power of the Daleks***, and the first tune – an untitled piece created by Troughton himself – comes shortly after this. Episodes two and six see him playing a snatch from* **'Mr Sludge the Snail'** *by Jenyth Worseley, and episode three contains* **'Can You Sew Cushions?'***, a traditional tune.*

Jamie and the Doctor. ▲
The Invasion.

The Doctor, Ben and Polly ▶
in the Vulcan colony. *The
Power of the Daleks.*

The Doctor in *The Mind* ▲
Robber.

One of the earliest ▶
publicity stills of the second
Doctor. *The Power of the
Daleks.*

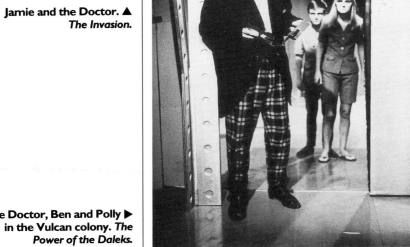

Accustomed to the first Doctor's fastidious operation of the TARDIS, Ben and Polly are quite taken aback when the newcomer, seemingly absorbed by his 500-Year Diary, suddenly announces that it is time to explore outside and, without looking, opens the doors. In response to his companions' cries of warning that they don't know where they have landed or whether or

not it is safe, the Doctor assures them that it is. He had already made sure; Ben and Polly just hadn't seen him do it. This is a fine early example of the second Doctor's modus operandi.

Initially, this new Doctor is characterised by his unpredictability and his resorting to foolery when faced with a difficult situation. At moments of stress, he often delves into his pocket and takes out a recorder, liberated from the TARDIS's storage trunk in his debut episode, proceeding to play a jaunty tune on it – and even, on occasion, dancing a little jig. However, doubts as to his credentials are quickly dispelled during the course of *The Power of the Daleks* as he and his companions get caught up in their latest adventure, battling to defeat a group of Daleks in their attempt to take over a human colony on the planet Vulcan. He demonstrates not only his predecessor's insatiable curiosity but also the same moral values. Ben and Polly are soon fully convinced that the stranger they met in the first episode is indeed the Doctor.

This new Doctor likes to create a smokescreen so that no one realises exactly what he is up to. His unassuming, sometimes clown-like behaviour keeps his adversaries – and sometimes even his allies – off balance. He deliberately leads people to underestimate his capabilities and intellect but he has a keen analytical mind and knows exactly what he is doing. This is well illustrated by a scene at the end of *The Power of the Daleks* when he appears somewhat bewildered and cowed at having 'accidentally' wiped out the colony's power supply while immobilising the Daleks. 'Did I do all that?' he innocently asks before whisking Ben and Polly back to the TARDIS. To Polly's later assertion that he did know what he was doing, his response is merely a wry grin and a chirpy tune picked out on his recorder.

Sometimes his deceptions take more elaborate forms. Particularly in his early stories, this Doctor proves himself a master of disguise and impersonation. *The Highlanders*, for instance, sees him adopting the guise of a German physician, Doctor von Wer, and dressing up as a washerwoman and as a Redcoat soldier. Similarly, in *The Underwater Menace* he passes himself off as a trader in the Atlantean market place. It is in *The Enemy of the World*, however, that the ultimate impersonation occurs: throughout this tale of intrigue and power plays, the Doctor manages to stay one step ahead of everyone else by exploiting his remarkable physical similarity to the villain Salamander.

In later adventures he makes less frequent use of this kind of subterfuge. He also becomes gradually less outlandish, both in tactics and in appearance. However, he still delights in confusing his opponents – deliberately failing a simple intelligence test set by the warlike Dominators, for example – and makes no attempt to correct others' misconceptions of him or of his actions.

Whereas the first Doctor tended to get caught up in situations, often against his wishes, the second favours a more interventionist role, making it his business to combat the various evils he encounters. As he says in *The Moonbase* : 'There are some corners of the universe which have bred the most terrible things. Things which act against everything that we believe in. They must be fought.'

Even so, the measures he takes are usually indirect rather than direct. He likes to catalyse activity, not to lead it. In *The Moonbase*, for example, he investigates the cause of a mysterious 'plague' which has stricken the human crew of a lunar base set up to help control Earth's weather, and discovers that there is poison in the sugar supply. Later, he deduces that the Gravitron – the weather-control device – could be used as a weapon to thwart a force of attacking Cybermen. However, having provided these answers, he then leaves it largely up to the humans to act upon them and in fact does very little which the humans could not have done for themselves, had they the initiative. It takes his intervention to prompt them into action. The second Doctor is a manipulator, using others without their realising it to gain the results he wants.

This method is well illustrated by events in *The Tomb of the Cybermen*. Here, having encountered an archaeological expedition excavating the Cybermen's tomb on the planet Telos, the Doctor again takes a back seat. However, despite his warnings to the archaeologists to be careful, it is clear that he is just as interested as they are in the tomb and its contents.

When the archaeologists gain access to the upper area of the tomb, their leader Professor Parry takes a cursory glance around and announces that the only door, apart from the one through which they have just entered, is a massive sealed hatchway leading to a lower level. The Doctor, however, contradicts him, explaining that there are two other exits, currently closed, which are operated from a control console. Manipulating some switches, he proves his point by causing the hidden doors to slide open. Kleig – another expedition member, who has his own reasons for wanting to discover the entombed Cybermen – is immediately suspicious, wondering how the Doctor knew about the controls. The Doctor retorts that he used his own special technique: 'Keeping my eyes open and my mouth shut!'

The second Doctor's powers of observation are no less acute than his predecessor's. In *The Ice Warriors*, when Leader Clent, the commander of a scientific base charged with using an ioniser device to resist the advancing glaciers of a new ice

The second Doctor and Thonmi (David Spenser) in the Tibetan monastery. *The Abominable Snowmen.*

Dr Who is our modern phoenix. At the end of nine hundred years, a strange psychological storm rejuvenated his form, changing his character in many ways. Overwhelmed by this strange force, he became a younger, indeed almost a new personality.

Our new Dr Who is more 'with it'; he is more 'switched on', more in tune with the Twentieth Century. There are, of course, still traces of his old personality and, characteristically he still wears the same clothes, which are a trifle baggy on his new figure.

He doesn't confide quite so much in his companions as he was wont to do. He's more introspective too, not quite so obvious as his old pre-change self. Much more devious in his thoughts and actions, he is also more logical and matter-of-fact.

In his new image he is inclined to be whimsical and, like Pan of old, he has a small musical pipe on which he tootles a merry tune now and again. It helps him to think and get his ideas straight. The ideas are, like the man, new, and one big change is that now he is more inclined to shape events to suit his own purpose rather than merely to let events overtake him.

He has all the scientific know-how of his old self. But he is more the man of action now. He will plunge into violent action like a twenty-year-old and he makes great use of his very great knowledge of human and alien nature. Sharp witted as ever, he cannot easily be fooled. He's smart and he knows it. He is just as irritable and touchy as ever, but he's faster on the uptake and very rarely taken by surprise.

Dr Who before rejuvenation was vague and absent-minded, but the now youthful doctor catches on more quickly, is more direct and impulsive and doesn't rely so much on inspiration - he shapes his own destiny... Now he's more closely involved in human affairs, even more curious about modern developments, and always ready and eager to reform or make trouble for any individuals he thinks are on the wrong wavelength.

From: **The Dr Who Annual** *published 1967. Author unknown.*

The Doctor with his 500- ▲ year diary. *The Power of the Daleks.*

The Doctor in the ioniser ▲ control room. *The Ice Warriors.*

age, gives him just forty-five seconds to deduce the cause of the global cooling and identify the correct solution, the Doctor passes the test with flying colours!

Clent is just one of a number of human establishment figures with whom the second Doctor comes into contact in his travels. Others include Hensell, Governor of the Vulcan colony in *The Power of the Daleks* ; the Commandant of Gatwick Airport in *The Faceless Ones* ; Robson, controller of a Euro-gas drilling operation in *Fury from the Deep* ; and Radnor, in charge of the T-mat travel system in *The Seeds of Death*. To characters such as these, who pride themselves on their well-ordered operations, the sudden arrival of a scruffy little stranger is cause for suspicion, if not down-right hostility – particularly if it happens to coincide, as it so often does, with the onset of some crisis or other. Although the Doctor is usually able to win them over in the end, if only by his force of personality and his obviously superior knowledge, they are frequently left be-wildered and exasperated by his unconventional methods, anarchic behaviour and conspicuous disregard for authority. He even seems to take a mischievous glee in running rings around them!

Even the Doctor's own companions are some-times left completely in the dark about his plans. Perhaps the most notable instance of this is in *The Evil of the Daleks*, when he pretends to collaborate with the Daleks in their use of his friend Jamie as a guinea-pig in an experiment to discover the 'human factor' – that elusive quality which has always enabled humanity to triumph over them in the past. So convincing is the Doctor's act – indicating that he does, perhaps, have a darker side to his nature – that even Jamie comes to suspect that he really has allied himself with the Daleks. It is only later, when he has succeeded in turning the Daleks' scheme against them, that the Doctor's true motives become clear.

For the most part this Doctor has a very good relationship with his companions. Less paternal-istic than his predecessor, he encourages them to take decisions and work things out for them-selves, rarely giving direct answers to their ques-tions. He even tolerates their occasional teasing, such as when Zoe chides him over his initial failure of an intelligence test in *The Krotons*.

A good example of his closeness to his com-panions can be seen in episode three of *The Tomb of the Cybermen*. When everyone settles down for the night in the main control room of the tomb, Victoria, the young orphan whom he and Jamie have recently befriended, finds herself unable to sleep, and he crosses to talk to her:

DOCTOR: Are you happy with us, Victoria?

VICTORIA: Yes I am. At least I would be if my father were here.

DOCTOR: Yes I know, I know.

VICTORIA: I wonder what he would have thought if he could see me now.

DOCTOR: You miss him very much, don't you?

VICTORIA: It's only when I close my eyes. I can still see him standing there, before those horrible Dalek creatures came to the house. He was a very kind man. I shall never forget him... never.

DOCTOR: No, of course you won't, but, you know, the memory of him won't always be a sad one.

VICTORIA: I think it will. You can't under-stand, being so ancient.

DOCTOR: Eh?

VICTORIA: I mean old.

DOCTOR: Oh!

VICTORIA: You probably can't remember your family.

DOCTOR: Oh yes I can, when I want to. And that's the point really; I have to really want to, to bring them in front of my eyes – the rest of the time they . . . they sleep in my mind and I forget. And so will you. (*Victoria looks doubtful*) Oh yes you will. You'll find there's so much else to think about, to remember. Our lives are different to . . . anybody else's, that's the exciting thing! Nobody in the Uni-verse can do what we're doing . . .

This is the only time that the Doctor ever mentions any family other than his grand-daugh-ter Susan, and the fact that he confides in Victoria is indicative of the strength of his affection for her. Certainly when she decides to part company with him, staying with the Harris family on Earth following the defeat of a parasitic weed creature in *Fury from the Deep*, he is visibly upset. As Jamie mopes over her departure, not caring where the TARDIS takes them next, the Doctor's forthright comment – 'I was fond of her too, you know, Jamie' – followed by his immediate activation of the controls, speaks volumes about his feelings on the matter.

Indeed, if the first Doctor was sometimes able to hide his true feelings with a show of bluster, the second is not. His expressive features bear wit-ness to a full range of emotions, through outrage

▲ Patrick Troughton poses for a publicity photograph in his original costume.

▲ The Doctor plays a tune on his recorder. *The Power of the Daleks.*

◄ The newly regenerated Doctor in the TARDIS. *The Power of the Daleks.*

Jamie, Zoe and the ▲
Doctor. *The War Games.*

The Doctor, Jamie and ▲
Zoe. *The Space Pirates.*

The Evil of the Daleks. ▲

to humility, from a vague uneasiness that something is wrong to a quiet satisfaction when everything goes right. When the beautiful Madeleine Issigri kisses him goodbye at the end of *The Space Pirates*, his face is a picture of bemusement. His tendency to slip quietly away at the end of an adventure seems to be motivated as much by his embarrassment at sentimental farewells as by his desire to avoid awkward questions. When his plans come to fruition, he prefers to leave others to do the celebrating for him.

Daleks, Cybermen, Yeti, Ice Warriors, Quarks and Krotons: all these foes and more the second Doctor faces during the course of his travels. Invariably he helps the oppressed to fight back against their oppressors, supplying solutions when needed and keeping silent when not.

In *The War Games* he encounters the Aliens, a race of beings who have abducted groups of soldiers from various wars throughout Earth's history in an attempt to create the ultimate army. Although he eventually foils this grandiose scheme, the Doctor is faced with the seemingly insurmountable problem of returning to their rightful times and places all the human soldiers left stranded in the Aliens' war zones. To solve this crisis, he is forced to take an unprecedented step: he calls on the help of his own people, the Time Lords. At last a little of the mystery surrounding his background is dispelled as he tells Jamie and Zoe why he first embarked on his travels:

DOCTOR: I was bored!

ZOE: What do you mean, you were bored?

DOCTOR: Well, the Time Lords are an immensely civilised race. We can control our own environment; we can live forever, barring accidents; and we have the secret of space-time travel.

JAMIE: Well, what's so wrong in all that?

DOCTOR: Well, we hardly ever use our great powers. We consent simply to observe and gather knowledge!

ZOE: And that wasn't enough for you?

DOCTOR: No, of course not. With a whole galaxy to explore? Millions of planets? Aeons of time? Countless civilisations to meet?

JAMIE: Well, why do they object to you doing all that?

DOCTOR: Well, it is a fact, Jamie, that I do tend to get involved in things...

The Doctor and Zoe on Beacon Alpha-4. *The Space Pirates.*

Once all the humans have been returned home and the Aliens' evil War Lord brought to justice, the Doctor is himself placed on trial before three high-ranking Time Lords, charged with repeatedly breaking his race's most important law of non-interference in the affairs of other planets. He mounts an eloquent defence, describing the many injustices he has had to combat and using a thought channel to display pictures of his most monstrous adversaries:

DOCTOR: All these evils I have fought, while you have done nothing but observe. True, I am guilty of interference, just as you are guilty of failing to use your great powers to help those in need!

This impassioned plea has some effect as the Time Lords accept that there is evil in the universe which must be fought and that the Doctor still has a role to play in that fight. However, they have no intention of setting him free. Having already returned Jamie and Zoe to their respective points of origin, they sentence him to a period of exile on the planet Earth in the twentieth century, during which time the secret of the TARDIS will be taken from him. And in preparation for his exile he must undergo a further change of appearance...

The Doctor's travels have, for the time being at least, come to an end.

CHAPTER TEN

Season Four: Out with the Old and In with the New

When *Doctor Who*'s fourth season got underway, at 5:50 pm on Saturday 10 September 1966, viewers could scarcely have suspected the major development which lay in store in just a few weeks' time with the transition from William Hartnell to Patrick Troughton.

The opening story of the season, *The Smugglers*, was in fact made at the end of the third production block, immediately after *The War Machines*. Its author, Brian Hayles, had been asked by story editor Gerry Davis to come up with an idea for an historical adventure and had decided that the seventeenth century would make a good setting. (Shortly afterwards he submitted a Second World War storyline entitled *The Nazis*, but this was rejected.) Davis agreed that smuggling would be a suitable theme to explore as this was in line with his desire for the series' historical stories to be based on identifiable, romantic areas of fiction – in this case, Russell Thorndike's *Doctor Syn* books.

To the mutual disbelief of newcomers Polly and Ben, the TARDIS arrives on the coast of seventeenth-century Cornwall. Here, pirates led by Captain Samuel Pike are searching for a hidden treasure while a smuggling ring masterminded by the local Squire is trying to offload contraband. The Doctor is kidnapped by Pike's men after inadvertently learning from churchwarden Joseph Longfoot, who is later murdered, a cryptic rhyme which holds the key to the treasure's whereabouts. Although he manages to escape, the Doctor is eventually forced to tell Pike the

rhyme's meaning – it refers to names on tombstones in the church crypt – and the treasure is uncovered. At this point the militia arrive, having been summoned by Revenue Officer Josiah Blake. A fight ensues in which Pike and many of his men are killed and the rest taken prisoner. The Doctor and his companions, meanwhile, slip back to the TARDIS.

The Smugglers was the first *Doctor Who* story for which the director and crew spent a period away from London on a location shoot – a week was spent in Cornwall. However, despite the impressive look of the production, this did nothing to halt a recent marked decline in the series' ratings, which fell to an average of 4.48 million viewers per episode – the lowest achieved by any Hartnell story – and an average television chart placing of 95th – again, the lowest of the Hartnell era.

The first Doctor, Ben (Michael Craze) and Polly (Anneke Wills). *The Smugglers.*

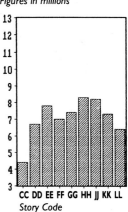

SEASON FOUR

CODE	TITLE
CC	**THE SMUGGLERS**
DD	**THE TENTH PLANET**
EE	**THE POWER OF THE DALEKS**
FF	**THE HIGHLANDERS**
GG	**THE UNDERWATER MENACE**
HH	**THE MOONBASE**
JJ	**THE MACRA TERROR**
KK	**THE FACELESS ONES**
LL	**THE EVIL OF THE DALEKS**

RATINGS

Figures in millions

Story Code: CC DD EE FF GG HH JJ KK LL

DOCTOR'S DEPARTURE

Although William Hartnell's departure from **Doctor Who** *was officially announced in August 1966, a newspaper report from December 1965 suggests that he had considered bowing out earlier. The short report appeared in* **The Manchester Evening News** *on 16 December saying that Hartnell was all set to quit. It went on to quote Hartnell as saying that he thought the programme could continue for another two years without him.*

PIPE MUSIC

The bagpipes heard at the start of every episode of **The Highlanders** *were played by Seumas MacNeill. The tune was entitled* **Pibroch.**

ATLANTEAN CHANT

The eerie atmospheric 'chant' heard in the temple of Amdo in Atlantis during **The Underwater Menace** *was in fact provided by the Cliff Adam Singers conducted by composer Dudley Simpson, who provided an electric organ accompaniment.*

SEASON FOUR:
EVENTS OF 10 SEPTEMBER 1966 – 1 JULY 1967

More US troops are sent to Vietnam as the war grows increasingly unpopular in the United States.

Francis Chichester completes his around-the-world solo yacht voyage.

Model Twiggy becomes the face of the 1960s.

The six-day war between Israel and Egypt is fought.

Tom (Mike Lucas), Jacob Kewper (David Blake Kelly) and the Squire (Paul Whitsun-Jones) with Polly and an injured Ben. *The Smugglers.*

Robert Jewell and John Scott-Martin are helped into Dalek casings. *The Power of the Daleks.*

Fortunately, this trend was reversed by the next story, *The Tenth Planet*, which introduced a popular new race of monsters devised by Gerry Davis and Kit Pedler as a potential replacement for the Daleks. Pedler's initial idea had been for a group of Star Monks inhabiting a world which appears to be Earth's twin – the tenth planet of the title. However, this idea had been modified in discussions with Davis to incorporate, in place of the Star Monks, a new threat which personified one of Pedler's own phobias – that of dehumanising medicine.

Pedler foresaw a time when replacing limbs and organs would become as commonplace as changing a shirt. As he told *Radio Times* in 1968: 'I was talking to my wife – she's a doctor too – in the garden. We were discussing spare-part surgery and conceived the idea of someone with so many mechanical replacements that he didn't know whether he was a human or a machine.'

'At the time,' he later wrote, 'I was obsessed as a scientist with the differences and similarities between the human brain and advanced computing machines, and I was thinking that although I could easily imagine a logical machine reasoning to itself and manipulating events outside it, by no stretch of the imagination could I visualise a machine producing a poem by Dylan Thomas. And so the Cybermen were born.'

The storyline for *The Tenth Planet* was developed jointly by Pedler and Davis. However, in view of Pedler's inexperience as a writer, Davis wrote most of the script. Davis received no writer's credit on the first two episodes because of the BBC's restrictions on story editors commissioning their own work, but his name did appear along with Pedler's on the last two as Pedler had to go into hospital while they were being written and this was judged a special case.

The TARDIS materialises in December 1986 at the entrance to a South Pole Space Tracking Station under the command of General Cutler. The scientists there are experiencing problems in controlling the return to Earth of a manned space capsule, and the Doctor realises that this is due to the gravitational pull of another planet which has entered the solar system and is now heading for Earth. His words are borne out when the base is invaded by a force of alien Cybermen.

The Cybermen's world, Mondas, is draining energy from ours, and the situation will soon become critical. Although Ben and Cutler manage to destroy the first wave of attackers, the base is then overrun by a second. However, one of the scientists, Barclay, suddenly realises that the invaders are susceptible to radioactivity, and using hand-held uranium rods, Ben and a group of the scientists are able to hold off and kill a number of

Director Christopher Barry discusses a scene with Patrick Troughton. *The Power of the Daleks.*

Cybermen. At the story's climax, Mondas disintegrates due to absorbing too much energy, and all the remaining Cybermen collapse and die, having been totally dependent on their planet.

The Cybermen were quickly taken to heart by the viewing public and it was not long before they were second in popularity only to the Daleks. Gerry Davis and Kit Pedler had succeeded in their aim of creating a new, memorable foe for the Doctor.

The first episode of *The Tenth Planet* went into the studio on 17 September 1966, launching *Doctor Who*'s fourth production block. For the whole of this block, the programme would be recorded on a Saturday rather than a Friday. A two-week gap followed the making of the fourth episode of *The Tenth Planet* and on 22 October 1966 Patrick Troughton stepped before the cameras to begin his run as the series' star.

After the regeneration scene, *The Power of the Daleks* saw the Doctor, Polly and Ben arriving on the Earth colony planet Vulcan for the start of a new adventure. The Doctor witnesses a murder and, investigating the body, discovers a pass badge which allows him unrestricted access to the colony. It transpires that the dead man was an Earth Examiner who had been secretly summoned by Deputy Governor Quinn to investigate the activities of a group of rebels, a problem regarded as insignificant by Governor Hensell. A scientist, Lesterson, has meanwhile discovered a

crashed space capsule containing inert Daleks which he is now in the process of reactivating. A horrified Doctor tries to warn of the consequences but is ignored when the Daleks claim to be the colonists' servants.

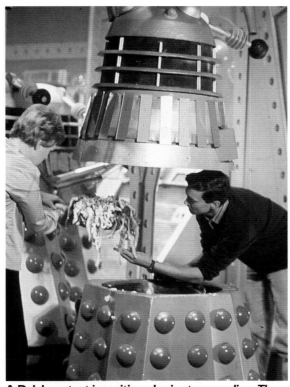

A Dalek mutant is positioned prior to recording. *The Power of the Daleks.*

PRODUCTION ROUTINE

*By the time of season four, the venue for **Doctor Who**'s weekly rehearsal period had changed to St Helen's Hall, St Helen's Gardens, London W10 – a church hall not far from Television Centre. All season four episodes up to and including part three of **The Moonbase** were recorded in Studio 1 at Riverside. The remainder were taped in Studio D at Lime Grove. The basic routine of rehearsal and recording was the same as for previous seasons, although there was no longer any particular day or time fixed for the three- or four-hour editing session which was needed to complete each episode: it would take place on either the Sunday, the Monday, the Tuesday or the Wednesday following recording, at whatever time of day an editing suite happened to be available. For episode four of **The Macra Terror**, a mobile Ampex editing unit was used.*

ELWYN JONES
WRITER

*Born in 1923, Elwyn Jones had an extremely distinguished TV career as a writer, script editor and producer. His most notable achievement was as prime mover behind and executive producer of the seminal BBC police series **Z Cars** and its **Softly, Softly** and other spin-offs. He also served the BBC as Head of Documentary Drama and, subsequently, as Head of Series. He died on 19 May 1982.*

MALCOLM HULKE
WRITER

*Malcolm Hulke did not begin writing professionally until he was in his thirties, and much of his work was in advancing the cause of television writing, through his talks and lectures and in particular his book **Writing For Television in the '70s**. Other books included **Cassell's Parliamentary Directory** and **The Encyclopedia of Alternative Medicine and Self Help**. For TV he wrote episodes of **Danger Man**, **Ghost Squad**, **Gideon's Way** and **The Protectors**. He was also script editor of **Crossroads** for many years, and novelised several plots from that series. His last **Doctor Who** script was **Invasion of the Dinosaurs** and his last novelisation was **The War Games**, completed just before his death on 6 July 1979.*

An original Cyberman on the set at Ealing. *The Tenth Planet.*

As the rebels grow in strength, their operations being covertly led by Head of Security Bragen, the Daleks take advantage of the colonists' naive trust to establish a reproduction plant, on a conveyor belt system, with which to increase their numbers. Their aim is total extermination of the humans. The Doctor eventually wins the day by turning the colony's power source against the Daleks, causing their destruction. The defeat of the Daleks, with whom Bragen and the rebels had allied themselves, gives Quinn an opportunity to re-establish control of the colony, Hensell having been killed earlier. The Doctor and his friends, meanwhile, slip back to the TARDIS.

The story's writer, David Whitaker, had originally submitted to Donald Tosh a storyline entitled *The New Armada*, which Gerry Davis had rejected when it was passed on to him, saying in a letter of 17 January 1966 – very shortly after he joined the series – that he didn't feel it was quite in line with the direction set down for *Doctor Who*

by the Head of Serials: 'We are looking for strong, simple stories. This one, though very ingenious, is rather complex with too many characters and sub-plots. To simplify it, as it stands, would reduce the plot to the point when it would be virtually a new creation.' However, Davis had gone on to write that he would like to meet up with Whitaker to talk over ideas, and had invited him to bring in a number of storylines in embryo form. It was out of these discussions that *The Destiny of Doctor Who*, as it was then called, was born, and was commissioned on 22 July 1966.

The Power of the Daleks was in some respects a very similar story to *The Tenth Planet*. In both cases, an isolated community inhabited by a small group of humans and commanded by a strong-willed but misguided authority figure is attacked and infiltrated by a race of terrifying alien monsters. These central story elements, which made for tense, claustrophobic and often very frightening situations, were later adopted by the production team as the basis of a successful formula which would be used time and again during seasons four and five. As Gerry Davis later explained, the justification for this was not only artistic but also monetary: 'My basic premise for *Doctor Who* stories in that era of minuscule budgets was to forgo the usual dozen tatty sets in favour of one major set around which we could concentrate the entire budget. This made a much more exciting and convincing central location for the drama.'

Most of the stories which took this standard form were sufficiently different in other respects to ensure that the similarity of their basic construction was not obvious. However, the second Cyberman adventure, *The Moonbase*, adhered so closely to the formula established in *The Tenth Planet* that it was all but a rewrite of the earlier story.

This time the TARDIS arrives not in the Antarctic but on the Moon, where a weather-control station under the command of a man named Hobson is in the grip of a plague epidemic – in reality the result of an alien poison planted by the Cybermen. Polly realises that as the Cybermen's chest units are made of some sort of plastic they must be vulnerable to attack by solvents. This is indeed the case, and all the Cybermen on the base are destroyed with a cocktail of chemicals sprayed at them from fire extinguishers. A second wave of Cybermen advances across the lunar surface but, prompted by the Doctor, Hobson uses the base's gravity-generating weather-control device to send them flying off into space.

Like *The Tenth Planet*, *The Moonbase* (at first called *The Return of the Cybermen*) was written as a joint effort between Kit Pedler and Gerry

Davis. Davis again wrote the lion's share of the script, but on this occasion received no on-screen credit for it.

The Cybermen of *The Moonbase* were somewhat different in appearance from those seen in *The Tenth Planet*. As the story's director, Morris Barry, remembers, he was given no clues as to what they should be like – his only reference point was the script: 'All I think I knew was that Cybermen actors had to be well over six foot two tall as a minimum – six foot four was fine – which made casting a bit of a problem. Once we had the actors, then their boots were blocked up by about four or six inches, which made them about six foot eight. On top were the helmets which made them very nearly seven foot tall. They were huge, really horrific.'

Eleven new Cyberman costumes were made for the story, the idea being to improve upon the originals in terms both of visual impact and of comfort for the actors. Gone were *The Tenth Planet*'s bulky constructions which had been so hot and cumbersome that actors had collapsed on set, and in their place came streamlined silver body-suits with much smaller chest units and lightweight fibreglass helmets.

An added touch was that each Cyberman had, covering its mouth on the inside of the helmet, a small metal plate, operated by the actor, which flipped open whenever it started to speak and closed again afterwards. This was helpful in indicating to the viewer which Cyberman was supposed to be talking, a function fulfilled by the

flashing lights on either side of a Dalek's dome, and also harked back to the technique used in *The Tenth Planet* where the actor would simply open his mouth in an 'O' shape and make no other lip movements.

In both stories, the voices themselves were provided not by the actors inside the Cyberman costumes but by specialist voice artists – Roy Skelton and Peter Hawkins on *The Tenth Planet*, Peter Hawkins alone on *The Moonbase* – sitting in another part of the studio and watching a monitor screen to synchronise the dialogue to the action. Whereas in *The Tenth Planet* the Cybermen had spoken in a disjointed singsong drawl, in *The Moonbase* a grating electronic monotone was

▲ Production assistant Edwina Verner and director Derek Martinus assist a Cyberman. *The Tenth Planet*.

◄ Two armed Daleks outside the capsule in which they were found. *The Power of the Daleks*.

The Doctor takes a stroll through the mercury swamp on Vulcan. *The Power of the Daleks*.

▲ Alexandra Tynan's original design sketch for a Cyberman from *The Tenth Planet*.

Algernon ffinch (Michael ▲
Elwyn). *The Highlanders.*

The Daleks in Lesterson's ▲
laboratory. *The Power of the
Daleks.*

Ben, Polly, Jamie and the ▲
Doctor on the Moon's
surface set at Ealing. *The
Moonbase.*

The Cybermen prepare to ▶
attack the lunar base. *The
Moonbase.*

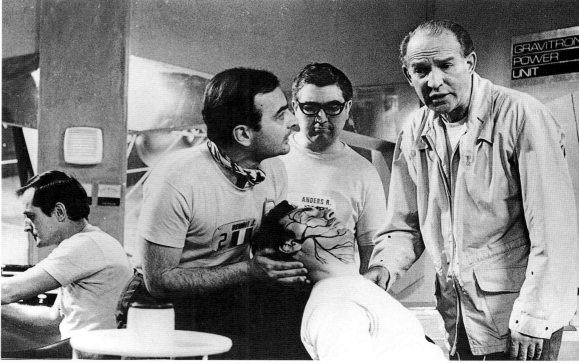

Benoit (Andre Maranne), Bob (Edward Phillips) and Hobson (Patrick Barr) with a victim of the 'plague'. *The Moonbase.*

adopted. As Hawkins recalls, this latter effect was achieved with the aid of a specially designed vibrating palate device placed inside his mouth: 'It was worked by a small buzzer powered by a battery pack. The trick was to mouth the words without speaking them. The mouth cavity modu-lated the buzzing into words. It wasn't much fun wandering around with damp leads hanging out of my mouth. I wasn't a pretty sight.'

After *The Moonbase* came *The Macra Terror*, another adventure following the same basic plotline. In this case the isolated community is a human colony which appears to be a happy place run along the lines of an enormous holiday camp but which has in fact been infiltrated and taken over by a race of giant crab-like creatures – the Macra. The brainwashed inhabitants are forced to mine a gas which is toxic to themselves but vital for their oppressors' survival. At one point Ben also comes under the Macra's malign influence and turns against his friends. However, he eventually regains his senses and under the Doctor's guidance destroys the gas-pumping equipment, killing the Macra and restoring the colony's freedom.

Writer Ian Stuart Black developed *The Macra Terror* out of the idea that different forms of life need different environments in which to survive. He had originally intended that the Macra would be 'insect men', although the story's work-ing title was, confusingly, *The Spidermen*, but this was vetoed by the production team.

With its central premise of an indoctrinated population slavishly repeating cheery jingles and mindless slogans and presided over by a figure-head Controller, Black's plot was reminiscent of George Orwell's *1984*. The sense of hidden menace was further enhanced by the fact that

Ben, the Doctor and Polly discover a cannon. *The Highlanders.*

The travellers arrive in Scotland in 1746. *The Highlanders.*

The Doctor exchanges his stovepipe hat for a tam o' shanter. *The Highlanders.*

much of the story was set at night, with the slavering Macra emerging out of the gloom and smoke to a pulsing, throbbing soundtrack, overlaid with slurping and sucking noises. The result was highly effective.

In fact, only one Macra prop was built, but with the use of ingenious camera angles and a number of trick effects director John Davies was able to create the impression that there were many. To give the prop the necessary mobility it was placed on the rear platform of a van. Its operator, Robert Jewell, stood inside it and moved the antennae, the claws and the mandibles.

The Macra Terror also heralded, for the first time since the series began, a new set of opening title graphics. This made use of the same howl-around effect as the original but was rather more complex. Again it was the work of graphic designer Bernard Lodge, who explains how it was made:

'An interesting thing happened while we were recording all the abstract images for the first set of titles. One of the production assistants put his face in front of the camera and this created an amazing effect: the image of his face tore away and distorted into feedback. I showed this to Verity Lambert at the time and said that we ought to use it, but she felt it was too horrible.

'A few years later, when we came to do the Patrick Troughton one, the producer Innes Lloyd asked for something along the same lines but different, so – with that earlier discovery in mind – I suggested that we incorporate a photograph of Patrick Troughton.

'I wondered about the shapes which came up on the screen; how the lettering generated its own feedback and how the photograph of Troughton would similarly generate feedback. I reasoned that using a simple abstract pattern would produce an effect which was predictable and, to a degree, controllable. I put up a caption card with some concentric squares on it and controlled the image so that we got something which was semi-rigid and semi-amorphous.

'The part where Troughton's face disappears looks electronic but was in fact done using a film wipe. This effect entails shooting a sequence where you start out with a black frame and then do something which gradually turns it into a white one: you print it up both as a negative and as a complementary positive, then these are used to print up the two halves of your wipe. The outgoing scene is gradually obliterated as the high contrast goes to black and the incoming one in a complementary way is gradually revealed. In this case, the sequence we shot was of a rough surface made out of ordinary white polystyrene, all crunched up. We lit it with a very hard side-light so that at a certain angle it gave just a white overexposed screen but then, as the polystyrene was slowly rotated, it sent out long shadows until they took over and the whole screen went black. You can in fact see a kind of gritty breaking-up in the finished sequence.'

▲ **Three of Alexandra Tynan's original costume designs for** *The Underwater Menace.* **From top: a fish person, an Atlantean girl, and an Atlantean man.**

PETER BRYANT
SCRIPT EDITOR/ PRODUCER

*Peter Bryant started out as an actor and, in the fifties, was one of the stars of the BBC soap opera **The Grove Family**. Later he took a temporary job as an announcer for BBC Radio, and this led to a permanent appointment. He also began to write radio scripts as a sideline. On the strength of this, and because he had a good theatrical background, he was transferred to the Radio Drama Department, where he worked as a script editor. Eventually he became head of the whole Drama Script Unit, as well as producing and directing. After about seven years he decided he would like to cross over to TV. He approached Head of Serials Shaun Sutton and was given an initial six-month attachment, assigned to work alongside departing story editor Gerry Davis on **Doctor Who**. He went on to become both script editor and producer of the series. After leaving the BBC in the early seventies he was involved in independent productions ranging from theatrical shows to TV commercials. He now works primarily as a literary agent.*

GEOFFREY ORME
WRITER

*Geoffrey Orme was already an established writer when he contributed **The Underwater Menace** to **Doctor Who**. He had begun his career in 1935 and worked mainly on comedy and thriller films until the sixties. These included **The Lost Load, Judgement Deferred, Miss Robin Hood, Devil on Horseback** and **Orders are Orders**. His TV work included **Ivanhoe, The Avengers** and **No Hiding Place**. He died in 1978.*

The Doctor's face as it ▲ appeared in the new title sequence.

The Laird (Donald Bissett), Jamie, the Doctor, Ben, Solicitor Grey (David Garth), the Sergeant (Peter Welch) and Perkins (Sydney Arnold). *The Highlanders.*

To accompany the new graphics, a rearranged version of the theme music was created by the Radiophonic Workshop. This was very similar to the original but had a somewhat quicker tempo and more overlaid sound effects.

With this change of title graphics and music *Doctor Who* moved a step further away from its roots; an even more important link had been severed earlier in the season with the transmission of *The Highlanders* – the last of the historical stories which had been such an integral part of the series' original format. Although just as popular with viewers as the science-based stories if the ratings and appreciation figures are anything to go by, the historicals were rather at odds with Innes Lloyd's preference for a more contemporary, action-orientated style, and he therefore decided to drop them.

The Highlanders (originally entitled *Culloden*) was commissioned from Elwyn Jones, a distinguished writer who had recently returned to a freelance career after a spell as the BBC's Head of Series. He had been introduced to Gerry Davis by Head of Serials Shaun Sutton, who had decided as a favour to find him some work. On learning that Jones had no particular idea for a story, Davis had suggested that something about the battle of Culloden might be suitable, Robert Louis Stevenson's *Kidnapped* being the source material he had in mind.

When Davis later checked to see how the scripts were progressing, he discovered that Jones

had been too busy working on the second season of *Softly, Softly* even to start them. Davis was therefore forced to write the story himself. As this was an emergency, he was again allowed an on-screen credit for his work, although Jones was credited as co-writer. Davis was very pleased with the finished result, mainly because he had a great deal of control over it and could ensure that it was a model example of how he thought a historical story should be done.

Arriving in Scotland in 1746, not long after the battle of Culloden, the Doctor, Polly and Ben become involved with a small band of Highlanders fleeing from the English Redcoats. The Doctor gains their trust by offering to tend their wounded Laird, Colin McLaren; but while Polly and the Laird's daughter, Kirsty, are away fetching water, he and the others are all captured by troops under the command of Lieutenant Algernon ffinch. Grey, a crooked solicitor who sells prisoners for transportation to slavery in the West Indies, then secures the group into his custody. However, after Polly and Kirsty blackmail ffinch into helping, the Doctor eventually wins the day by smuggling arms to the Highlanders, who are being held on board a stolen ship, the *Annabelle*. Grey and the ship's unscrupulous captain, Trask, are overpowered and the vessel returned to its rightful owner, MacKay, who agrees to take the Scots to safety in France.

Another notable aspect of *The Highlanders* is that it introduced a new companion for the Doctor: Scottish piper James Robert McCrimmon,

An Atlantean fish person. *The Underwater Menace*.

MORRIS BARRY
DIRECTOR

Morris Barry studied at the Embassy School of Acting in London following school and then worked in repertory until the Second World War, when he joined the army. Almost eight years later, having been promoted to Major, he returned to acting, winning roles not only in the theatre – where he began to direct – but also in radio and films. In the mid-fifties he joined the BBC, first as a temporary floor manager and then as a production assistant in the TV Drama Group. After eighteen months he began directing, his early credits including **Starr and Company**, **Compact** *and his work for* **Doctor Who**. *Later he continued a successful career as a director and a producer, including on* **Spy Trap**, **Poldark** *and* **Count Dracula**. *Having been with the BBC for 22 years, he left to become a freelance director, TV tutor and actor, taking roles in* **Blake's 7** *and the 1979* **Doctor Who** *story* **The Creature from the Pit** *and many other programmes. He is now retired.*

or Jamie. Although destined to become one of the series' best remembered and most popular regulars, he was not originally intended as such: he started life as just a minor, one-off character in Davis's story. However, impressed with the performance and personality of Frazer Hines, who played the role, the production team decided that he would make an excellent foil for the Doctor. Consequently Davis rewrote the concluding scenes and Jamie joined the Doctor, Polly and Ben on their travels.

As Jamie was such a late addition to the regular character line-up, the stories immediately following *The Highlanders* had to be hastily amended to incorporate him. This was done for the most part by pairing him off with one of the other companions – usually Ben – and splitting the dialogue between them, although in *The Moonbase* he was simply rendered unconscious for the best part of three episodes.

During the late spring and summer of 1966, while commissioning scripts for season four, Gerry Davis had considered a number of storylines

▲ The Cybermen outside the BBC's Television Film Studios at Ealing.

▲ One of designer Ken Sharp's corridor sets for *The Macra Terror*.

The Macra prop. *The Macra Terror*.

◀ The Pilot (Peter Jeffrey) and Ola (Gertan Klauber) in the colony. *The Macra Terror*.

Alexandra Tynan's ▲ original costume design for Ruth Maxtible. *The Evil of the Daleks.*

The Dalek Emperor. ▲ *The Evil of the Daleks.*

CASTING A COMPANION

Deborah Watling was a very late choice for the part of Victoria. The actresses who originally auditioned for the role were Paula Challoner and her sister, who were seen twice, the second time on 3 April 1967, by director Derek Martinus. Then, on 10 April, a further six actresses auditioned. These were Celestine Randall, Elizabeth Knight, Gabrielle Drake, Tracy Rogers, Lanse Traverse and Denise Buckley. Buckley was offered the part and accepted, but three days later, on 13 April, Innes Lloyd confirmed that the role was to go to Deborah Watling instead.

Maxtible (Marius Goring) and Waterfield (John Bailey). *The Evil of the Daleks.*

submitted by freelance writers. Some of these, including *The Herdsmen of Aquarius* by Donald Cotton, *The Evil Eye* by Geoffrey Orme and three – *The Heavy Scent of Violence, The Man from the Met* and *The Hearsay Machine* – by George Kerr, proved unsuitable, but one which was taken forward was *The Imps* by William Emms, writer of season three's *Galaxy 4*. This concerned an alien spore being brought to Earth aboard a passenger space-liner. Upon arrival at a space-port, the intervention of some imp-like beings who can pass through solid objects results in the spore germinating into a race of hostile plants, which terrorise the isolated community.

When *The Imps* fell through at the scripting stage, its intended director, Julia Smith, was asked to take on a different project instead. This was Geoffrey Orme's *The Underwater Menace*, which had been commissioned by Gerry Davis on 16 August 1966 and initially planned for the slot immediately after *The Power of the Daleks*. The order of the stories was changed in October 1966 as Hugh David, the director assigned that slot,

Victoria and Jamie ▶ encounter a Dalek in the hallway of Maxtible's house. *The Evil of the Daleks.*

considered *The Underwater Menace* (originally entitled *Under the Sea* and then *The Fish People*) impossible to make on *Doctor Who*'s limited budget. Consequently the story David was given to direct was *The Highlanders*, which was originally to have followed Orme's.

The Underwater Menace sees the TARDIS arriving on an extinct volcanic island. Before long, the travellers are captured by guards and taken into the depths of the Earth, where they find a hidden civilization – the lost city of Atlantis. A deranged scientist, Professor Zaroff, has convinced the Atlanteans that he can raise their city from the sea, but in truth he plans to drain the ocean into the Earth's molten core so that the resultant superheated steam will cause the planet to explode. The Doctor manages to foil Zaroff's plan, but only at the cost of breaking down the sea walls and flooding the city. Zaroff drowns, but everyone else escapes.

As Hugh David had predicted, this production stretched *Doctor Who*'s resources to the limit and at times this was apparent on screen. Despite some fine location filming, good special effects and amusing dialogue, the overall style was somewhat akin to that of a far-fetched fifties B-movie. The story even had its own archetypal mad scientist in Professor Zaroff (played with great gusto by Joseph Furst), whose original motivation – a sort of warped revenge for the deaths of his wife and children in a car crash – was lost between storyline and final script with the result that he appeared to be acting purely on an insane whim. All that was learnt of his background was that he was a brilliant scientist, a specialist in seafood production, who had disappeared some twenty years earlier, believed kidnapped and since presumed dead.

The 'monsters' of the piece, the Fish People – humans transformed into aquatic creatures with surgically implanted artificial gills – were an interesting concept, but again a difficult and expensive one to realise, the result being their costume and make-up was rather limited.

Doctor Who's cast and crew had taken a short Christmas holiday between recording of the last episode of *The Highlanders* on 24 December 1966 and the first of *The Underwater Menace* on 7 January 1967, but this meant that the remaining episodes of the season had to be made only one week ahead of transmission, a precarious situation which allowed absolutely no room for manoeuvre.

The season's penultimate story, *The Faceless Ones* by David Ellis and Malcolm Hulke, begins with the TARDIS materialising in London 1966 on a runway at Gatwick airport! While hiding from the airport authorities, Polly witnesses a murder in one of the hangars and she and Ben are kidnapped by the perpetrators. Investigating, the Doctor and Jamie discover that Chameleon Tours, the company which owns the hangar, is a front for a race of aliens who have lost their identity in a planetary accident and are now abducting thousands of teenaged holiday-makers in order to use their bodies as patterns for their own. The Doctor rescues the abducted humans from the Chameleons' space station and gives the aliens some ideas for a more acceptable solution to their problem.

Shortly before teaming up with Malcolm Hulke, David Ellis had submitted three *Doctor Who* storylines of his own, *The Ocean Liner*, *The Clock* and *The People Who Couldn't Remember*, which had all been rejected by Gerry Davis. As Hulke recalled, *The Faceless Ones* (originally entitled *The Chameleons*) had then come about as a result of a chance meeting between the two writers during preparations for a Writers Guild Award Ball:

'Both being writers, we started telling each other stories. Eventually I put up an idea – nothing to do with *Doctor Who* – he elaborated on it, and we decided to work it out together. So we collaborated over the next few weeks and worked out a film story, which we never sold. Then I think it was David who said "Why don't you and I have a stab at *Doctor Who*?" As I'd written for the series before (*The Hidden Planet*), we got in touch with Gerry Davis. We discussed it with him, and he said that he would like a story set in a big

department store. So we worked out a story called *The Big Store*, in which the Chameleons posed as shop dummies. Gerry was quite pleased with this but then the producer said "Big stores are out! Try an airport!" So we started again and the final story came out of that.'

The production team requested the change in the story's setting for the simple reason that they had recently obtained permission to do some filming at Gatwick Airport – a major coup for the series. The location work added a tremendous sense of scale to the production, director Gerry Mill making full use of the terminal building and runway areas where the crew was allowed to shoot. The finished programmes also made ingenious use of some stock footage of airport operations.

The Chameleons themselves were a very sinister race, provoking feelings of paranoia (any character could suddenly be revealed to be a Chameleon 'duplicate') and the classic fear of loss of identity; and their actual appearance was kept concealed until relatively late in the story, with only the occasional glimpse of a hand or the back of a head to whet viewers' appetites.

The Faceless Ones was also the last story to feature Ben and Polly. They drop out of the action early on and don't reappear until the end of the sixth and final episode, when they decide to part company with the Doctor and Jamie as they are

▲ The model set of the Dalek Emperor's control room, complete with Louis Marx toy Daleks. *The Evil of the Daleks.*

▲ Filming for *The Evil of the Daleks* at the Kendal Avenue location. The TARDIS is loaded onto the Leatherman lorry and stolen.

CASTING

Often, directors would have several ideas as to who might play a given part. By way of example, Derek Martinus considered the following artistes for **The Evil of the Daleks**:

Waterfield	
	Maurice Denham
	Hugh Burden
Maxtible	
	Lee Montague
	Roy Dotrice
	Paul Hardwicke
Toby	Robert Gartland
	Paul Dawkins
	Christopher Benjamin
Kennedy	
	James Beck
Perry	John Carlin
Molly	Carole Mowlam
	Marty Cruickshank
	Lucy Fleming
Ruth	Isobel Black
Terrell	Barrie Ingham
	John Kelland
Kemel	John Maxim

Story editor Gerry Davis and director Derek Martinus on set with the Dalek Emperor. *The Evil of the Daleks.*

RECORDING

There were only two significant examples of out-of-scene-order recording in season four. The first was in part four of **The Tenth Planet,** *when some sequences involving dry-ice effects were left until last to be shot. Vision mixer Shirley Coward and director Derek Martinus also recall that the regeneration sequence was the first thing to be done on that episode's recording day, although this was not planned in the camera script. The second example was in part four of* **The Faceless Ones,** *when a scene showing the character Jenkins being duplicated by the Chameleons was recorded just after the one which would follow it on transmission.*

WITH EFFECT FROM...

From **The Evil of the Daleks** *onwards, the BBC's Visual Effects Department took full responsibility for designing* **Doctor Who's** *effects (this task had previously fallen to the Design Department).*

THE ORIGINAL EVIL

David Whitaker's original two-sheet synopsis for **The Evil of the Daleks,** *dated 4 January 1967, tells a rather different story to that finally transmitted. It starts with the TARDIS being stolen by Waterfield because the Daleks are holding his daughter hostage. Waterfield lures the Doctor and Jamie to his two-man time machine and then takes them back to 1880 where they are confronted by the Daleks. He subsequently persuades the Doctor to take him back to 20,000 BC where they capture a caveman called Og. Og is brought back to 1880 and studied by Waterfield. Meanwhile Jamie is taken to Skaro where he meets Victoria. The Daleks take over the study of Og and learn what it is that makes mankind tick. They plan to return to the past to destroy it. After a battle with the Daleks, the story ends back in Victorian London.*

The Doctor and Jamie at Gatwick Airport. *The Faceless Ones.*

now back in their own time. As Anneke Wills recalls, she and Michael Craze were both asked to stay on but declined to do so as they were concerned about typecasting. Michael Craze, on the other hand, maintains that they were not offered new contracts and other people's recollections seem to confirm this. As Malcolm Hulke expressed it, 'The producer had rather gone off them as actor and actress, as I recall.' Having already been paid to rework their story once to alter the setting from a department store to an airport, Ellis and Hulke then had to perform a further rewrite for which they were paid another fee.

In the absence of Ben and Polly, Jamie was the sole companion for most of the story, although along the way he made friends with Samantha Briggs, the sister of one of the kidnapped teenagers. Samantha had been thought of as a potential new companion, but Innes Lloyd could not persuade Pauline Collins to continue in the role.

The Faceless Ones ends with the discovery that the TARDIS has disappeared, which acts as an effective lead-in to the following adventure, David Whitaker's *The Evil of the Daleks*, commissioned on 24 January 1967.

The TARDIS has been stolen by an antique dealer, Edward Waterfield, who lures the Doctor and Jamie into a trap. They are transported back to Waterfield's own time, 1866, where his daughter Victoria (Deborah Watling) is being held hostage by the Daleks to ensure his co-operation. The Daleks force the Doctor to monitor Jamie's performance of a test – the rescue of Victoria – with the supposed intention of identifying 'the human factor': that special quality possessed by humans which enables them always to defeat the Daleks. The Doctor goes along with this scheme and implants the human factor into three test Daleks with the result that

they become friendly and playful.

Everyone is transported to the Daleks' home world Skaro where the Doctor discovers to his horror that the Daleks' true aim has been to isolate not the human factor but 'the Dalek factor' – the impulse to destroy – and to implant it into humans. The massive Emperor Dalek informs him that his TARDIS will be used to spread the Dalek factor through all time. However, by a ruse, the Doctor is able to infuse many more Daleks with the human factor. A civil war breaks out between the two Dalek factions and they are apparently all destroyed, the Doctor looking down upon their city and commenting that this is 'the final end'. As Waterfield has been killed saving his life, he offers Victoria a place aboard the TARDIS.

David Whitaker had already begun writing his scripts for *The Evil of the Daleks* when the decision was made to drop Polly and Ben in *The Faceless Ones*. Consequently he was paid an additional fee to rework the first two episodes, in the process building up Victoria from a one-off character into a potential new regular.

The story as transmitted was full of terror and excitement, with strong characterisation and a suspenseful, twisting plot. Widely acclaimed as a highlight of the season, it benefited from Derek Martinus's experienced direction and some memorable performances, notably by John Bailey as Waterfield and Marius Goring as his alchemist partner Theodore Maxtible.

After a period of relative stability for the series' production team, *The Evil of the Daleks* saw the departure of story editor Gerry Davis, who left at the end of May 1967, partway through its run, and moved on to another show, *First Lady*. He had actually been asked to become producer of *Doctor Who* – Innes Lloyd now being keen to leave the series, feeling that he had contributed all he could to it – but did not want to do so. His successor as story editor was Peter Bryant who had been trailing him as an assistant since around March. Bryant was also seen as a potential replacement for Lloyd, and was in fact credited as associate producer on *The Faceless Ones*. At the same time as he took over from Davis as story editor, Bryant brought in a new assistant of his own, his friend Victor Pemberton, who had previously had a small acting role in *The Moonbase* at a time when he was working as a bit-part player while trying to establish himself as a writer.

Transmitted on 1 July 1967, the last episode of *The Evil of the Daleks* brought *Doctor Who's* fourth season to an end after an unbroken run of 43 weeks.

CHAPTER ELEVEN

Season Five: Year of the Monsters

When *Doctor Who* returned at 5:50 p.m. on Saturday 2 September 1967 after eight weeks off the air, it was in a somewhat healthier state than it had been a year before. The changes made by producer Innes Lloyd and story editor Gerry Davis had succeeded in revitalising the series, and this was reflected in a ratings increase from an average of around five million viewers per episode at the start of season four to an average of around seven million at the end, accompanied by a rise of about ten percentage points in the average appreciation figure, which now hovered around the 55 mark. A critical change of lead actor had been successfully accomplished, a period of experimentation had led to a strong new format, and now two promising new companions had been introduced. A firm foundation had been established which could now be built upon.

The season's opening story, *The Tomb of the Cybermen*, by Kit Pedler and Gerry Davis, saw the return of the silver cybernetic giants for their third appearance in a year. When the TARDIS materialises on the planet Telos, the Doctor, Jamie and Victoria meet an Earth archaeological expedition, led by Professor Parry, who are excavating a tomb rumoured to contain the last remains of the extinct Cybermen. Two of the human party, Klieg and Kaftan, have their own reasons for wanting to get into the tomb – they secretly plan to revive the Cybermen and use the creatures' strength, allied to the intelligence of their own Brotherhood of Logicians, to create an invincible force for conquest. However, it transpires that the tomb is actually a giant trap designed to lure suitable humans into the Cybermen's clutches, for con-

version into Cybermen. After fending off an attack by Cybermats, small but deadly cybernetic creatures which home in on people's brainwaves, the Doctor eventually defeats the revived Cybermen, led by their formidable Controller, by

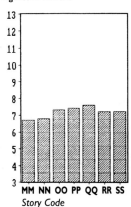

Director Morris Barry on the Ealing tomb set during rehearsals for *The Tomb of the Cybermen*.

RATINGS

Figures in millions

Chart: bar graph with vertical axis from 3 to 13, horizontal axis labelled MM NN OO PP QQ RR SS.

Story Code

The Cyberman ▲
Controller's helmet on
display in 1978.

A Cybermat. *The Tomb* ▲
of the Cybermen.

SEASON FIVE:
EVENTS OF 2
SEPTEMBER 1967 –
1 JUNE 1968

First prototype of Concorde is
shown to the public.

The first heart transplant takes
place in South Africa.

American civil rights leader
Martin Luther King is
assassinated.

Yuri Gagarin, the first man in
space, dies in a plane crash.

The first decimal coins (5p and
10p) are minted and issued.

**The upper storeys of the tomb are absent on the
smaller set at Lime Grove. *The Tomb of the Cybermen.***

returning them to hibernation and re-sealing the
tomb. In the process, the Controller is apparently
destroyed.

The Tomb of the Cybermen (originally entitled
The Cybermen Planet and later *The Ice Tombs of
Telos*) was the last story of *Doctor Who*'s fourth
production block, its final episode being recorded
on Saturday 22 July 1967; and it saw Peter Bryant,
after only four weeks as the series' official story
editor, being temporarily elevated to the position
of producer while his assistant Victor Pemberton
took the story editor's credit. This came about
simply as a result of Bryant asking Innes Lloyd if
he could handle a story by himself. 'Innes knew
that I wanted to be a producer,' he remembers,
'and by then I had a pretty solid background in the
business, one way and another; I had all the
qualifications one needs to be a producer. I'd
done it all. So Innes said "Yes, fine, sure." I think
he may also have felt that since he wanted to leave
the programme at that point, if he had someone
ready to take over from him it would be a lot
easier.'

Bryant passed this early test with flying colours
as *The Tomb of the Cybermen* proved to be an
extremely popular story, not only with the general viewing audience but also with the series'
creator, Sydney Newman. 'The morning after the
first episode went out,' Bryant explains, 'I had a
marvellous telephone call – I've never forgotten
it – from Sydney Newman. He just phoned me up
to say that he'd seen it and how great he thought
it was. That was terrific, very nice – the kind of
thing Sydney did. Great guy.'

The production was certainly a memorable
one, due in part to some impressive set-design
work by Martin Johnson. Particularly complex
was the construction of the Cybermen's hibernation area for the film inserts shot at Ealing. This
consisted of several tiered rows of chambers, each
just large enough to house one actor in full
Cyberman costume, and the whole 29-foot-tall
structure was supported on a scaffold framework.
Over the front of each chamber was placed a thin

sheet of plastic, sprayed with a stencil of a
specially designed cybersymbol, creating a mem-
brane which the Cyberman would break through
in the scene where the creatures are revived. The
Controller had a separate chamber of his own
behind a large hinged door at the base of the
structure. The front of the door bore a bas-relief
of the cybersymbol produced from polystyrene.

With a plot containing elements taken from
many 'Egyptian mummy' horror films, *The Tomb
of the Cybermen* can also be seen as something of
a landmark in the series' gradual move towards a
more graphic and adult style. Indeed, the level of
violence in the story formed the basis of discussion in the first programme of the BBC's new
viewers' comment show *Talkback*, broadcast
at 6:25 p.m. on Tuesday 26 September 1967,
when one participant expressed particular concern about a scene where Kaftan's manservant
Toberman, having been partly cybernised, struggles with a Cyberman and repeatedly strikes its
chest unit, causing foam to ooze forth. Kit Pedler
was one of the guests on hand to speak in *Doctor
Who*'s defence.

The effectiveness of *The Tomb of the Cybermen* can be attributed in part to the fact that its
central plot was a variation on the successful
formula established the previous season – although in this case it is the small group of humans
which is trying to gain access to the aliens' base
rather than the other way around! The following
story, *The Abominable Snowmen* by Mervyn
Haisman and Henry Lincoln, also followed the
standard formula, the isolated community in this
instance being a remote Tibetan monastery in the
thirties.

**A headless Yeti poses with the TARDIS. *The
Abominable Snowmen.***

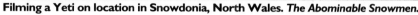
Filming a Yeti on location in Snowdonia, North Wales. *The Abominable Snowmen.*

The Doctor stops off at the monastery in order to return a sacred bell, the ghanta, which he was given for safe-keeping on a previous visit. There he meets an Englishman named Professor Travers (portrayed by Jack Watling, father of Deborah who played Victoria), who is on an expedition to track down the legendary Abominable Snowmen, or Yeti. Although Travers achieves his goal, it transpires that the Yeti roaming the area are disguised robots which scare away or kill anyone foolish enough to approach them.

Unbeknown to the Doctor, the High Lama Padmasambhava, an old friend of his, has been taken over by a nebulous alien being, the Great Intelligence, and is controlling the Yeti's movements with models on a chessboard. The Intelligence's aim is to create a material form for itself and take over the Earth, and Padmasambhava has been tricked into providing the gateway for it. The Doctor eventually banishes the Intelligence back to the astral plane, allowing Padmasambhava, his life extended far beyond its natural length, to die in peace. The story ends with Travers at last sighting a real Yeti: a timid creature, much less bulky than the robots, which scurries off with him in pursuit.

The exterior scenes for *The Abominable Snowmen* were filmed in Snowdonia, North Wales – another of the major location shoots during *Doctor Who*'s first six years. A whole week was spent at the location, although the filming was somewhat hampered by bad weather. When it

came to the studio work, the first two episodes were made on consecutive days – Friday 15 and Saturday 16 September 1967. Throughout the remainder of this unbroken 45-week production block, episodes would be made on Fridays and, in the case of those transmitted as season five, three weeks and one day ahead of transmission.

Although Innes Lloyd's name had disappeared from the programme's credits during Peter Bryant's trial run as producer on *The Tomb of the Cybermen*, things were back to normal for this story, with Lloyd as producer, Bryant as story editor and Pemberton as uncredited assistant story editor. However, Lloyd was still looking to leave the series at the earliest opportunity, and was grooming Bryant as his successor.

The production team were so pleased with *The Abominable Snowmen* that on 27 September 1967, before it was even transmitted, they commissioned writers Mervyn Haisman and Henry Lincoln to come up with a sequel. Jack Watling returned as Travers in this second Yeti tale, *The Web of Fear*, but as the setting was some forty years after the adventure in the Himalayas he now had to play the part as an old man, complete with spectacles and a bushy beard.

The Doctor, Jamie and Victoria arrive in a London of the near future to find it in the grip of the Great Intelligence's second attempt to take over the Earth. A deadly web is enveloping the

▲ A Cyberman emerges from his frozen tomb on Telos. *The Tomb of the Cybermen.*

Eric Klieg (George ▲ Pastell) and Professor Parry (Aubrey Richards). *The Tomb of the Cybermen.*

Frazer Hines relaxes on a ▲ Yeti costume. *The Abominable Snowmen.*

LOCATIONS

The Tomb of the Cybermen
Gerrards Cross Sand and Ballast Co., Buckinghamshire

The Abominable Snowmen
Nant Ffrancon Pass, Snowdonia, Wales; Ogwen Lake, Snowdonia, Wales

The Enemy of the World
Littlehampton, West Sussex; Villiers House, Redhill, Surrey

The Web of Fear
Greenwich Footway Tunnel, London; Old Covent Garden, London

Fury from the Deep
Radio 390 Offshore Platform, Red Sands, Thames Estuary; Margate Beach, Kent; Fields near Denham Aerodrome, Buckinghamshire

Special effects designer Michealjohn Harris and set designer Martin Johnson spray fake snow on the tomb set. *The Tomb of the Cybermen.*

Kaftan (Shirley Cooklin) on location for *The Tomb of the Cyberemen.*

city, and Travers, who, by reactivating a Yeti control sphere, inadvertently opened the way for the Intelligence to return, is acting as scientific adviser to an army unit trying to combat the menace. He is assisted by his daughter Anne. The troops are operating from the now-deserted London Underground system, but their task is made hazardous by marauding Yeti and the lethal, foam-like web which is systematically engulfing the tunnels. In addition, as the Doctor soon realises, someone in their midst is acting as a controlled agent of the Intelligence.

Although a number of other people come under suspicion, including the soldiers' officer Colonel Lethbridge-Stewart, the unwilling traitor is eventually revealed to be the seemingly dependable Sergeant Arnold. This discovery comes too late, as Travers and Victoria have been taken hostage and the Doctor is forced to give himself up. The Intelligence's aim is to drain the Doctor's mind and a special helmet is placed on his head for that purpose. However, the Doctor has managed to 'cross the wires' on this device, and he almost succeeds in draining the Intelligence until, much to his frustration, he is 'rescued' by his well-meaning friends. He has at least broken the Intelligence's link with Earth for now.

The director of *The Web of Fear* was Douglas Camfield. He initially considered shooting some of the story on location inside the Underground itself, but this idea had to be dropped when he was told by London Transport that he could do so only on payment of a very high fee and, even then, only between two and five in the morning. Apart from a few scenes filmed in a pedestrian tunnel in Greenwich which had been built in a similar style, all the action set on platforms and in tube tunnels had therefore to be taped in the recording studio. Designer David Myerscough-Jones had some sets made which, when fully dressed and lit, proved highly convincing – so much so that when the story was transmitted, London Transport accused the BBC of having carried out unauthorised filming on their premises!

The Web of Fear bears a number of plot similarities to Nigel Kneale's classic *Quatermass and the Pit* – and particularly to the Hammer Films adaptation of it, which had been released the previous year. Both have as their main setting the London Underground; both involve an attack by a disembodied alien force capable of exerting an influence over people's minds; both depict the efforts of a military operation to defeat the menace; and both have a distinguished scientist and his young female assistant working alongside the principal hero.

Quatermass and the Pit's overbearing army officer, Colonel Breen, is paralleled in *The Web of Fear* by the admittedly rather more sympathetic Colonel Lethbridge-Stewart, who would later become a very significant character in *Doctor Who*'s history. This part was originally to have been played by David Langton, but when Langton pulled out it was offered instead to Nicholas Courtney who had initially been cast in the more minor role of Captain Knight. It was Camfield who added the 'Stewart' to the Colonel's name – in the scripts it was simply Colonel Lethbridge – as he felt that the officer should be an anglicised Scot in the General 'Mad Mitch' Mitchell mould.

Patrick Troughton poses in the rain with two headless Yeti. *The Abominable Snowmen.*

The *Quatermass* overtones, coupled with Camfield's own love of gothic horror, helped to ensure that *The Web of Fear* was very much in line with the current trend towards a more adult, horrific style. This trend was reflected in all aspects of the production: for example, the Yeti costumes were slightly remodelled for their second appearance as it was thought that their original design had made them look a little too cuddly. The version seen in *The Web of Fear* was slimmer and more menacing, with large glowing eyes.

Following the Cybermen and the Yeti came another race of classic *Doctor Who* monsters, the Ice Warriors, making their debut appearance in the story of the same name. Although originating from the planet Mars, Brian Hayles's creations were far removed from the little green men of popular science fiction. True, they were green (although viewers could not have known this!), but they were far from little, towering around seven feet tall and clad in bulky carapace-like armour.

The Doctor, Jamie and Victoria arrive on Earth in AD 3000 and find the planet in the grip of a new ice age. Scientists in a base commanded by Leader Clent are using an ioniser device to try to halt the advance of a glacier. However, a dangerous complication arises when they discover, frozen in the ice face, the body of a giant reptilian warrior. Brought back to the base and thawed out, the creature is revealed to be Varga, the leader of an expedition from Mars whose spaceship landed on Earth many centuries ago and has been buried in the glacier ever since. As Varga sets about freeing his comrades from the ice and formulating a plan to conquer the Earth – Mars itself is now a dead world – the humans are faced with another problem: if the Martians' ship has an atomic reactor, continued operation of the ioniser could cause a catastrophic explosion – and yet, if the ioniser is not used, the base risks destruction by the glacier.

The scientists' computer, on which they rely for

▲ Victoria and Jamie encounter Professor Travers for the first time. *The Abominable Snowmen.*

MUSIC

Story	Composer
The Tomb of the Cybermen	Stock
(various tracks and composers)	
The Abominable Snowmen	No Music
The Ice Warriors	Dudley Simpson
(singer: Joanne Brown)	
The Enemy of the World	
Stock (Miraculous Mandarin, Music for String Instruments, Percussion and Celeste by Bartok)	
The Web of Fear	Stock
(including Music for String Instruments, Percussion and Celeste by Bartok)	
Fury from the Deep	Dudley Simpson
The Wheel in Space	
Brian Hodgson and Stock (Tranquil Scene by Moneta Eagles)	

▼ Professor Travers (Jack Watling). *The Web of Fear.*

Anne Travers (Tina Packer) is menaced by a re-styled Yeti. *The Web of Fear.* Inset: One of David Myerscough-Jones's London Underground sets.

Leader Clent (Peter ▲ Barkworth). *The Ice Warriors.*

Miss Garrett (Wendy ▲ Gifford). *The Ice Warriors.*

REPEAT OF THE DALEKS

When **The Evil of the Daleks** *was repeated, some additional dialogue was recorded by Patrick Troughton and Wendy Padbury and overdubbed at the start of the first episode to reinforce the link with* **The Wheel in Space.** *This ran as follows:*

DOCTOR: *Now as I remember, Zoe, it all started when Jamie and I discovered somebody making off with the TARDIS.*

ZOE: *But what about those Daleks you showed me?*

DOCTOR: *We're coming to that, Zoe. Just let me show you the story from the beginning...*

Another unscheduled change in the repeat came towards the end of episode four when a technical fault resulted in a break in transmission. A brief musical interlude followed, until the fault was rectified.

advice on all their decisions, is unable to solve the dilemma without further information, and it appears that disaster is imminent. However, supported by the Doctor, the disaffected scientist Penley, who has never approved of humans being dependent upon a computer, decides to take the risk of activating the ioniser. There is an explosion, but only a minor one which destroys the Ice Warriors and, at the same time, checks the ice flow.

Another of the aliens-infiltrate-an-isolated-scientific-base stories, *The Ice Warriors* was also reminiscent of the 1951 Howard Hawks film *The Thing from Another World* in which scientists discover an alien spacecraft frozen in a glacier. Brian Hayles's inspiration for the Ice Warriors came from reading a news report about a mammoth discovered buried in the ice in Russia. However, the way he saw the creatures was not quite how they turned out on screen. His scripts made only passing references to their being reptilian, placing much more emphasis on their having cyborg-like electronic attachments. The credit for their eventual appearance is due largely to season five's costume designer, Martin Baugh, who had also been responsible for the Yeti. Rather than giving the Ice Warriors conventional clothing, he commissioned a firm of boat builders to make fibreglass shells which would be their heads and bodies. The legs and arms were moulded in heavy latex rubber and strapped on to the actors. Bernard Bresslaw recalls being quite taken aback when he first saw the costume he was to wear as Varga, having assumed that he would be clad in more traditional Viking-style armour.

The scenes of the frozen landscape of Britain were shot mainly on film at Ealing and the sets were constructed primarily of polystyrene. The use of the more flexible and controllable medium of film, and the extra space available at Ealing, gave director Derek Martinus the opportunity to create a very realistic setting – at one point he even arranged for a live grizzly bear to be brought into the studio, to be seen attacking Jamie and the scientist Penley!

One of the many reasons Patrick Troughton had been chosen to play the second Doctor was that Innes Lloyd believed an actor of his calibre would help to attract other top names to the show. This was certainly borne out on *The Ice Warriors*, which featured such distinguished and well-known performers as Peter Barkworth (Clent), Peter Sallis (Penley), Angus Lennie (Storr) and Bernard Bresslaw (Varga).

Troughton's own skills as a character actor were certainly much in evidence in the next story, David Whitaker's *The Enemy of the World*, in which he was given the opportunity to play not

Varga (Bernard Bresslaw) inside the ioniser base. *The Ice Warriors.*

only the Doctor but also the villain, Salamander – a scheming megalomaniac.

When the TARDIS lands on an Australian beach, the Doctor, Jamie and Victoria find them-

Salamander (Patrick Troughton). *The Enemy of the World.*

Zondal (Roger Jones) stands in front of the sonic cannon. *The Ice Warriors.*

▲ Giles Kent (Bill Kerr). *The Enemy of the World.*

▲ Nicholas Fedorin (David Nettheim). *The Enemy of the World.*

▲ Fariah (Carmen Munroe). *The Enemy of the World.*

selves being shot at by men in a hovercraft. A young woman, Astrid, rescues them in a helicopter and takes them to meet her boss, Giles Kent, from whom the Doctor is amazed to learn that he is the double of the scientist and politician Salamander. Salamander has discovered a means of storing solar energy and then distributing it to strategic points on each continent, thus ending starvation and poverty in a world currently ravaged by earthquakes, volcanoes and other seemingly natural disasters. To most of the Earth's populace he is a hero, but Giles, Astrid and others believe him to be using his popularity to establish himself as an all-powerful dictator.

The Doctor refuses to intervene until he has hard evidence to support Kent's claims. Eventually, having impersonated Salamander to gain access to his research station, he uncovers the truth. It transpires that Salamander and Kent had once worked together. Almost five years before, they convinced a group of people undergoing an endurance test in a bunker beneath the research station that a war had broken out on the surface. It is these people who, deceived into thinking that they are striking back against an evil enemy, have been engineering the so-called natural disasters which have allowed Salamander to seize power. Having quarrelled with Salamander, Kent is now trying to kill him and take his place. His treachery having been exposed, Kent blows up the research station. Salamander, meanwhile, flees to the TARDIS, where he tries to convince Jamie and Victoria that he is actually the Doctor. When the

Doctor himself arrives, Salamander activates the dematerialisation control. However, he neglects to close the doors first, and is sucked out into the vortex, the three travellers almost sharing his fate.

Its lack of alien monsters made *The Enemy of the World* the odd story out in season five. In style and plotting, it was much closer to a James Bond-type spy thriller than to a traditional *Doctor Who* idea, Salamander, with his grandiose scheme for world domination, being cast from the same mould as Dr No and Ernst Blofeld. The inclusion of such action-adventure hardware as a hovercraft and a helicopter helped bolster this impression and the Doctor himself was rather less central to the action than usual. There were fewer scenes than there should have been of the Doctor and Salamander confronting each other, as the camera being used to film the split screen effect jammed in the studio. The fact that a story which departed so far from the norm was still successful is a good illustration of just how wide the possibilities were within *Doctor Who*'s basic framework.

The Enemy of the World was Innes Lloyd's last story as *Doctor Who*'s producer, as he had finally been granted his wish to move on to other projects. As planned, Peter Bryant then took over from him. However, Victor Pemberton had by this time become aware that he was not cut out for the story editor's job. He returned to freelance writing and the post went instead to Derrick Sherwin, who up until this time had been an actor and a freelance writer. Shortly afterwards, Terrance

PRODUCTION ROUTINE

*All season five episodes up to and including part five of **Fury from the Deep** were recorded in Studio D at Lime Grove, as was part one of **The Wheel in Space**. Part six of **Fury from the Deep** and part three of **The Wheel in Space** were made in Television Centre Studio 1, parts two and four of **The Wheel in Space** in Television Centre Studio 3 and parts five and six of **The Wheel in Space** in Riverside Studio 1.*

RECORDING

*Although most season five episodes were shot in sequence and continuously wherever possible, there was a marked trend towards increased use of out-of-sequence recording. Episode three of **Fury from the Deep** and episode six of **The Wheel in Space**, for example, were shot largely on a set-by-set basis rather than a scene-order basis. Episode five of **The Abominable Snowmen** was also unusual in having ten planned recording breaks. The biggest departure from the norm, however, came on **The Enemy of the World**. Due mainly to Patrick Troughton's dual role in this story, a considerable amount of out-of-sequence and discontinuous recording was done – particularly on episodes three and six. Also, on a number of this story's episodes, adjustments were made to the studio day's schedule to allow a longer time than usual for recording; and episodes four and five were both edited on the same day – 1 January 1968 – in a session lasting from 10:30 a.m. to 9:30 p.m.*

MERVYN HAISMAN
WRITER

*Mervyn Haisman began his career as an actor, running his own theatre company before moving on to work in insurance for ten years and finally taking up writing. His first television work was for **Doctor Finlay's Casebook**. Henry Lincoln had also started as an actor and, at the time he and Haisman met up, he had just finished writing for **Emergency Ward 10**. Together they worked out an idea for the Yeti, which, as Patrick Troughton was a friend of Lincoln's and had told them the sort of thing the production team were after, they knew would get a favourable reception. Following their work for **Doctor Who**, the writing partnership dissolved and they went their separate ways. Haisman has since script-edited **Sutherland's Law** and written for **The Onedin Line**, **Squadron** and **Jane** amongst others.*

The Euro-gas refinery control room set at Ealing. *Fury from the Deep.*

Dicks – another freelance writer – was invited by Sherwin, an acquaintance of his, to come in as a new assistant story editor.

The penultimate story of season five was *Fury from the Deep* (originally entitled *Colony of Devils*), commissioned from Victor Pemberton himself. 'I tried not to use my influence or anything,' he recalled in a 1987 interview. 'I actually said "I've got an idea; can I come and talk to you about it?" I talked to Peter and Innes and they said "Yes, do it."'

The story opens with the TARDIS making an unusual landing on the surface of the sea, just off the east coast of England. After rowing ashore in a rubber dinghy, the travellers are shot with tranquilliser darts and taken prisoner by security

The Doctor and Victoria listen to the strange heart beat sound emanating from the pipeline. *Fury from the Deep.*

guards, having unwittingly arrived in the restricted area of a gas refinery. Whilst held at the refinery base the Doctor is informed that there have been a number of unexplained problems with the pressure in the feed pipes from the off-shore drilling platforms. Although he and his companions are initially under suspicion, it soon becomes apparent that something much more sinister is at the root of the trouble.

It is later revealed that one of the rigs has sucked up a parasitic form of seaweed. This is able to protect itself by releasing poisonous gas or a strange kind of foam which allows it to take control of the minds of those it touches. The weed spreads rapidly, and seems set on establishing a huge colony centred around the rigs. However, the Doctor makes the chance discovery that it is very susceptible to high-pitched noise; consequently he is able to use the amplified sound of Victoria's screams to destroy the parasite. At the story's conclusion, Victoria elects to stay with the family of Harris, one of the refinery workers. Although sharing Jamie's sadness at her departure, the Doctor is understanding of her decision to settle down to a more peaceful life.

Deborah Watling had originally auditioned for the part of Polly in 1966 but producer Innes Lloyd had suggested that she needed a little more experience before taking on such a role. The following year, once she had gained that experience, he had been happy to cast her as Victoria. However, she had now come to the end of her

Victoria, the Doctor and Jamie arrive in the restricted area of the weed covered beach. *Fury from the Deep.*

contract and decided to move on to other challenges.

Victor Pemberton based *Fury from the Deep* in part upon his 1966 radio serial *The Slide* (an earlier version of which had been seen but turned down by *Doctor Who* story editor David Whitaker in 1964). Due to disagreements with Derrick Sherwin, who had performed some quite significant rewrites on his scripts, Victor Pemberton reportedly chose at one point to distance himself from the production. In the event, however, he was pleased with the end result.

One change made to the story involved the way in which the weed creature was ultimately defeated: at first it was to have been destroyed by the amplified sound of Jamie playing the bagpipes rather than of Victoria screaming. The revised version served as a much more fitting exit for Deborah Watling, who had made her decision to leave the series quite late in the day, leading Pemberton to make some last-minute amendments.

The season ended as it had begun: with a Cyberman story. *The Wheel in Space*, David Whitaker's second contribution to the season, came from an idea of Kit Pedler's entitled *The Space Wheel*. The scripts were commissioned on 14 December 1967 with a delivery date of 31 January 1968. However, by that deadline, Whitaker had submitted only the first two episodes, causing Peter Bryant concern. After discussions with Whitaker, Bryant insisted that parts three and four

should be delivered on the agreed date, although he gave him until Friday 2 February to deliver parts five and six.

The TARDIS materialises on board a spaceship, the Silver Carrier, where the Doctor and Jamie are attacked by a servo robot, apparently its only occupant. Fortunately, Jamie manages to contact a nearby space station known as the Wheel and to summon help. Both travellers are then transported to the station. Meanwhile, the Silver Carrier discharges some Cybermats which also travel to and enter the station. The Wheel's Controller, Jarvis Bennett, decides to destroy the Silver Carrier, and as the TARDIS is still over there Jamie sabotages the laser to prevent this. The Cybermats make their way to the Wheel's store of bernalium, a material essential to the laser's operation, and destroy it, thus leaving the station defenceless against an approaching meteorite storm. As there is a further supply of bernalium aboard the Silver Carrier, two of the Wheel's crew are dispatched to obtain it. However, they have walked into a carefully prepared trap: when they arrive they find two Cybermen on board, and fall under their hypnotic control. They then return to the Wheel, bringing with them the Cybermen, concealed in the crates of bernalium.

The Cybermen take over a large part of the station, their intention being to use its direct radio link with Earth as a beacon for their invasion fleet.

Zoe is unaware of the approach of the Cybermen (Jerry Holmes and Gordon Stothard). *The Wheel in Space.*

VICTOR PEMBERTON
WRITER/STORY EDITOR

*Victor Pemberton's career started in radio when a friend, David Spenser, challenged him to write a play because he was criticising another. The result was **The Gold Watch**, the first of many radio scripts. His first television script was for Rediffusion's **Send Foster**, which concerned the exploits of a junior reporter on a local newspaper. He also worked as an actor to supplement his writing income and this led to director Morris Barry casting him in **Doctor Who (The Moonbase)**. After a brief stint writing and story-editing **Doctor Who**, Victor contributed to **Timeslip** and **Ace of Wands** and wrote numerous other scripts for TV and radio. In 1976 he wrote **Doctor Who and the Pescatons**, an original adventure on an LP record, which he novelised for Virgin Publishing in 1991. He also produced **Fraggle Rock** and now runs his own production company, Saffron.*

DERRICK SHERWIN
SCRIPT EDITOR/ WRITER/PRODUCER

*Derrick Sherwin worked initially as a junior set designer and scenic artist in the theatre. This led to a number of other jobs including scene shifter, stage manager and lighting designer. Finally, interrupted only by a two-year spell in the Royal Air Force, he became an actor – a profession he was to pursue for many years in theatre, films and television. Eventually, while continuing to act, he also began to work as a freelance writer, mostly on TV plays and series such as **Z Cars** and **Crossroads**. Late in 1967, he was interviewed by BBC Head of Serials, Shaun Sutton, and offered the job of assistant story editor on **Doctor Who**. After **Doctor Who**, he worked on a number of other BBC series before leaving to found an independent production company. In the early eighties he ran the very first computer animation company, Electronic Arts, before returning to independent TV production. He has also continued to work as a freelance writer in England and America.*

HENRY LINCOLN
WRITER

Born in London in 1930, Henry Lincoln began writing in his late twenties and has since gained more than one hundred TV credits. Although his early work was in drama – much with co-writer Mervyn Haisman – an interest in ancient Egypt led him to become increasingly involved in documenting historical mysteries. Since 1969, the main focus of his work has been a particular enigma concerning a strange 'treasure' apparently discovered in the 1890s at the French village of Rennes-le-Chateau. This formed the basis of three documentaries – **The Lost Treasure of Jerusalem?** *(1972),* **The Priest, the Painter and the Devil** *(1974) and* **The Shadow of the Templars** *(1979) - which he wrote and presented for BBC2's* **Chronicle** *series. It was also the subject of his 1982 book* **The Holy Blood and the Holy Grail** *(co-written with Michael Baigent and Richard Leigh), which became an international best seller, as did its follow-up,* **The Messianic Legacy**. *Lincoln has also written poetry and lectured extensively.*

OPERATION WEREWOLF

Around the time of season five, a storyline entitled **Operation Werewolf** *was apparently submitted to the* **Doctor Who** *production office. Written by Robert Kitts and* **Doctor Who** *director Douglas Camfield, it concerned a Gestapo scheme to win the Second World War by using a crude form of matter transference – sending German soldiers to England armed with gas-filled V rockets – and by brainwashing allied troops. The Doctor, Jamie and Victoria were to have teamed up with the French Resistance, exposing one of the British officers as a spy and ultimately defeating the scheme just as the D-Day landings began. According to Kitts, Innes Lloyd was interested in the story – which would have been a six-parter – but it ultimately fell through without being commissioned.*

Frazer Hines and Patrick Troughton pose for a publicity photograph with the Servo Robot. *The Wheel in Space.*

Wendy Padbury as Zoe in her debut story. *The Wheel in Space.*

The Doctor sends Jamie and a young astrophysicist named Zoe Herriot over to the Silver Carrier to fetch the TARDIS's vector generator rod while he sets about freeing the Wheel's crew from the Cybermen's control. All the Cybermen on the station are killed. The Doctor then installs the rod from the TARDIS in the now-repaired laser, making it powerful enough to destroy the Cyberfleet. An approaching force of space-walking Cybermen is also vanquished.

The Doctor is preparing to leave when he discovers Zoe hiding on board the TARDIS, hoping to join him and Jamie on their travels. To give her an idea of what she might be letting herself in for, he uses a thought visualiser to project on the TARDIS's scanner screen an account of what happened during his last encounter with the Daleks...

Zoe was devised as the new companion to succeed Victoria. The part was first offered to Pauline Collins (who had already been invited to take on a regular role in the series when she played Samantha Briggs in the previous season's *The Faceless Ones*), but she turned it down. Eventually the role went to Wendy Padbury. The name 'Zoe' was provided by Peter Ling, who had used it in his storyline for *The Fact of Fiction* which formed the basis for season six's second story, *The Mind Robber*.

Although *The Wheel in Space* brought season

five officially to an end, its last episode being transmitted on 1 June 1968, the closing scene led directly on to a repeat of *The Evil of the Daleks* over the next nine Saturdays, including a two-week gap between episodes three and four to allow for the BBC's extended coverage of the Wimbledon tennis tournament – the first repeat of a complete story, and the only one ever to be incorporated into the fiction of the series itself.

It has been reported that *The Evil of the Daleks* was intended to be the very last Dalek story, their creator Terry Nation having apparently withdrawn his permission for the creatures to appear in *Doctor Who* as he hoped to launch them in their own series in the USA. Some doubt is cast on this, however, by the fact that less than six months later, while season five was being made, the production team actively discussed the possibility of doing a story featuring both the Daleks and the Cybermen – an idea taken sufficiently seriously for Terry Nation to be contacted in December 1967 in an attempt to sound out his views. Strangely, nothing came of these discussions.

Season five exhibited a uniformly high standard of writing, direction, production and acting, and has since become widely regarded as one of the very best in *Doctor Who*'s long history. However, the only true constant in *Doctor Who* is change, and the series' ingredients were already being remixed for the following season.

CHAPTER TWELVE

Season Six: The Journey Ends

After the widely acclaimed success of season five, season six – the first episode of which was transmitted at 5:15 p.m. on Saturday 10 August 1968 – saw something of a downturn in *Doctor Who*'s fortunes. Certainly it was a rather fraught and chaotic time behind the scenes, with a number of unexpected difficulties arising during the course of the year.

The problems began with the season opener, *The Dominators* (which was made as the pe-nultimate story of the fifth production block, immediately after *The Wheel in Space*). Writers Mervyn Haisman and Henry Lincoln on this occasion delivered their draft scripts extremely late, and script editor Derrick Sherwin, unhappy with their content, decided to do a major rewrite, cutting the serial from six episodes to five in the process. Very dissatisfied with the end result, Haisman and Lincoln insisted on the use of a pseudonym, Norman Ashby (made up of the forenames of their respective fathers-in-law).

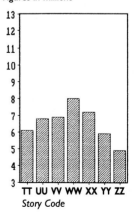

SEASON SIX	
CODE	**TITLE**
TT	THE DOMINATORS
UU	THE MIND ROBBER
VV	THE INVASION
WW	THE KROTONS
XX	THE SEEDS OF DEATH
YY	THE SPACE PIRATES
ZZ	THE WAR GAMES

RATINGS

Figures in millions

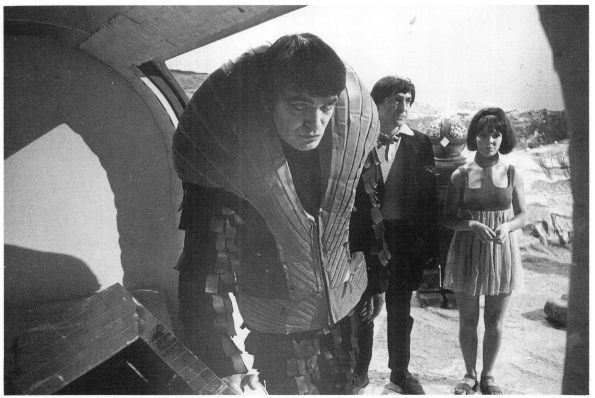

Dominator Rago (Ronald Allen) examines the Dulcian shuttle craft while a Quark guards the Doctor and Zoe.
The Dominators.

The Doctor and Zoe in ▲ the Dulcian war museum. *The Dominators.*

The interior of the ▲ Dominators' space craft. *The Dominators.*

Teel (Giles Block) and Kando (Felicity Gibson) are menaced by two Quarks. *The Dominators.*

'I found Mervyn and Henry tough guys to work with,' recalls Sherwin. 'They were aggressive writers, insofar as they were very difficult to convince that they had made a wrong move if something needed adjusting or a piece of dialogue needed changing. They fought for every dot and comma. It was not a happy relationship, in fact, they hated my guts! I was a very hard taskmaster.'

Haisman and Lincoln, for their part, felt that Sherwin had completely altered the basis of their story, which under its original title, *The Beautiful People*, had been conceived as a comment on the hippie movement. 'We were right in the middle of it then,' Haisman later said, 'and in our story we wanted to examine what happens to a completely submissive society – one which has lost the desire or the need to fight – when it is suddenly overrun. Do they remain true to their ideals, or do they have to set aside their ideals and fight? It's a question which we simply wanted to examine.'

In the final version of the story, the TARDIS materialises on the planet Dulkis, currently under threat from two alien Dominators. Aided by their robotic servants, the Quarks, and slave workers drawn from the native Dulcian population, the Dominators set about drilling bore holes, through which they plan to fire rockets into the planet's molten core. Their intention is then to drop an atomic seed capsule into the resulting eruption, turning Dulkis into a radioactive mass – fuel for the Dominators' space fleet. The pacifistic Dulcian Councillors refuse to retaliate, although Cully, the rebellious son of their leader Senex, has already joined forces with the time travellers. The Doctor eventually defeats the Dominators by intercepting the seed capsule as it is dropped and placing it on board their ship, which is then destroyed shortly after takeoff. Dulkis suffers only a minor volcanic eruption as a result of the rockets fired into its magma.

Even after *The Dominators* was broadcast arguments continued between Haisman and Lin-

Toba (Kenneth Ives) and Rago. *The Dominators.*

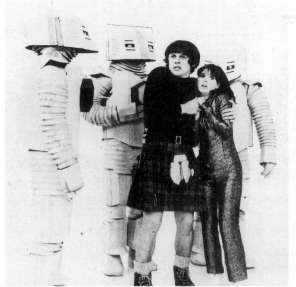

Jamie and Zoe are captured by the White Robots. *The Mind Robber.*

The Master of the Land of Fiction (Emrys Jones). *The Mind Robber.*

▲ D'Artagnan (John Greenwood). *The Mind Robber.*

▲ Rapunzel (Christine Pirie). *The Mind Robber.*

▲ Blackbeard (Gerry Wain). *The Mind Robber.*

coln and the BBC. Without the writers' knowledge, permission had been given for the Quarks to be featured in one of the *TV Comic Doctor Who* strip stories, and this gave rise to a dispute as to who owned the rights. One consequence of these ongoing disagreements was that a planned third Yeti tale, which had been at the storyline stage, fell through. This story, at one point thought of as Jamie's swansong, would have been set in and around a Scottish castle, the laird of which was under the control of the Great Intelligence.

While *The Dominators* was, in the event, a rather lacklustre start to the season – due in part to the problems over the scripts – *The Mind Robber* (originally called *The Fact of Fiction* and later *Manpower*) was a different matter altogether. Quite unlike any previous *Doctor Who* story it told of a dream-like world where fictional characters are real. The writer was Peter Ling, co-creator of the soap operas *Compact* and *Crossroads*, who explained how it had been commissioned:

'It all really came about as a result of a railway journey. Terrance Dicks and Derrick Sherwin were working on *Crossroads* and *Doctor Who* at that time – although how they found time to do both I don't know! During that time when we were all commuting to Birmingham I got to know them and they suggested I wrote a *Doctor Who* story. My first reaction was "Oh no, I couldn't possibly do that – it's not my cup of tea and I don't know anything about science fiction." In the end I did what must have been one of the least SF-orientated stories they made.

'*The Mind Robber* was about literature, not science – a planet where fantasy exists. I think they thought at the time, "This is a bit of a dodgy one – it may not work but it will be fun to do." I

don't think they thought of it as the direction in which they wanted to take the series.'

Part of the inspiration for the story was Ling's observation that many fans of soap operas such as *Crossroads* come to believe that the characters are in fact real people.

The Mind Robber begins with the Doctor having to activate the TARDIS's emergency unit to escape the lava flow caused by the volcanic eruption at the end of *The Dominators*. The ship is lifted out of the space/time dimension and arrives in an endless void where the Doctor, Jamie and Zoe are menaced by strange White Robots. Having regained the safety of the TARDIS, the travellers believe they have escaped, but suddenly the ship disintegrates! They find themselves in a land of fiction, where they are hunted by toy soldiers and encounter characters such as Rapunzel and Lemuel Gulliver.

This domain is presided over by a man known only as the Master, a prolific English writer from 1926, who is in turn controlled by a computer, the intelligence responsible for which has brought him here to exploit his near-boundless imagination. Now, however, the Master is desperate to escape and wants the Doctor to take his place. The Doctor's mind is forcibly linked to the computer but he gains a degree of control as a result and is able to engage the Master in a battle of wills using a variety of fictional characters. Zoe and Jamie meanwhile succeed in overloading the computer and, in the confusion, the White Robots destroy it, finally freeing the Master.

Like *The Dominators*, *The Mind Robber* underwent a number of major changes at the scripting stage. It was originally commissioned on 31

Jamie and the Doctor. ▲
The Mind Robber.

THE DOMINATORS SOUNDS

In preparing the sound effects for
The Dominators, *Brian Hodgson
took the unusual step of basing most
of them around the voice of actress
Sheila Grant. Thus the Dominators'
space craft effects and the Quark
exterminations, voices and operating
'hum' were all modulations of
Grant's voice.*

Wendy Padbury, Frazer Hines and Patrick Troughton on location for *The Invasion*.

January 1968 as a six-parter, and five scripts had
been delivered by 9 April. A decision was then
taken to shorten it to a four-parter. Subsequently
the shortening of *The Dominators* from six episodes to five meant that there was a spare slot to
be filled before the end of the production block
of which *The Mind Robber* was the last story,
completing its studio work on Friday 19 July 1968.
Derrick Sherwin added a completely new opening episode to Ling's story, extending it to five;
because of this, for the only time in the series'
history, no writer's credit appeared on screen for
that episode.

In putting together this extra episode, Sherwin
had something of a resource problem, as he later

explained: 'We had already spent all the money.
I had no sets, no visiting characters and no new
monsters. All I had was a white cyclorama cloth,
lots of smoke, the three regulars, the TARDIS prop
and what was left of the tatty TARDIS interior set
– and out of that I had to construct an episode! I
also used some old robot costumes that I found
dumped in a storeroom.'

These robot costumes in fact originated from
one of BBC2's *Out of the Unknown* science-fiction
plays, *The Prophet*, which had been transmitted
on 1 January 1967. (*Doctor Who* later returned the
favour as the *Out of the Unknown* episode 'Get

Jamie (Hamish Wilson) ▶
**the Doctor and Zoe meet
Lemuel Gulliver (Bernard
Horsfall) and a clockwork
soldier. *The Mind Robber*.**

**The Doctor, Zoe and Jamie are captured by clockwork
soldiers in the forest of words. *The Mind Robber*.**

The Cybermen descend the steps near St Paul's Cathedral. *The Invasion.*

▲ Two shots of the helicopter used during location filming for *The Invasion*. The UNIT soldier is Captain Turner (Robert Sidaway).

Off My Cloud', broadcast on 1 April 1969, featured both the TARDIS police box and the Daleks, making their first appearances on colour TV.)

Another change which Sherwin had to make to *The Mind Robber* was due to an unforeseeable crisis which arose while it was in production: Frazer Hines caught chicken pox, requiring him to be absent from the whole of episode two. Luckily, the fantastical nature of the story meant that Sherwin could easily insert a scene in which the Doctor is challenged to assemble a jigsaw puzzle of Jamie's face and gets it wrong, resulting in a temporary change of appearance for his companion. Until Hines's return, midway through episode three, Jamie was then played by a different actor, Hamish Wilson.

While season six made use of a far greater variety of settings and plots than had the largely Earth-bound, formulaic season five, it also featured fewer monsters. This was not so much an artistic decision on the production team's part as a matter of economic necessity: the programme's budget would no longer run to the cost of creating large numbers of convincing alien costumes. Even so, of the seven stories in the season, there were still three which could be considered traditional monster tales.

The first of these was *The Invasion*, which was conceived by the production team as a sequel to season five's *The Web of Fear*. The return of Professor Travers in that earlier story had shown that popular and well-written humanoid characters could be brought back for guest appearances with just as much success as the monsters. It was in fact intended that both Travers and his daughter Anne would appear once more in *The Invasion*, but this idea had to be dropped and two very similar characters substituted when the artistes concerned proved to be unavailable. One character from *The Web of Fear* who did make a comeback was Lethbridge-Stewart, now promoted to Brigadier and portrayed as before by Nicholas

Courtney. This time he was placed at the head of a special new military and scientific organisation, UNIT – the United Nations Intelligence Taskforce – which was to become an integral part of *Doctor Who*'s format in the early seventies.

The Invasion also had the same director as *The Web of Fear*, Douglas Camfield, whose tight direction and expert knowledge of all matters military helped to make *The Invasion* one of the highlights of the season.

The Invasion differed from *The Web of Fear* in one important respect: it featured not the Yeti but an even more popular race of monsters, the Cybermen. The basic story idea was conceived by their co-creator Kit Pedler, who was paid a copyright fee for the use not only of the Cybermen but also of the Cybermats, even though the latter did not appear in the final version of the story, and the scripts written by Derrick Sherwin. Sherwin had by this stage effectively become co-producer of *Doctor Who* with Peter Bryant, leaving Terrance Dicks to take over as script editor proper. A young writer named Trevor Ray was brought in to replace Dicks as assistant script editor.

When the TARDIS becomes invisible on materialising in twentieth-century England, the Doctor calls at Professor Travers's London home to seek his help in repairing the faulty circuits. However, it is some four years since their last meeting and Travers and Anne are now away in America. In their absence the house has been let to a compu-

SCHEDULED BREAK
To allow for coverage of the Olympic Games in Mexico, there was a two-week gap in transmission between the end of **The Mind Robber** *and the start of* **The Invasion**.

◄ Three clockwork soldiers (Paul Alexander, Ian Hines, Richard Ireson). *The Mind Robber.*

◄ Members of the public watch as a Cyberman is filmed emerging from the sewers. *The Invasion.*

A shot from model Isobel Watkins's (Sally Faulkner) portfolio. *The Invasion.*

A Cyberman emerges ▲ from the London sewers. *The Invasion.*

The Cybermen advance on the UNIT troops. *The Invasion.*

Gia Kelly (Louise Pajo). ▶ *The Seeds of Death.*

ter scientist, Professor Watkins, and his niece Isobel. Isobel reveals that her uncle has recently disappeared, and the Doctor offers to help track him down, starting at the place where he last worked – the London HQ of International Electromatics, the world's major supplier of electronic equipment.

On meeting IE's managing director, Tobias Vaughn, the Doctor is immediately suspicious. His doubts are confirmed after he becomes reacquainted with Lethbridge-Stewart and learns that there have been other mysterious disappearances at the IE premises. Investigating further, he discovers that Vaughn is in fact in league with the Cybermen, who are planning an invasion of Earth, but is also plotting against them in order to seize power for himself. Watkins is being held prisoner by Vaughn and forced to develop the cerebration mentor, a machine designed to generate emotional impulses which can be used as a weapon against the Cybermen.

The Cybermen immobilise most of Earth's population, sending a hypnotic signal through special circuits incorporated in all IE equipment, and launch their invasion. However, the Doctor has managed to protect himself and his friends from the Cybermen's signal and, with help from an embittered Vaughn, the aliens' scheme is eventually defeated.

The Invasion (which, like *The Moonbase*, had the working title *The Return of the Cybermen*) was originally planned as a six-part story but extended to an eight-parter at the scripting stage. As the first entry in *Doctor Who*'s sixth production block (studio recording for which began on Friday 20

Slaar (Alan Bennion). *The Seeds of Death.*

Zoe and the Doctor tend to an unconcious Vana (Madeleine Mills). *The Krotons.*

MUSIC	
Story	**Composer**
The Dominators	none
The Mind Robber	Stock
	(Symphony No 7 in
	E Major by Bruckner)
The Invasion	Don Harper
	(John Baker provided
	the muzak playing in
	Vaughn's offices; other
	musical stings were provided
	by Brian Hodgson)
The Krotons	none
The Seeds of Death	
	Dudley Simpson
The Space Pirates	
	Dudley Simpson
	(vocal: Mary Thomas)
The War Games	
	Dudley Simpson

September 1968), it benefited from a larger location film allocation than usual. Particularly memorable were the scenes of the Cybermen bursting forth from their base in the London sewers to take over the city. With the co-operation of the Ministry of Defence, director Douglas Camfield was also able to use the 2nd Battalion of Coldstream Guards for a day's filming at Acton, which increased still further the realistic feel of the piece.

The other returning monsters of the season were the Ice Warriors, who made their second appearance in Brian Hayles' *The Seeds of Death* which had been in development since the beginning of 1968 and originally had the title *The Lords of the Red Planet.* Terrance Dicks worked quite closely with Hayles on his scripts for this story as the original drafts were not quite what was required, and he is listed on BBC documentation as co-author of episodes four to six. On screen, he was credited simply as script editor. Derrick Sherwin's name did not appear, although he was in fact still working alongside Peter Bryant as co-producer.

This time the TARDIS brings the Doctor, Jamie and Zoe to Earth in the twenty-first century, where they learn that human society is now reliant on T-Mat – a matter-transmitting device which beams people and freight instantly to destinations all around the globe, using a Moon relay station. The system is currently malfunctioning and the travellers agree to pilot an obsolete rocket to the Moon station to investigate. To their horror, they find the place overrun by Ice Warriors preparing an invasion.

To weaken Earth's resistance the Warriors are using the T-Mat to send Martian seed pods to selected points on the planet's surface. These pods emit a fungus which draws oxygen from the surrounding atmosphere, making it lethal to humans but ideal for the Martians themselves. The travellers use the T-Mat to get back to Earth, where the Doctor discovers that the only thing that can destroy the pods is water. At the local weather-control bureau, having disposed of an Ice Warrior left on guard there, he adjusts the instruments so as to cause a downpour, thus ending the threat of the pods. He then returns to the Moon where, by a ruse, he is able to misdirect the Martian invasion fleet into a close orbit around the Sun, where it will be destroyed. The remaining Ice Warriors on the Moon are also killed.

◀ **The Doctor and Tobias Vaughn (Kevin Stoney) prepare to confront the Cybermen with the cerebration mentor.** *The Invasion*

Hermack's 'V' Ship. ▲

Caven's Beta Dart docks ▲
with Beacon Alpha-1.

Beacon Alpha-1. ▲

The 'V' Ship docks with ▲
Beacon Alpha-4.

**All the above photographs
were taken during the model
filming for *The Space Pirates*.
Models designed and
directed by John Wood.**

A Kroton en route to attack the TARDIS. *The Krotons.*

In this second Ice Warrior story, two new levels of the Martian hierarchy were introduced: a commander, Slaar, and the Grand Marshal of the invasion fleet. Their costumes differed from those of the basic Warrior, being much less bulky and boasting a larger, high-domed helmet which in the Grand Marshal's case had a glittery appearance. The Ice Warriors themselves, of which three were seen, wore costumes parts of which were re-used from their debut story, an important economy measure at a time when, as Terrance Dicks puts it, '*Doctor Who* was quite seriously underbudgeted.'

Although by no means as extensive as in the case of *The Invasion*, there was a certain amount of location work done for *The Seeds of Death*. As the story's director, Michael Ferguson, recalls, this led to a rather amusing incident:

'We did some location shooting on Hampstead Heath and there was a very tall actor playing one of the Ice Warriors. I remember I was filming when suddenly there was a terrible crash. Somebody had been driving past in their car and been

so astonished by the sight of an Ice Warrior, casually leaning against a tree, smoking a cigarette with a cigarette holder, that they had neglected to notice that they were just about to run into the car in front!'

Season six's other monster tale was *The Krotons* by Robert Holmes, a name new to *Doctor Who*. Holmes had originally submitted an earlier version of the story, then entitled *The Space Trap*, to BBC2's *Out of the Unknown*. However, as it could not be used on that series it had been passed on to Derrick Sherwin, who in turn had handed it to Terrance Dicks, then still working as an assistant. 'I liked the idea,' recalls Dicks, 'but because at that time we did not have a slot for it, I was told I could commission it as a four-parter in reserve, or as one for the next season. Either way there was no particular haste as no one was in a hurry for it. I worked on it with Bob Holmes in a very leisurely fashion and it became a sort of hobby for me, to keep me out of mischief. With some pride I can say it was the first completely independent thing I had ever done on *Doctor Who*.'

At this time a script for a proposed comedy-based story entitled *The Prison in Space*, commissioned by then script editor Peter Bryant on 4 June 1968 from writer Dick Sharples, turned out to be unsuitable. 'David Maloney had just joined as director,' says Dicks, 'only one and a half scripts were in, and everybody hated them. Panic and despair quickly ensued, with all concerned daily getting more and more disgruntled. I did some work on it, but it was, with hindsight, a doomed project from the start. Eventually we all got together around a table for a "What are we going to do?" meeting, at which point I said I had a very good four-part script already in the cupboard which we could use instead. David said, "Let me see it." He went away only to call back a short time

Dervish (Brian Peck) and Caven (Dudley Foster). *The Space Pirates.*

Major Ian Warne (Donald Gee) and General Nikolai Hermack (Jack May). *The Space Pirates.*

Zoe, Jamie and the Doctor in the Gonds' Learning Hall. *The Krotons.*

later pronouncing *The Krotons* to be workable.'

In this story, the Doctor, Jamie and Zoe arrive on the twin-sunned world of the primitive Gonds, who are ruled and taught in a form of self-perpetuating slavery by the alien Krotons, crystalline beings whose ship, the Dynatrope, crash-landed here thousands of years ago after being damaged in a space battle. The Krotons are at present in suspended animation awaiting a time when they can be reconstituted by absorption of mental energy. To this end the two most brilliant Gond students are periodically received into the Dynatrope, apparently to become 'companions of the Krotons' but in truth to have their mental energy drained before being killed. When the Doctor and Zoe take the students' test, their mental power is sufficient to reanimate the Krotons. However, the Doctor discovers that the aliens' life system is based on tellurium and, with help from the Gond scientist Beta, he is able to destroy them using a variant of sulphuric acid, which acts as a poison to them.

The last-minute nature of *The Krotons* was perhaps apparent at times from the transmitted episodes, particularly where the Krotons themselves were concerned. Their limitations were certainly recognised by the production team, as Terrance Dicks recalls: 'We were underbudgeted, so with the little money we could give them it was hardly surprising that Visual Effects could not make the Krotons live up to our expectations. The

director, David Maloney, had to do some camera script rewrites himself when it became obvious that they could do little more than stand still and loom menacingly. So where the script might have read "Kroton moves forward and fires gun", David amended it to read, "Kroton stands still and fires gun".'

Whatever drawbacks the Krotons might have had, producer Peter Bryant was in no doubt that the commercial success of *Doctor Who* relied to a large extent on its monsters. Seeing that part one of *The Krotons* had gained an audience of nine million viewers, compared with an average of under seven million for some recent stories, he wrote a memo on 21 January 1969 to BBC Enterprises, bemoaning the cost of creating such alien creatures and explaining that, as he had no budget left, the next six months' worth of *Doctor Who* had been planned with no monsters at all. His point was that if Enterprises wanted to be able to market the show, they should be prepared to contribute some money towards creating its most marketable assets. His memo provoked no concrete reaction.

The series' ratings had in fact been climbing since the beginning of the season, from an average of 6.1 million viewers per episode for *The Dominators* to an average of 8.0 million per episode for *The Krotons* – the best achieved since season four's *The Macra Terror.* Similarly, the average appreciation figures had risen from 53

Lady Jennifer Buckingham ▶
(Jane Sherwin) driving her
ambulance in the First
World War zone. *The War
Games.*

The travellers arrive on Beacon Alpha-4. *The Space
Pirates.*

ROBERT HOLMES
WRITER

*Robert Colin Holmes was the
youngest ever commissioned officer in
the Queen's Own Cameron
Highlanders, serving in Burma. After
demob he joined the police and
passed out top of his year at Hendon
Police College. He eventually moved
to court work, and left the force to
become a court reporter and
journalist. His work as a sports
reporter took him to the Midlands,
where he became the final editor of
John Bull Magazine, at the same
time submitting material to Granada
TV for **Knight Errant**. Other early
TV work included **Emergency
Ward 10**, **Ghost Squad**, **Public
Eye**, **Undermind** (his first science
fiction) and **Intrigue**. His first work
for **Doctor Who** was a commission
to write **The Space Trap**, later
retitled **The Krotons**. Subsequently
he went on to become one of the
series' most popular writers,
responsible for more than a dozen
televised stories. He also had a
successful period as **Doctor Who**'s
script editor between 1974 and
1977. He scripted much TV drama
during the seventies and eighties,
including a **Wednesday Play** (**The
Brilliant New Testament**) and
episodes of **Doomwatch**, **Dr
Finlay's Casebook**, **Dead of
Night**, **The Regiment**, **Warship**,
Spy Trap and **Dixon of Dock
Green**, and he adapted the BBC's
1981 science-fiction thriller serial
The Nightmare Man from David
Wiltshire's novel. He was working on
further **Doctor Who** episodes when
he died, after a short illness, on 24
May 1986.*

per cent for *The Dominators* and 52 per cent for *The Mind Robber* to 57 per cent for *The Seeds of Death* and *The Krotons* – second only in the Troughton era to the 58 per cent gained by *The Wheel in Space*. However, in terms of its average position in the weekly TV chart, perhaps the best guide to a series' popularity, *Doctor Who* was faring less well. It had dropped from 55th place for *The Dominators* to 65th for *The Invasion*, and although *The Krotons* saw a brief resurgence to 60th, the downward trend then resumed, with a sharp drop to 83rd for the season's penultimate story, *The Space Pirates*, and 81st for the final one, *The War Games*. After *The Krotons*, the average ratings and appreciation figures also turned downwards, reaching low points of 4.9 million viewers per episode and 54 per cent respectively for *The War Games*. Peter Bryant's apprehension about the season's latter months was well founded.

The story originally intended to follow *The Seeds of Death* was *The Dream Spinner* by Paul Wheeler, commissioned by Derrick Sherwin on 18 July 1968. However, this subsequently fell through and, having been impressed by his scripts for *The Krotons*, the production team then asked Robert Holmes to make a second contribution to the season – *The Space Pirates*.

When the TARDIS materialises in Earth's future on a navigation beacon far out in space, the Doctor, Jamie and Zoe get involved in a struggle between the International Space Corps and a group of space pirates plundering Argonite. The ISC, led by General Hermack, are convinced that the pirates' mastermind is Milo Clancey, an inno-

cent yet eccentric space-mining pioneer, while the true culprit is in fact a man named Caven. Caven is assisted by Madeleine Issigri, daughter of Clancey's one-time partner Dom who, unbeknown to her, is his captive. When Madeleine discovers Caven's full treachery she sees the error of her ways and helps to bring him to justice.

The Space Pirates was very much a product of its time. With the Apollo moon landings only a few short months away and public interest in space travel at an all-time high, it was an obvious idea for *Doctor Who* to attempt a space opera. A particularly notable feature of the story was its extensive model work, involving a number of detailed spaceship miniatures. These scenes were shot in such a way as to exhibit the same strong contrasts between light and dark as the pictures being sent back from the Apollo missions. For the sake of added realism, as most viewers would by now have been well aware that a trip from the Earth to the Moon would take two days, the script was careful to emphasise the long journey times involved in travelling between the various different locations in which the story was set. This had the perhaps unintended additional effect of slowing up the action, with the result that *The Space Pirates* provided a very noticeable contrast to the fast-moving style of the preceding story, *The Seeds of Death*.

The final story of season six, *The War Games* by Malcolm Hulke and Terrance Dicks, was possibly its most important. Not only did it mark the end of an era in every sense of the phrase, it also laid the foundations for *Doctor Who*'s future.

Like *The Krotons* and *The Space Pirates*, it was a production which came about due to problems on other scripts. By October 1968, Malcolm Hulke had been commissioned to write a breakdown for a four-part serial intended to be the penultimate one of the season. Derrick Sherwin, meanwhile, had been working for some six months on a story of his own which was planned as the season's six-part finale. In the event, Sherwin's story fell through around the end of 1968, and Terrance Dicks was given the task of working with Hulke to extend his original idea into an epic ten-part adventure with which to fill the gap.

One task which Hulke and Dicks knew they had to accomplish in their story was writing out the second Doctor, as Patrick Troughton had now elected to leave the series. In addition, they had to provide a suitable exit for his two companions, Jamie and Zoe, as Frazer Hines and Wendy Padbury had decided that it would be best if they bowed out at the same time. Also, owing to the last-minute nature of the project, the two writers had to complete their ten scripts at the rate of about one every two days in order to get them ready in time for the story's production.

The TARDIS arrives in what appears to be no-man's-land on a First World War battlefront. In reality, however, this is not even Earth: it is an alien world split into a number of different zones, in each of which a fierce war is being waged. The wars are controlled by a race known only as the Aliens, who have gathered soldiers from many periods of Earth's history, brainwashed them and put them to battle with the aim of forming an invincible army from the survivors. With this army, they then plan to take over the galaxy. The Aliens' War Lord is assisted by a Security Chief and a War Chief, the latter of whom the Doctor quickly recognises as a member of his own race, the Time Lords. The War Chief has in fact provided the

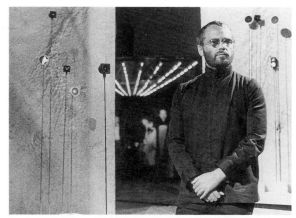

The War Lord (Philip Madoc) on trial by the Time Lords. *The War Games.*

Aliens with the time vessels, SIDRATs, which are essential to their scheme; but he secretly plans to double-cross them and seize power for himself.

When the War Lord learns of the War Chief's duplicity he has him shot down by guards. By this time, however, with the aid of a band of human resistance fighters who have shaken off the Aliens' control, the Doctor has already managed to put a stop to the war games. Unfortunately, he has no way of returning all the human soldiers to their proper times and places, so he has no choice but to call on the Time Lords for help. As the story moves towards its conclusion, we finally learn some of the secrets of the Doctor's past which

TERRANCE DICKS
SCRIPT EDITOR/ WRITER

Born in East Ham, London, in 1935, Terrance Dicks was educated at the local grammar school and went on to read English at Downing College, Cambridge. After two years' national service in the army, he got a job as an advertising copywriter. This lasted for five years, during which time he started writing radio scripts as a sideline. Eventually he switched to full-time freelance writing, first on plays and comedy series for radio and then in television on programmes like **The Avengers** *and* **Crossroads.** *Following some five years as script editor on* **Doctor Who**, *ending in 1974, he returned to freelance writing. Later he produced some of the BBC's classic serials. Aside from his contributions to the* **Doctor Who** *TV series, he has also written two spin-off plays,* **Doctor Who and the Daleks – The Seven Keys to Doomsday** *in 1974 and* **Doctor Who – The Ultimate Adventure** *in 1989 – and well over fifty novelisations. Today he is one of the UK's most prolific authors of children's fiction.*

PETER LING
WRITER

Peter Ling started his writing career whilst in a sanatorium recovering from tuberculosis, contracted at the age of sixteen towards the end of the Second World War. He began sending material on spec to several TV comedians – one of whom was Jon Pertwee – and later wrote comedy linking material for a BBC magazine series called **Whirlygig.** *It was here that he met up with Hazel Adair, with whom he later collaborated on an early BBC soap opera,* **Compact.** *They also developed* **Crossroads** *for Lew Grade, and Ling was to work on this for 23 of its 24 years. After* **The Mind Robber** *he suggested one further* **Doctor Who** *idea – about a planet on which time runs backwards – but this was rejected as being too complex to realise.*

Jamie, Zoe and the Doctor held prisoner in the cellar of a chateau. *The War Games.*

PRODUCTION ROUTINE

The studios used for recording season six were:

The Dominators:
Parts one and two in TC4, parts three to five in TC3.

The Mind Robber:
Parts one, two and five in TC3, parts three and four in Studio D, Lime Grove.

The Invasion:
All in Studio D, Lime Grove.

The Krotons:
All in Studio D, Lime Grove.

The Seeds of Death:
All in Studio D, Lime Grove.

The Space Pirates:
Part one in Studio D, Lime Grove, parts two to four and six in TC4, part five in TC6.

The War Games:
Parts one, two and four in TC4, parts five, eight and ten in TC8, part seven in TC1 and part nine in TC6. Details for parts three and six are currently unknown.

TC = Television Centre

RECORDING

*Season six saw a further increase in out-of-scene-order recording. Episodes five, seven and eight of **The Invasion** and episodes two to six of **The Seeds of Death** were all taped using this technique. In addition, the beginning of **The Mind Robber** part three was recorded at the end of part two's studio day, so that actor Hamish Wilson, standing in for the ill Frazer Hines, would not have to return the following week; and the absent Hines's single scene for part two was recorded as a video insert immediately before the shooting of part five. Another change this season was that the studio day was generally scheduled to finish at 10:00 p.m. rather than 9:45 p.m. each week, giving an extra fifteen minutes recording each day.*

Zoe, the Doctor and Jamie say their farewells at the end of *The War Games.*

have been kept shrouded in mystery over the past six years. Having unavoidably revealed his position to the Time Lords, he is taken prisoner, placed on trial and subsequently sentenced to exile on Earth. Jamie and Zoe, meanwhile, are sent back to their own points of origin.

Before being dispatched to begin his exile, the Doctor is told that he must again take on a new appearance. A number of possible choices are displayed on a large screen, but none of them meets with his approval. Suddenly, to his indignation, the Doctor is himself up on the screen, and his image begins to break up and revolve as the Time Lords trigger his second regeneration. The final image is of the protesting figure of the Doctor, his face in shadow, slowly spinning off into blackness.

The producer's credit on *The War Games* went to Derrick Sherwin as Peter Bryant was by this time becoming gradually less and less involved with *Doctor Who*, having been assigned to troubleshoot an ailing BBC series entitled *Paul Temple*. Later, Sherwin would move across to join him on that show. Peter Bryant's last credit as producer was therefore on *The Space Pirates* (for which Sherwin had returned temporarily to script-editing duties as Terrance Dicks was so busy on *The War Games*).

During the latter stages of season five, it had been necessary for the regular cast to give up some of their weekends for location filming. After

a while they had protested about this, and it had been agreed that time would in future be specially set aside for location work. Mainly for this reason, there had been a two-week break in recording between *The Invasion* and *The Krotons*, a three-week break between *The Krotons* and *The Seeds of Death* and further breaks of two weeks each between *The Seeds of Death* and *The Space Pirates*, and *The Space Pirates* and *The War Games*. Also, the regulars appeared only in film insert sequences in part six of *The Space Pirates*, as they were already away on location for *The War Games* when that episode was recorded. This was the only time apart from season three's *Mission to the Unknown* that none of the regulars was present in the studio for recording of an episode. Thus by the time of *The War Games* (the latter episodes of which were made on Thursdays rather than Fridays) episodes were once again being recorded only a week in advance of transmission. The final episode of the production block and indeed of the season was recorded on Thursday 12 June 1969 for transmission on Saturday 21 June.

The exit not only of Patrick Troughton but also Frazer Hines and Wendy Padbury brought the second Doctor's era to a very final conclusion. For viewers there was no cushion of a staggered departure of their favourite characters – all were gone in one fell swoop. In the meantime, the Saturday evening slot would be filled by a new imported American science-fiction series called *Star Trek*.

CHAPTER THIRTEEN

The Companions

The Doctor has always had a companion (or companions) on his travels, and it seems that he, like the humans he so admires, is a social animal. What's more, the companions serve a vital dramatic function in the telling of the stories. For one thing, the presence of someone in whom the Doctor can confide enables the writer to give explanations by way of their dialogue, without having to resort to voiceovers or clumsy techniques such as characters thinking out loud. The companions also represent an important point of audience identification, which cannot really be said of the Doctor himself.

Another factor relates to the continuous recording method used in the sixties. To keep breaks to a minimum, scripts had to be structured so as to allow a smooth transition from scene to scene, and in most cases this required at least four characters. While two actors performed a scene on one set, another two would position themselves on the next, ready for the cameras to cut to them; then, while the second pair played out their scene, the first would move to new positions (perhaps on a different set), and so on. The more characters there were, the easier it became to avoid a recording break. For example, actors who had to make costume or make-up changes during the course of an episode could do so without the need for an interruption if the writer was able to focus attention elsewhere for a few scenes. This is one of the main reasons why *Doctor Who* had as many as four regular characters to start with but progressively fewer as more sophisticated editing techniques became available.

When the programme started, viewers were introduced to the Doctor's then only companion, his grand-daughter Susan (Carole Ann Ford). At the outset, she is attempting to pass herself off as an

CAROLE ANN FORD
SUSAN FOREMAN

*Carole Ann Ford was born in June 1940 and first appeared in a film at the age of eight. Following acting and elocution lessons, she started doing commercials and walk-on work, and her first proper role was in the play **Women of the Streets**. She continued working in theatre, film (including **Day of the Triffids**) and television (including **Emergency Ward 10**, **Moonstrike**, **Compact** and **Man on a Bicycle**). After leaving **Doctor Who**, Carole worked mainly in the theatre. Following the birth of her second daughter, Tara, she decided to put her career on hold and has acted only occasionally since – though she did reprise her role as Susan in the twentieth-anniversary **Doctor Who** story **The Five Doctors**.*

WILLIAM RUSSELL
IAN CHESTERTON

*Russell Enoch – who also works under the name William Russell – was born on 19 November 1924 and became interested in acting at an early age. He was involved in organising entertainments during his national service in the Royal Air Force and then, after university, went into repertory theatre. He appeared in **Hamlet** in London's West End and won a number of film roles, usually as a dashing hero. Notable TV work followed in **The Adventures of Sir Lancelot** for ITV and **Nicholas Nickleby** and **David Copperfield** for the BBC, shortly after which he was cast as Ian Chesterton in **Doctor Who**. He later continued a successful acting career, particularly in the theatre, and for a time held a senior post in the actors' union, Equity. In recent years he has been a member of the Royal Shakespeare Company.*

William Hartnell and Carole Ann Ford (Susan) in *The Sensorites*.

William Russell (Ian) in *Marco Polo*.

JACQUELINE HILL
BARBARA WRIGHT

Born in 1931, Jacqueline Hill trained at the Royal Academy of Dramatic Art and made her stage debut in London's West End in **The Shrike**. *Many more roles followed, including, on TV,* **Shop Window**, **Fabian of the Yard** *and* **An Enemy of the People**. *It was around this time that she married top director Alvin Rakoff, who cast her opposite Sean Connery in one of ABC TV's* **Armchair Theatre** *plays. She was asked to play Barbara Wright in* **Doctor Who** *after she and producer Verity Lambert, whom she knew socially, discussed the role at a party. Soon after leaving the series in 1965 she gave up acting to raise a family. However, she resumed her career in 1979 and gained further TV credits on, amongst other programmes,* **Romeo and Juliet**, **Tales of the Unexpected**, *and the 1980* **Doctor Who** *story* **Meglos** *(as a character called Lexa).*

MAUREEN O'BRIEN
VICKI

After studying for a teaching diploma at the Central School of Speech and Drama, Maureen O'Brien became a founder member of the Everyman Theatre in her native Liverpool. About three months later she was persuaded to audition for the part of Vicki in **Doctor Who**. *She was reluctant to accept the role, but did so partly to be with her London-based boyfriend (later her husband). It was a decision she later regretted as, although she liked the people she worked with, she did not enjoy the job and the enormous publicity it brought her. After leaving* **Doctor Who** *she worked as a supply teacher at a girl's school in Kennington, then returned to the theatre. This was followed by a three-year spell in Canada. Since returning to the UK in the mid-seventies, she has had further success in theatre, TV, radio and film, and as a writer of crime fiction.*

JACKIE LANE
DOROTHEA 'DODO' CHAPLET

In 1963, young actress Jackie Lane was playing the part of a secretary in **Compact** *when she was offered the part of the Doctor's grand-daughter, Susan, but decided that she did not want to be tied down to a year's contract. In 1966, however, having had only sporadic work in between, she accepted an offer from John Wiles, who had seen her as a Cockney character in a play, to portray Dorothea Chaplet. When, four months later, her contract expired, it was not renewed. She then gave up acting, and went to work as a secretary in the Australian embassy in Paris. She returned to England some time later and is now head of an acting agency's voice-over department.*

Maureen O'Brien (Vicki), William Hartnell and Peter Purves (Steven) in *The Time Meddler*.

ordinary Earth schoolgirl, but her teachers cannot help but notice that there is something distinctly unusual about her. While in some subjects she appears lamentably ignorant – mistakenly suggesting, for example, that England has a decimal currency in 1963 – in others she excels. As Ian Chesterton, her science master, remarks, 'She lets her knowledge out a bit at a time so as not to embarrass me.' The title of *Doctor Who*'s first episode, *An Unearthly Child*, is indeed an eloquent description of this strange human/alien girl.

Susan appears physically to be a child of about fifteen, the age her teachers believe her to be, but her mental capacity is far more developed than most humans could ever hope to achieve. How she and her grandfather came to embark on their travels in the first place is never explained, although William Hartnell and Carole Ann Ford decided to assume in their own minds that they had fled from some disaster on their home planet and had been unable to return because of the TARDIS's unreliability.

Understandably, Susan is the person towards whom the Doctor shows the greatest affection. There is a strong bond between them, and only once do we ever see them quarrel, in the third episode of *The Sensorites*. Here, Susan protests that the Doctor is treating her like a 'silly little child' when he chastises her for making decisions on her own accord during her telepathic communications with the Sensorites. 'I won't be pushed aside,' she tells him. 'I'm not a child any more, grandfather, I'm not!'

Although this rift is quickly healed, the Doctor is furious with the Sensorites for having created it: 'In all the years my grand-daughter and I have been travelling, we have never had an argument. And now, you have caused one!' Nevertheless, he is not insensitive to the fact that Susan is growing up; and when she falls in love with David Campbell during *The Dalek Invasion of Earth*, he realises that the time has come for her to settle down and find roots of her own. At great emotional cost to himself, he leaves her behind on Earth so that she can start a new life with David.

Indeed, when he abducts Ian (William Russell) and Barbara (Jacqueline Hill) in *100,000 BC* it is largely out of concern for Susan, as she has childishly threatened to leave the TARDIS and go off with the two strangers.

Ian is a very pragmatic, down-to-earth character. On first entering the TARDIS, he is totally incredulous. Barbara, on the other hand, although no less astonished by what they have discovered, is more ready to accept what the Doctor and Susan are telling them: 'I just believe them, that's all,' she stammers when pressed on the matter.

Ian's logical, scientific mind and Barbara's training as a history teacher stand them in good stead during their later adventures. Barbara is able to see for herself some of the times and places she has previously taught about, such as France during the Reign of Terror. It is however a source of frustration to her that she and her fellow travellers are unable to alter the course of history, as she discovers to her cost when, although warned against it by the Doctor, she tries to put an end to the Aztec practice of human sacrifice.

The original TARDIS team is in many ways a very effective one. As required for good drama, there are strong bonds between the characters. Ian and Barbara, for instance, are not only friends and colleagues but also products of the same society,

Jean Marsh (Sara Kingdom) in *The Daleks' Master Plan*.

Adrienne Hill (Katarina) in *The Daleks' Master Plan*.

PETER PURVES
STEVEN TAYLOR

*Peter Purves was born in New Longton, Lancashire on 10 February 1939. After leaving school he took a four-year teacher training course. In 1961, after only one year as a teacher, he turned to acting, initially with the Barrow-in-Furness Repertory Company and later with the Wimbledon Theatre Company. His first TV role was in **Z Cars** and more TV work followed, including a play called **Girl in the Picture** and an episode of **The Villains**. In 1965 he auditioned for the part of a Menoptra in the **Doctor Who** story **The Web Planet**, but was turned down. However, the director, Richard Martin, later cast him as Morton Dill in **The Chase**, and this led to him playing Steven Taylor. After **Doctor Who**, Purves eventually became a regular presenter on the children's magazine programme **Blue Peter**. More presenting work followed, primarily on sports-based programmes, and it is for this that he is now best known. He has also been managing director of a video production company.*

ADRIENNE HILL
KATARINA

*Plymouth-born Adrienne Hill trained in acting at the Bristol Old Vic, then spent some time with the Old Vic Company in London, followed by eight years' work in repertory theatre. Having been spotted by **Doctor Who** production assistant Viktors Ritelis while understudying for Maggie Smith in a play called **Mary, Mary**, she was invited to audition for the role of Princess Joanna in **The Crusade**. Although she did not win that part, director Douglas Camfield remembered her and cast her as Katarina. In the late sixties she had continued success, particularly in radio, and landed a regular role in the BBC's **Waggoner's Walk**. She then moved abroad with her husband when his work took him first to Holland and later to the USA. In the late seventies, after her marriage broke up, she returned to England and studied for a degree. During the eighties she launched a new career as a drama teacher, while continuing to do occasional acting work.*

able to support and sympathise with each other. Similarly, there is a clear tie between the two teachers and Susan, their former pupil. The family relationship between the Doctor and Susan provides a powerful link in their case. Not only are there bonds, there is also room for conflict, another prerequisite for satisfying drama. Sometimes, it is Ian and Barbara who stick together in an argument against the Doctor; on other occasions, Barbara and Susan are in opposition to the Doctor and Ian; and various other permutations arise during the course of the stories.

Where Ian, Barbara and Susan succeeded perhaps less well as characters was in the area of audience identification. Ian and Barbara can in some ways be seen as harking back to the rather stuffy parental characters of earlier children's television drama. While young viewers would no doubt have come across many teachers like these in their own schools, they could hardly be expected to identify with them. Susan, on the other hand, was young enough for children to identify with, but she was an alien with a mysterious background and latent telepathic powers, all of which tended to distance her from their everyday experience. This may be one reason why the character who succeeded her in the TARDIS was a rather more conventional one.

It is in *The Rescue*, the story immediately following Susan's exit, that the Doctor meets the young orphan girl Vicki (Maureen O'Brien), to whom he is delighted to offer a place aboard the ship. While Vicki can never replace Susan, she does help to fill a gap in his life after his grand-daughter's departure.

Like Susan, Vicki is a young girl from the far future. There, however, the similarity ends. A much less intense and serious character than Susan, she is lively, high-spirited and effusive, acting as a good sparring partner for the Doctor in semi-humorous stories like *The Romans*. She can also be strong-willed and capable, as she demonstrates in helping the Xerons to rebel against their Morok oppressors in *The Space Museum*. On the other hand, she has a tendency towards silliness; and in some of her later stories her character does seem to have been rather neglected by the series' writers. In addition, Ian and Barbara do not have quite the same bond with Vicki as they had with Susan. Certainly at the end of *The Chase*, when the opportunity presents itself for them to return to their own time on Earth, they have no hesitation in taking it.

Astronaut Steven Taylor (Peter Purves), the successor to Ian and Barbara, echoes Ian's original disbelief of the TARDIS's capabilities: when Vicki tells him that its initials stand for Time and Relative Dimensions in Space, he replies with the acronym IDBI, standing, as he explains, for 'I Don't Believe It'. However, he quickly settles down to a life of time and space travel. A much more straightforwardly heroic character than Ian, Steven makes a solid and dependable, if somewhat headstrong and argumentative, companion for the Doctor.

When Vicki falls for Troilus in ancient Troy (*The Myth Makers*), it is a clear sign that she is growing up. This is confirmed at the end of the story as she elects to leave the TARDIS and stay behind with her new love, despite the danger of their situation. The Doctor and Steven are subsequently joined by the Trojan handmaiden Katarina (Adrienne Hill) and then by the Space Security Service agent Sara Kingdom (Jean Marsh), but both die during *The Daleks' Master Plan*. It is not until the end of the following story, *The Massacre of St Bartholomew's*

JEAN MARSH
SARA KINGDOM

*Born in London in 1939, Jean Marsh became interested in showbusiness while taking dancing and mime classes as therapy for a childhood illness. After attending a charm school and working as a model, she started acting in repertory and took voice lessons. Her repertory work was supplemented by a number of film appearances as a dancer. She then spent three years in America, appearing in Sir John Geilgud's Broadway production of **Much Ado About Nothing** and numerous TV shows, including an episode of **The Twilight Zone**. Returning to London, she won roles on stage, film and TV. It was during this period that she appeared in **Doctor Who**, first as Princess Joanna in **The Crusade** and then as Sara Kingdom in **The Daleks' Master Plan**. In the late sixties she co-created and starred in LWT's **Upstairs, Downstairs**. Since then, she has maintained a very busy career in the theatre, on TV – including a starring role in the US sit-com **9 to 5** – and films such as **Return to Oz** and **Willow**. Recently she co-created another successful TV series, **The House of Elliot**.*

ANNEKE WILLS
POLLY

*Born in 1943, Anneke Wills made her acting debut aged eleven in a film called **Child's Play**. She then studied at a drama school, the Arts Educational, for about four years, winning many children's TV and theatre roles. Subsequently she enrolled at the Royal Academy of Dramatic Art, but did not complete the course. More TV work followed, including roles in **Armchair Theatre**, **The Saint** and **The Avengers**. In 1966 she was cast as Polly in **Doctor Who** (her then husband, Michael Gough, having recently played the Celestial Toymaker). Later she won another regular role in the crime drama **Strange Report**. She then gave up acting and moved to Norfolk, where she ran a craft shop. Around 1979 she left England and lived at various times in Belgium, India – where she stayed in a religious retreat and returned to the stage in some Shakespeare productions – and in the USA. She has now settled in Canada, where she has directed a production of the play **Rashomon**, but works mainly as an interior decorator.*

Jacqueline Hill (Barbara) in *The Aztecs*.

Eve, that a permanent replacement for Vicki is introduced.

Dorothea Chaplet (Jackie Lane) – Dodo for short – is another young orphan, whom the Doctor inadvertently carries off in the TARDIS. Like Vicki, she is someone he can look after and fuss over in the absence of his grand-daughter. Indeed, he even tells Steven how much Dodo reminds him of Susan, although to an objective observer the resemblance is only slight.

Dodo was the first of many trendy young companions from contemporary England and the fact that she occasionally wore a miniskirt was considered quite daring at the time. There was, however, a limit to how far the BBC establishment would allow things to go: although Dodo was originally supposed to be a Cockney, the production team were instructed that she had to deliver her lines in standard 'BBC English'. Consequently, as the early scripts had been written with a Cockney in mind and as Jackie Lane had already started to rehearse as a Cockney, Dodo had a rather variable accent during the first few episodes.

Steven and Dodo made a spirited team but were never quite as effective as the original line-up of regulars. They had little in common with each other or with the Doctor, and their only real bond was that they were all travellers together aboard the TARDIS. They were also depicted largely as stereotypes, with little attempt being made to develop their characters.

When producer Innes Lloyd and story editor Gerry Davis assessed the situation, they decided that a change was called for. It was, they felt, rather too obvious that Jackie Lane was older than the

character she was portraying: what was needed was someone younger and perhaps more sophisticated. Steven, on the other hand, was too stolid and unvarying: a more quirky, rough-and-ready character would be better. Accordingly, Steven and Dodo were written out in consecutive stories – *The Savages* and *The War Machines* – and two new companions, more in line with the production team's intentions for *Doctor Who*, were introduced. These newcomers were Ben Jackson (Michael Craze) and Polly (Anneke Wills), the original character sketches for whom were as follows:

Ben

24, Able Seaman (Radar), Cockney. Father, now dead, was wartime sailor and peacetime dock-crane driver. Mother married again to unsympathetic step-father. Ben trained at sea school from age of 15, having previously stowed away on cargo ship for adventure and to get away from unhappy home. Enjoys all sports, especially boxing and athletics – interested in all things mechanical and electrical and in true Naval fashion can turn his hand to most things, including basic cooking and sewing.

A realist, down to earth, solid, capable and cautious. Inclined on occasions to be shy.

Polly

24, private secretary to scientist. Father, country doctor in Devon, four brothers (one older – three younger). Happy and conventional middle-class background, she has never been tied to her mother's apron strings – they never know when to expect her home but when she arrives they are happy to see her. Has been, in turn, a travel courier – done a small amount of modelling (which she found irksome to her intelligence and feet).

She loves sports cars, watching motor racing, skiing, clothes, swimming – pet hates: pomposity, deb's delights, conforming and officials (police to ticket collectors).

Intelligent, imaginative, impulsive, inclined to act first, think later. She is totally undomesticated, cannot sew, knit or cook.

The two characters have, on the face of it, little in common except perhaps a taste in entertainment, as they meet in The Inferno nightclub where Ben's chivalrous instincts lead him to protect Polly from the attentions of a loutish youth. However, it is often said that opposites attract, and by the end of their debut story, *The War Machines*, Polly and Ben are the best of friends.

What Polly and Ben did have in common was that they were both very up to date, swinging sixties characters, along the lines of those seen in recent film successes such as *Georgy Girl* and *Alfie*. Whereas only a few months before the BBC had found it unacceptable to have a Cockney character as a regular aboard the TARDIS, attitudes had now changed.

Polly's character was nevertheless at odds with one prevailing trend, as Anneke Wills explains: 'At the time, I remember, *The Avengers* was very popular, and we'd had Honor Blackman in her black leather gear, chucking people over her shoulder and so on. The trend was towards these kind of macho heroines. I wanted to go against that and make Polly a complete coward! I just decided that whenever Polly encountered a monster she was going to scream and say "Let's run away, let's hide" rather than being the brave one.'

The fact that Polly and Ben were such contemporary characters did not always work in their favour. Once removed from the present-day setting of their debut adventure, *The War Machines*, they tended to seem a little out of place. Although the balance of the characters was perhaps rather better after the Doctor transformed into his more mischievous second incarnation, the production team still felt that it was not quite right. Consequently, when the opportunity arose to add a third companion, they took it almost on the spur of the moment and James Robert McCrimmon began his adventures aboard the TARDIS.

With Jamie (Frazer Hines), *Doctor Who* hit upon a winner. True, he had nothing in common with Ben, Polly or the Doctor, but in his favour were an innocent and receptive manner, a stubborn refusal to be beaten by anything, and a fierce loyalty to and trust in the Doctor.

Once Jamie had become established, Ben and Polly were quickly and abruptly written out, making their final appearance in *The Faceless Ones*. Having been absent for most of the story, they come

Deborah Watling (Victoria) in *The Abominable Snowmen*.

running in at the conclusion, excited that they are back home and able to continue with their own lives. Meanwhile, out of their shadows at last, Jamie has had an opportunity to shine. The writers of *The Faceless Ones*, David Ellis and Malcolm Hulke, clearly recognised that his innocence and his ignorance of all things technical could be used to good effect, providing several light-hearted moments and some entertaining banter between him and the Doctor, and this continued into the next story, *The Evil of the Daleks*, with Jamie playing Watson to the

MICHAEL CRAZE
BEN JACKSON

*Michael Craze was born on 29 November 1942 in Cornwall and got into acting quite by chance as, at the age of twelve, he discovered through Boy Scout Gang Shows that he had a perfect boy soprano voice. This led him to win parts in **The King and I** and **Plain and Fancy**, both at Drury Lane, and **Damn Yankees** at the Coliseum. Once he had left school, he went into repertory and got into TV through his agent. His first television was a show called **Family Solicitor** for Granada which was followed, amongst others, by a part in ABC TV's 1960 series **Target Luna** (written by Malcolm Hulke and Eric Paice and produced by Sydney Newman). When he was twenty Michael wrote, directed and acted in a film called **The Golden Head** which won an award at the Commonwealth Film Festival in Cardiff. Following **Doctor Who**, Michael worked on several ITV productions, including one episode (**The Last Visitor**) of Hammer Films' first TV series **Journey to the Unknown** in 1968. In the eighties Michael acted only occasionally and also managed a pub.*

FRAZER HINES
JAMES ROBERT McCRIMMON (JAMIE)

*Frazer Hines was born on 22 September 1944 in Horsforth, Yorkshire. He studied acting at the Corona Academy and made his professional debut at the age of eight. By the age of fifteen he had appeared in six films. Further stage, TV and film work followed. After his three-year stint as Jamie in **Doctor Who** he resumed the life of a jobbing actor until 1972, when he was cast in the soap opera **Emmerdale Farm** as Joe Sugden – a role he has played ever since. In between making episodes of **Emmerdale**, as it was renamed in the eighties, he has continued a career in the theatre and made occasional appearances in other TV shows, including two **Doctor Who** reunion stories, **The Five Doctors** and **The Two Doctors**. He is also a noted amateur jockey.*

Jackie Lane (Dodo) and Peter Purves (Steven) in *The Celestial Toymaker*.

DEBORAH WATLING
VICTORIA WATERFIELD

*Born on 2 January 1948, Deborah Watling grew up in an acting family. She attended stage school after failing her O level exams, but left after three weeks and got herself an agent. She then landed the part of Alice in a BBC play **The Life of Lewis Carroll**. This was followed by other roles, including film parts, with Cliff Richard in **Take Me High** (1973) and with David Essex in **That'll Be The Day** (1973). She was offered the role of Victoria in **Doctor Who** as Innes Lloyd had remembered the **Radio Times** cover for **The Life of Lewis Carroll** and asked Deborah to play the part. Following **Doctor Who**, Deborah opened her own boutique before landing a part in **The Newcomers**. Since then she has appeared in numerous TV roles including **Danger UXB**, **Rising Damp** and **Doctor in Charge** and has done much work in the theatre.*

WENDY PADBURY
ZOE HERRIOT

*Born in 1948, Wendy Padbury trained at the Aida Foster Stage School and made her TV debut on the BBC arts programme **Monitor** soon after starting the course. More TV work followed, and by the age of seventeen she had landed a regular role in the ATV soap opera **Crossroads**. Soon after this, she applied for the role of Zoe in **Doctor Who**. After several rounds of auditions and a screen test at Lime Grove, she was given the job. Although the production team tried to persuade her to stay on at the end of season six, and she was tempted to do so, she decided to leave at the same time as her co-stars Patrick Troughton and Frazer Hines. She then worked in the theatre and in the early seventies appeared in three seasons of the Southern TV children's series **Freewheelers**. Since the mid-seventies she has divided her time between raising a family and continuing her acting career.*

Anneke Wills (Polly) and Michael Craze (Ben).

Doctor's Holmes as they unravel the clues which lead them to Waterfield's antique shop.

The Doctor and Jamie certainly make a very effective double act but *Doctor Who* without a female companion was virtually unthinkable, and the character of Victoria Waterfield (Deborah Watling) was introduced. After the death of her father at the end of *The Evil of the Daleks*, Victoria, like Vicki before her, becomes an orphan with nowhere to go and the Doctor is pleased to welcome her aboard the TARDIS.

In Jamie and Victoria, the series found its most successful team since the departure of the original three companions. Although born over a century later than Jamie, Victoria has had a sheltered up-bringing, as one would expect of a refined young lady of the Victorian era, and she shares some of his innocence and naivety. They can be seen as a pair of babes in the wood to whom the Doctor gives his guidance and protection.

Victoria is a fine foil for Jamie. Although a little prim and proper, she is also resourceful and independent, hampered only by her lack of knowledge of all things modern. On the surface she appears fearless, but in a dark room full of cobwebs she will scream the roof down at a touch of the smallest spider. On her travels with the Doctor she encounters menaces far greater than spiders and spends a good deal of her time screaming!

In the end, the seemingly endless battles with hideous alien monsters all become too much for the sensitive Victorian girl and given the opportunity to stay with a friendly family in reasonable peace and safety, she reluctantly decides to do so. Jamie is distraught and even the Doctor is moved – they have both developed a great affection for the girl.

Victoria's successor, Zoe Herriot (Wendy Padbury), is a very different sort of character. A no-nonsense, highly intelligent astrophysicist from the twenty-first century, she has previously relied on logic to see her through, and her world is shattered by the arrival of the Doctor who advises her that 'logic...merely enables one to be wrong with authority'. Once the Doctor has engineered the defeat of the Cybermen in *The Wheel In Space*, Zoe stows

Frazer Hines (Jamie) in *The Highlanders*.

Wendy Padbury (Zoe) in *The Wheel in Space*.

away on board the TARDIS in the hope of gaining an opportunity to broaden her horizons. During her travels with the Doctor she is also able to show him that logic can sometimes work: in *The Invasion*, she wipes out an entire Cyberman invasion fleet with a few well-placed missiles. She also gets plenty of opportunities to demonstrate her great mathematical abilities and her photographic memory.

Jamie and Zoe make another very successful team: Zoe has an air of superiority and indefatigable logic while Jamie's ability to believe almost anything he is told stands him in good stead. The two friends are eventually forced to part company with the Doctor when the Time Lords return them to the moment in time just before each embarked on their travels with the Doctor, thus erasing from their memories all but their very first adventure with him.

At the end of the sixties, the Doctor tumbled away, en route to exile on Earth. All his many and varied companions to date had brought out new facets of his character, and some had even made the alien Time Lord seem more human and vulnerable. They had also been very popular characters in their own right and, in fulfilling their essential dramatic role, an integral part of *Doctor Who*'s appeal.

CHAPTER FOURTEEN

The Adversaries

It has been said that you can judge a man by the quality of his enemies and this is certainly true of the Doctor. Throughout his first two incarnations, he came up against a whole host of different foes which made a vital contribution to *Doctor Who*'s success in the sixties.

The Doctor's enemies can be divided into three groups: villains, monsters and opponents who may not necessarily be villainous or monstrous, yet still endeavoured to make the Doctor's life more difficult.

Aside from the monstrous Daleks, human or humanoid villains are the most common adversary faced by the Doctor in the sixties. Perhaps the best example is the power-mad Mavic Chen (Kevin Stoney) from *The Daleks' Master Plan*. Chen is the Guardian of the Solar System in the year 4000, but he desires ultimate power over the whole of the galaxy. As the epic plot of *The Daleks' Master Plan* moves towards its finale, Chen becomes more and more megalomaniacal, his lust for power growing ever stronger. His twisted motivation and egomania is perfectly revealed in this scripted speech, cut from the final televised version of *The Daleks' Master Plan* but reinstated in John Peel's 1989 novelisation:

'The Day of Armageddon is drawing close . . . The whole history of mankind will be snuffed like a candle in a gale. When I return it will be with a power that no human has ever known. Power absolute. Then Earth can start again, but without the shackles of infantile philosophies like democracy. It will be a new and virgin land that can be shaped... moulded... fashioned into the image that I design. I will be its life blood . . . I its creator . . . I its God!'

This desire to be treated as a god is a characteristic shared with many other human villains such as the second Doctor's double Salamander (Patrick Troughton) from *The Enemy of the World*, the War Chief (Edward Brayshaw) – a renegade Time Lord – from *The War Games* and Tobias Vaughn in *The Invasion*. There are many similarities between the characters of Mavic Chen and Tobias Vaughn, not least that they were both played by the same actor,

Kevin Stoney. Both are in league with a race of alien monsters – the Daleks and the Cybermen respectively – and both use their positions of authority to aid their allies' plans: Chen uses his rank as Guardian to cover up the theft of the taranium element the Daleks need to power their time destructor while Vaughn uses his position as head of a huge electronics conglomerate, International Electromatics, to arrange for tiny microcircuits which have the ability to render the population of Earth unconscious to be placed in all their products, thus leaving the planet open to the Cybermen's invasion.

Vaughn uses his urbane charm to disarm his opponents, although he is often overtly condescending and clearly considers himself above most

▲ **Tobias Vaughn (Kevin Stoney).** *The Invasion.*

Mavic Chen (Kevin Stoney). *The Daleks' Master Plan.*

The evil Celestial ▶ Toymaker (Michael Gough), an eternal being who entraps unwary travellers in his games. *The Celestial Toymaker.*

DALEK DESIGN

The Daleks were designed by Raymond P. Cusick of the BBC Design Department, working from writer Terry Nation's description of them as '...hideous, machine-like creatures. They are legless, moving on a round base. They have no human features. A lens on a flexible shaft acts as an eye. Arms with mechanical grips for hands. . .The creatures hold strange weapons in their hands.' Nation also told Cusick that he envisaged the Daleks gliding about like the Georgian State Dancers who performed dances in which their feet were hidden beneath long flowing skirts. Unhappy with the idea of a 'man in a silver suit', Cusick decided – in discussions with director Christopher Barry and associate producer Mervyn Pinfield – that the actor operating the Dalek should be completely enclosed. He drew a sketch of a man seated in a chair and added a smooth outline around it; this formed the basis of the Dalek shape. Although he also discussed his ideas with Jack Kine and Bernard Wilkie of the Visual Effects Department, the only significant contribution they made was to suggest a slatted base section rather than a smooth one as Cusick had intended. This was in the mistaken belief that it would make the Daleks easier to construct. The props were made by Shawcraft Models (Uxbridge) Ltd – the freelance firm responsible for most of the specialist work on **Doctor Who** *at this time – under the supervision of manager Bill Roberts.*

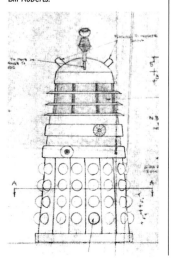

of humanity. He is a man of means and has accumulated his wealth through his business acumen. Like Chen he enjoys a position of considerable power, yet he craves even more and contacts the Cybermen in an attempt to gain the ultimate power – control of the Earth. Vaughn even undergoes partial cybernisation to help achieve his objective.

Vaughn's vision of a world united under his rule does not differ much from Chen's. Like Chen before him, Vaughn tries to persuade the Doctor that his plans are all in the best interests of Earth:

'You think I'm mad, that all I want is power for its own sake . . . No . . . the world is weak, vunerable, a mess of uncoordinated and impossible ideals. It needs a strong hand . . . a single mind . . .a leader.'

Chen and Vaughn also share a contempt for those with whom they ally themselves, plotting to seize power themselves. However they both make a fatal error in believing that they are fully trusted by their co-conspirators. Neither Daleks nor Cybermen believe in trust and both have the same method of dealing with traitors.

In the characters of Chen and Vaughn we can see strong influences of what the programme's writers perceived the state of the real world to be in the sixties. Only two decades after the end of the Second World War, the public could still strongly identify with dictatorial villains. The Cold War was at its height, the Soviet Union and its satellite countries being seen as examples of a system of government which took away all personal freedoms.

In both cases the Doctor's intervention in the well-laid plans for world or universal domination results in pushing the villain concerned right over

the edge into insanity, revealing the basic fictional truth that in the end villains, however intelligent and cunning they are, always underestimate those who resist their schemes. And in particular they underestimate the Doctor.

Although not a power-driven dictator, an interesting rogue is the Celestial Toymaker (Michael Gough) from the third season story of the same name. Unlike most villains, he does not seek to dominate the world or the galaxy; his motives are altogether more sinister. The Toymaker is an immortal being who brings the TARDIS into his own dimension of fantasy and forces the Doctor and his companions, Dodo and Steven, to play some deadly games in order to regain the TARDIS and their freedom. The games are heavily stacked against the time travellers, whom the Toymaker fully intends to add to his collection of subjects – or playthings – which include the many other travellers who have lost at his games.

The Doctor has encountered the Toymaker before and he knows the dangers:

DOCTOR: This place is a hidden menace – nothing is just for fun!

STEVEN: What's the idea of it?

DOCTOR: He's trying to get us into his power, that's why we've got to fight him.

The Toymaker is one of the most evil beings that the Doctor ever encounters, as the deadly games he devises have no point to them other than to entrap their hapless players. The Toymaker gains simple amusement from watching his victims struggle like rats in a laboratory maze.

TOYMAKER: You're so innocent, Doctor. The last time you were here I hoped you'd stay long enough for a game but you had hardly time to turn around.

DOCTOR: And very wise I was too. Hmm? You and your games are quite notorious. You draw people here like a spider does to a fly.

TOYMAKER: How absurd. It amuses me to give amusement.

DOCTOR: And should they lose the game they play, you condemn them to become your toy forever. Hmm?

TOYMAKER: That is one of my rules, certainly. But if they win, they're perfectly free to go.

DOCTOR: And if I refuse?

TOYMAKER: Then you lose by default. Is that what you choose?

DOCTOR: No, I do not.

The Doctor manages to defeat the Toymaker by solving the complex strategy of the trilogic game, and by finding a solution to the Toymaker's 'heads I win, tails you lose' scenario. This results in the destruction of the Toymaker's realm of fantasy but, as the Doctor explains, the Toymaker himself cannot be destroyed and will continue to entrap the unwary as he rebuilds and repopulates his world.

Other villains have rather more modest goals. Greed, for instance, is the primary motivation behind the actions of characters as diverse as the callous businessman Forester in *Planet of Giants*, the pirate Captain Pike in *The Smugglers* and the corrupt solicitor Grey in *The Highlanders*. Still others, such as Bennett in *The Rescue*, appear to have a psychopathic streak, or even – as in the case of *The Underwater Menace*'s Professor Zaroff – to be completely deranged.

In many of the historical adventures, the TARDIS crew arrive in the camp of one of two opposing factions, such as the Greeks and the Trojans at the seige of Troy (*The Myth Makers*) or the Crusaders and the Saracens in the middle of the Holy Wars (*The Crusade*). They become entangled in the plots and counterplots between the leaders of the opposing factions, whose careful plans for power are often threatened by the arrival of the Doctor and his companions. It is usually the leaders' attempts to get rid of the TARDIS crew that alert the Doctor to the machinations that are occurring around him. In *The Aztecs*, the Aztec priest Tlotoxl (John Ringham) does his best to rid himself of the interfering Doctor. His motivation is simply that he does not want any outside interference in his position of power within the Aztec community – as High Priest it is his job to organise and provide the sacrifices that placate the sun god and make the crops fruitful. If there were to be no sacrifices then his power base would simply crumble away. His acts are those of self-preservation rather than studied malice.

The humans the Doctor encounters tend to be villains by circumstance, but the humanoid aliens are villains by nature. Races such as the Moroks (*The Space Museum*), the Dominators and the Drahvins (*Galaxy 4*) are all vicious and uncaring species who enslave others to their will as a matter of course. As the Doctor is a crusader for the enslaved and downtrodden, he naturally sets out to defeat their aims for conquest.

The Drahvins are a particularly interesting example of this type of villain, as they are a race of beautiful women who use their appearance to fool the unwary about their true nature, whereas their enemies, the Rills – hideously ugly creatures by Earth standards – are a peace-loving species. The moral of *Galaxy 4* is that appearances can be deceptive and that communication is the key to understanding.

Villainous humanoids aside, it is the monsters which made the greatest impact on *Doctor Who* and

its audience. One dictionary definition of a monster is 'something misshapen, abnormal, out of the ordinary course of nature, an abnormally cruel or depraved person.' Monsters tend to be hideous to look at, ruthless in their persecution of all other life forms but their own and without any notion of decency or fair play. The Daleks are therefore the ultimate monster. Just why these tin dustbins on wheels successfully scared a generation has been asked many times. Much of their appeal must come from their total inhumanity; the fact that they don't look like an actor wearing a costume adds greatly to their scare factor.

The Daleks lifted *Doctor Who* from a mildly interesting semi-educational teatime adventure series into a nationwide, and later worldwide, hit. From their first appearance at the beginning of episode two of *The Daleks*, the subsequent furore drastically altered the production team's view of the programme's future direction. Over the next six years, a stream of new monsters would be introduced in an attempt to emulate the success of the Daleks. Voords, Mechanoids, Zarbi, Chumblies, and many others tried but never quite captured the public's imagination in the same way. But one monster did succeed.

The Cybermen are the ultimate nightmare of medical science gone mad and much of their success can be attributed to the many stories they appeared in during seasons five and six. Unlike the Daleks, who appeared approximately once a year during the sixties and looked pretty much the same throughout, the Cybermen's appearance changed every time we saw them. The Cybermen in *The Tenth Planet* are so different from those in *The Moonbase* that only the distinctive handlebar-like

▲ The Aztec priest Tlotoxl (John Ringham), is motivated by self preservation rather than evil intent. *The Aztecs.*

◄ The Daleks, *Doctor Who*'s archetypal monster. *The Evil of the Daleks.*

▲ The Drahvins, beautiful but deadly aliens. *Galaxy 4.*

▲ The Ice Warriors, a war-like race who originated on Mars. *The Ice Warriors.*

CYBERMAN DESIGN

*In the original script for their debut story, **The Tenth Planet**, the Cybermen were described as 'tall, slim, with one-piece, close-fitting silver mesh uniforms. Their faces and heads are normal but under the hair on the head is a shining metal plate stretching from centre hair-line to occiput (this could be disguised by a hat). Their faces are all rather alike, angular and by normal definitions good-looking. On the front of their trunks is a mechanical computer-like unit consisting of switches, two rows of lights and a short, moveable proboscis. They all carry exotic side arms. At the shoulder joints there are small, ram-like cylinders acting over the joints themselves. Instead of flesh there is a transparent, "arm-shaped" forearm covering containing shining rods and lights, but there is a normal hand at the end of it.' Costume designer Sandra Reid (who now works under the name Alexandra Tynan) was briefed on cybernetics by writer Kit Pedler and then created costumes based on her interpretation of his ideas. Certain aspects such as the moveable proboscis were dropped for cost reasons. It was also decided that the best way to realise the Cybermen's faces was to have them wearing grey jersey masks. Holes trimmed with silver vinyl were added for the eyes and mouth, and silver make-up applied to disguise the actor's own features underneath.*

pipes that run from the sides to the top of the head mark them as even belonging to the same race.

Where the Daleks play on our fear of the inhuman and the unlike, the Cybermen play on the greater fear of becoming inhuman and unlike, transformed into a silver zombie, robbed of all emotion, lacking everything that humans value in life. In *The Tomb of the Cybermen* we are allowed a glimpse of how the original Cybermen, the Mondasians, created machines capable of taking any human and cybernising them. To bring this point home, Toberman, one of the archaeological party of humans who uncover the Cybertombs, becomes partly converted. Trapped between species, his still-human brain allows him to sacrifice himself to save the remaining humans.

The Cybermen are just one of a great number of monstrous creations which appeared during the Troughton era. In fact, the last three years of the sixties were typified by the many and varied creatures battled by the second Doctor. Macra, Yeti, Ice Warriors, weed creatures, Krotons, and of course, the Daleks came up against the Doctor. Some returned for a second bout – including a race of creatures that were destined to become the programme's third most popular monsters: cruel Martian invaders, the Ice Warriors.

Originally from Mars, the Ice Warriors had spread out through the galaxy, and eventually abandoned their home planet, which was rapidly becoming too warm for them to survive there. One of their scout ships lands on Earth, which is where the Doctor first encounters them in the year 3000 (*The Ice Warriors*). The Doctor confronts them again when they attack the Earth in the twenty-first century (*The*

Seeds of Death). In the latter story, the Warriors have seized control of the Moon relay station of the T-Mat matter transport system used to transfer food and materials globally. By stopping the transmissions the Warriors cause starvation and shortage, but this is just the first stage of their plan: they intend to make the Earth suitable for them to live on by changing its climate.

Their creator, Brian Hayles, developed the Warriors as a class-bound race. In *The Ice Warriors* we are introduced to the Warrior class: tall, imposing creatures, covered from head to foot with tough scaly armour. For their following appearance, in *The Seeds of Death*, Hayles introduces two further classes. There is the commander, a more slightly built Martian with no body armour. A tall domed helmet covers his head. The commander, unlike the Warrior, has no inbuilt weaponry. The third strata of Ice Warrior society is the Grand Marshal class. Seen only on a monitor link with the invading Martian fleet, the Marshal looks similar to the commander, but his helmet is more lavishly decorated, and he speaks normally, without the hissing wheeze that typified the Warriors, and caused by the unfamiliar Earth air.

If enemies such as the Ice Warriors, the Daleks, and the Cybermen are the epitome of evil monstrousness, there is another group of the Doctor's opponents who are not inherently evil: beings whose goals simply happen to be the opposite of the Doctor's. Take, for example, the Monk (*The Time Meddler*). He is a member of the Doctor's own race, unnamed at the time. He too has a TARDIS and uses it to roam the galaxy, but whereas the Doctor interferes only when he encounters injustice, the Monk delights in rewriting history by altering already established facts, and these small alterations send ripples through time until some critical event is changed: he might give a gun to a Stone Age man, thus bringing forward all resultant inventions until we potentially end up with the atomic bomb being developed in medieval times.

Another example of the misguided is the tragic case of the Chameleons (*The Faceless Ones*). Here we are introduced to a race of creatures who have lost their own identities through a horrific accident. The psychological impact of this happening is almost unthinkable and so there is no small wonder that the Chameleons choose a somewhat drastic solution to their problem – the kidnap of teenaged humans from whom the Chameleons could steal identities. As the Doctor points out to them, there are other solutions, and indeed he helps them to find one that does not involve the act of interplanetary terrorism that they had been pursuing.

The monsters and other adversaries are as much a part of *Doctor Who* as the Doctor himself, and form the backbone to its lasting popularity. Today it is mainly the monsters that people remember, not the history, the companions, the plots or the moral stance.

CHAPTER FIFTEEN

Now on the Big Screen . . . in Colour!

When discussing the popularity of *Doctor Who* during the sixties it is easy to concentrate solely on the TV productions. But the programme's success can perhaps be better measured by the penetration of *Doctor Who* and Dalek phenomena in other leisure markets. At that time, television was very much a luxury item; far more accessible than the TV series itself were the toys and games, the books and magazines, the comic strips and the newspaper articles. Perhaps of greatest importance, however, were the cinema films released in 1965 and 1966.

These were both based around the popularity of the Daleks, but the first approach from a film company to adapt a *Doctor Who* story had occurred in July 1964. The Walt Disney Production Company had been interested in obtaining the film rights to John Lucarotti's *Marco Polo* adventure, and it is not known why this option was not taken up or, it appears, even discussed further.

▲ Jennie Linden (who played Barbara) with Peter Cushing.

▲ The Doctor, Barbara and Susan (Roberta Tovey). *Dr. Who and the Daleks.*

The Doctor (Peter Cushing) and Ian (Roy Castle). *Dr. Who and the Daleks.*

A selection of front-of- ▲ house posters, the bottom one from the film's Spanish release. *Dr. Who and the Daleks.*

A French film poster for ▲ the second film *Daleks' Invasion Earth 2150 AD.*

The Doctor and Ian remove a Dalek creature from its casing. *Dr. Who and the Daleks.*

After these initial enquiries, it was perhaps to be expected that someone would want to take the Daleks on to the big screen, and the approach eventually came from film financier Joe Vegoda and producer Milton Subotsky. In 1964, Vegoda drew Subotsky's attention to the Daleks and to the possibility of making a cheap film to capitalise on their television success.

In December 1964, discussions with the BBC and Terry Nation were concluded and a contract signed for the first film, *Dr. Who and the Daleks*, to be based on Terry Nation's scripts for their debut story, *The Daleks*. Although for one film only, the contract did contain a clause to the effect that one further film could be made if the first was successful. The film was officially underway: an Aaru production for Regal International release, with

A group of Thals, aided by Ian and Barbara, try to enter the Dalek city. *Dr. Who and the Daleks.*

The Daleks in the control centre of their city. *Dr. Who and the Daleks.*

Subotsky and Max J. Rosenberg producing and Joe Vegoda executive producing. After completing the script, Subotsky contacted Gordon Flemyng to direct and filming started at Shepperton Studios on 8 March 1965.

One of the early decisions made by Subotsky was to bring in a star name to play the Doctor, making it easier to sell the film to America. Peter Cushing fitted the bill admirably. The remainder of the cast were chosen by Gordon Flemyng in consultation with Subotsky, as Flemyng explains: 'The casting of Roy Castle (in only his second film performance) was a hangover from Milton's involvement with the

The Doctor, Susan, Ian and Barbara inside the Dalek city. *Dr. Who and the Daleks.*

The Daleks' flying saucer sits amongst the rubble of London. *Daleks' Invasion Earth 2150 AD.*

▲ **An Australian poster for** *Dr. Who and the Daleks.*

pop industry. He felt very secure in that field and had a tendency to return there if in doubt. In the second film we cast Bernard Cribbins for the same reason.'

One of the main changes from the TV series was in the Doctor's background. The character Cushing played was a human who had constructed his TARDIS time machine himself and in a radical departure from the TV series, the interior of the time ship was completely remodelled. Flemyng explains that this was as much to do with the process of film-making as with trying to be different from what had gone before:

'Because the film was being made for the wide screen, we wanted to make everything bigger and better. We wanted you to feel that when you went into the TARDIS, it was huge. It was supposed to have been cobbled together by the Doctor in his back garden and we made the wires and lights multicoloured so it would all seem bolder than the TV version.'

One of the contributing factors to the look of the film was an idea brought in by Flemyng: 'I had gone into the viewing room to see the rushes from the previous day but the person who had been in before me had been viewing his material through an anamorphic (wide-angle) lens. They had forgotten to take the anamorphic lens out of the projector, and all my rushes had this strange, unearthly quality, with all the angles not quite right and the pictures looking wrong somehow. I decided that we could use this effect in the film and so all the scenes in which we wanted the forest to look strange and

alien, we filmed without the anamorphic lens on the camera, while the rest was filmed with the lens on. The distortion achieved was enough to give the film the alien look I was after.'

Robomen, humans whose minds are controlled by the Daleks, are used to enforce the Daleks' will among the people of Earth. *Daleks' Invasion of Earth 2150 AD.*

▲ **The British front-of-house poster for** *Daleks' Invasion Earth 2150 AD.*

Frankly I find the TV pieces ludicrous beyond measure and aimed, one sometimes imagines, at morons: the same story on the screen, with a generally higher level script, greater production qualities, colour and a sense of healthy humour (the film I find is always chuckling at its own ridiculousness, while the TV serial seems to take itself seriously) allied to far better performances generally, makes the movie quite good clean and simple fun, which I'm sure the youngsters will lap up.
F. Maurice Speed
From review of 'Dr. and the Daleks' What's On (25 June 1965)

'In colour and on the wide screen', proclaims the poster for *Dr. Who and the Daleks* (Studio One, 'U'), no doubt to point the advantages of the film over the children's television serial from which it derives.

On the other side of the balance-sheet, I might mention it lasts nearly an hour and a half against just under half an hour on TV, reminding us that some prescriptions are more effective in small doses.
Patrick Gibbs
From 'Kid's Stuff' The Daily Telegraph (25 June 1965)

This riot of pseudo-scientific invention has all the appeal that the television serial had - with the added advantage of colour. The all-metal city of the Daleks, with its fascinating 'scientific' trimmings and its electronically-operated sliding doors, emerges as a marvel of ingenuity.
From 'Dr. Who and the Daleks' Berkshire Chronicle (6 August 1965)

The Doctor is held captive. *Daleks' Invasion Earth 2150 A.D.*

In films, as in TV, the Daleks posed certain problems. 'They couldn't go up stairs and they couldn't travel on anything that wasn't smooth,' remembers Flemyng. 'Bill Constable, the designer, having taken on board that information, built sets that facilitated them as opposed to humans. For example, the doors in their city opened from the centre and were wide at the bottom, narrow at the top – Dalek shaped. The city was designed by Daleks for Daleks.'

The Dalek saucer. *Daleks' Invasion Earth 2150 A.D.*

The Doctor and Barbara at the Doctor's house. *Dr. Who and the Daleks.*

To operate the Daleks, Flemyng hired the experienced BBC operators, but as he had more Daleks than the BBC, more operators were required. 'What we needed were fairly small but quite strong people. We chose dancers because they fitted this brief. It was actually quite tiring to move those things around all day!'

A major modification to the Daleks for the film was that the extermination effect was changed to a powerful blast of smoke from the gun.

'That was a fire extinguisher!' laughs Flemyng. 'We used that simply because we couldn't afford to add a ray to the film and it wouldn't have been good enough to just have people fall down. We wanted something that could be seen.'

Another reason was given by Subotsky in an interview for *Kinematograph Weekly* in April 1965: 'We were going to have them [the Daleks] shooting out flames, but John Trevelyn, the censor, thought children were frightened of flames. So we went to the other extreme and armed them with fire extinguishers!'

This determination that the film should appeal to children was confirmed by Flemyng: 'We were quite definitely going for a "U" certificate and if it hadn't received a "U" certificate it wouldn't have succeeded. Most children went to see those films without adults, because they could shout and scream and cheer and do what they liked, and that was most emphatically the market we were aiming for. For example, we had a huge problem over whether we were going to actually show what was inside the Dalek. No one had ever shown what a Dalek looked like, and we decided that it was basically a brain, an intelligence with no recognisable features.

'I remember going to talk to the censor about what I was going to show when I took the lid off this thing and how I might be able to get round not showing it. Because what the censor was saying was, you are not to show it. If you show something and it's a problem to us, we're going to cut it out, because this is a young person's film. Ultimately we

The Doctor tries to force Alydon (Barrie Ingham) to defend himself. *Dr. Who and the Daleks.*

decided it was a brain with one arm, because it had to have the means to operate the machine – firing the gun and steering – and we showed the claw hand on the end of the arm.'

The first Dalek film received a lot of publicity while it was in production and when it opened at Studio 1 in London's Oxford Street on 24 June 1965. F. Maurice Speed, writing in *What's On*, commented that it was 'a sort of deluxe version . . . of the famous television serial and proves again, if any additional proof were needed, how much more entertaining is the large screen.' Patrick Gibbs in the *Daily Telegraph* wrote 'Very immoral, the way [the Doctor] overcomes his allies' tendency to pacifism and we are left with the idea that might is right, which will perhaps upset those in ivory towers but hardly ruffle practical parents.' Writing in the *Chronicle and Echo*, Ron Thompson predicted ' . . . that "Dr. Who and the Daleks" will be one of the most popular films of the year.'

Once the money started rolling in, and with no sign of the Daleks' popularity declining at the end of 1965, the option of making a second film was exercised by Vegoda and Subotsky. Originally titled *Daleks Invade Earth 2150 A.D.*, it was made as *Daleks' Invasion Earth 2150 A.D.* Filming started, again at Shepperton, on 31 January 1966, and completed on 22 March.

This time the budget was bigger, and the script chosen to form the basis for the film was Terry Nation's second Dalek story for the TV programme, *The Dalek Invasion of Earth*.

Gordon Flemyng was again directing: 'I think people very quickly realised they'd got a moneymaker on their hands and the second film was made in a hurry to cash in on it before it stopped.'

Peter Cushing returned as the Doctor with Roberta Tovey as his grand-daughter, but this time the romantic leads were taken by Jill Curzon as Louise – the Doctor's niece – and comedy actor Bernard Cribbins as Tom Campbell, a bumbling policeman who stumbles into the TARDIS after failing to prevent a raid on a jewellery shop.

The increased budget allowed for some location work and Flemyng remembers one scene involving a Dalek and the Thames: 'We laid tracks down into the water when the tide was out and positioned a weighted Dalek on them, attached to a line. We then waited for the tide to come in and pulled the Dalek out of the water using the line. For that scene the Dalek was operated by remote control and wires.'

The other major location shots – the streets of London and the mine in Bedfordshire – were in fact filmed on the back lot at Shepperton. Flemyng explains that his crew didn't travel far to the locations because of the Daleks. 'We couldn't go very far because we couldn't make the Daleks work – they wouldn't run on anything other than a smooth surface. On the back lot at Shepperton we could put down camera tracking for them to run on and prepare the set accordingly. In the film, if you see a Dalek moving through rubble, then the rubble is either in the foreground or the background.

The red Dalek plunges out ▲ of control. *Daleks' Invasion Earth 2150 A.D.*

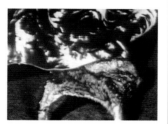

The claw of a Dalek ▲ creature. *Dr. Who and the Daleks.*

The interior of the ▲ TARDIS. *Dr. Who and the Daleks.*

The TARDIS in the ▲ petrified forest. *Dr. Who and the Daleks.*

Hopefully the audience doesn't realise this and the trick works.'

One of the most notable aspects of the second film is the effects work, in particular the impressive Dalek spacecraft – built by Ted Samuels at Shepperton's own Visual Effects unit – first seen hovering over London and which later ferries the Daleks to their mine. The climax of the film sees the ship crashing spectacularly as the mine is destroyed.

'I remember that those scenes were complex and difficult,' says Gordon Flemyng. 'Difficult, because we had limited facilities. We couldn't keep reshooting until we were totally happy. There were a number of model shots which we could afford to do a couple of times but after that we had to fake it. Although the film had a relatively bigger budget than the first, it was mostly eaten up by the sheer number of effects and the location work.'

Because of its greater cost, and the fact that, by 1966, the Dalek boom was slowly winding down, the second film did not do as well as hoped. Subotsky has said that, although he later had a screenplay for a third film (called *Doctor Who's Greatest Adventure* in which two Doctors appear together with some giant monsters), they couldn't obtain the rights from the BBC. Gordon Flemyng, however, does not recall any discussions concerning a third film.

Daleks' Invasion Earth 2150 A.D. premiered in June 1966 and went on general release on 5 August. Like its predecessor, it received a great deal of publicity. Cecil Wilson of the *Daily Mail* wrote:

The travellers try to get into the TARDIS, which has been partially buried by rubble. *Daleks' Invasion Earth 2150 A.D.*

'Mingled with the pleasure of seeing [the Daleks] perish is the chilling thought that they will be back before long, to glide and grunt their way through another Dalek picture.' The letters page of *Film Review* was alive with criticisms: 'What is an actor like Peter Cushing doing in a film of this calibre? It is pitiful,' commented M Fisher from London while J Miles, also of London, wrote: 'To me this was the film of the month.' Most publicity was provided by the breakfast cereal Sugar Puffs – who may also have provided some of the film's finance as a large advertising poster for the cereal is seen prominently in the film – who ran a 'Win a Dalek' competition on the back of all their packets.

As films which were conceived as a means of making money, and which were made cheaply and quickly for a children's market, both stand up well today as another interpretation of the *Doctor Who* myth.

The Daleks prepare to extract the molten core of Earth. *Daleks' Invasion Earth 2150 A.D.*

CHAPTER SIXTEEN

The Curse of the Daleks

Following their TV debut (*The Daleks*) in December 1963 and their return appearance (*The Dalek Invasion of Earth*) in November 1964, the Daleks eclipsed *Doctor Who* itself to become one of the great British success stories of the early sixties. The public had taken to them like a duck to water; and the entertainment industry latched on to them just as wholeheartedly, seeing in them a great deal of money just waiting to be made.

1965 saw the coming to fruition of most of these ideas and spin-offs: *Dr. Who and the Daleks,* the first of the two cinema films, toys and games, and the first Dalek stage play.

Produced by John Gale Productions Ltd, directed by Gillian Howell and designed by Hutchinson Scott, *The Curse of the Daleks* opened on Tuesday 21 December 1965 at Wyndham's Theatre in London's Charing Cross Road and ran for two weeks over the Christmas holiday period. The script was credited to David Whitaker and Terry Nation, although in fact Nation had little to do with it — after completing his episodes of the TV story *The Daleks' Master Plan* Nation had taken a break from *Doctor Who* work, allowing Whitaker, the series' first story editor, to write much of the Dalek spin-off material of this era.

The Daleks were very much the stars of the stage

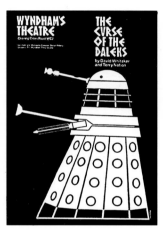

▲ The cover of the theatre programme for *The Curse of the Daleks.*

DALEK TALES

The Curse of the Daleks featured four unknown Dalek operators who were less than happy with their role in the play, as these quotes from an unknown source show: 'It's incredibly boring. There's four of us doing it and we're all sick of it. I think all the cast were sick of it by the time we had finished rehearsals. The trouble with this show is that there is no humour in it. Not one joke – just these things. You wouldn't think that thing cost £150 would you? Still, we come off at the end of the week.'

'It's awful. You have your feet on the floor and push yourself along. That's all we have to do – we don't speak at all; the man who does the voices for the BBC put them on tape for us and the stage manager just flicks on the tape.'

The Daleks pictured outside the Strand Theatre, London, to promote *The Curse of the Daleks.*

THE DALEKS
BY DAVID
WHITAKER

As you know, Terry Nation discovered and translated the Dalek Chronicles. The story of how those Chronicles came to light is interesting in itself. This is how it was.

About two years ago, I was at home writing when Terry telephoned me and asked if he could talk over something. I was delighted to hear from him and agreed at once. An hour later we settled down in chairs with a tray of coffee and sandwiches between us. Terry took a small cube from his pocket and handed it to me, asking for my opinion of it.

I examined it curiously. It was twice the size of a lump of sugar, entirely made of glass except for a small collection of little compartments at its centre. I shook my head in bewilderment and returned it to him, confessing myself baffled.

'I found it in my garden,' he said, 'and, out of curiosity, I drilled a hole through to its centre. A number of slivers of metal fell into the palm of my hand. I magnified them and found them to be microfilms.'

It was then that he told me of the planet called Skaro, set in the next Universe but one, and of the races inhabiting it, the kindly, graceful and peace-loving people called the Thals. I learned of dead forests and a lake of mutations, a brilliant city rising out of a desert. And I heard of the other race on that planet, the inhuman, terrifying creatures called Daleks – sworn enemies of all humanity.

If you wonder why it is that all the adventures and stories of the Daleks are set well into the future, you must realise that what Terry discovered are capsules containing histories of the future. What curve of Time is responsible for this, neither of us can tell you. Are the glass cubes sent down by some friendly planet deliberately, as a warning to us? Or has some Dalek History museum exploded violently in space, showering the stream of time by accident with information the Daleks must want to keep secret? Who can say? Perhaps it is enough that we do know, and can prepare ourselves.

Since that day, more of the little cubes have come to light and Terry and I have sometimes worked together, so anxious has our world become to know as much about the alien race as it can. This play you are to see, for example, is the result of our collaboration – a translation we have worked on from a cube discovered in Kensington Gardens. We both believe there are other glass cubes in existence, hidden, perhaps, in a clump of grass or lying at the base of a tree. When you are out in your garden or in the park, do remember to keep your eyes open, won't you?

From 'The Curse of the Daleks'
Stage Play Programme

play; the Doctor did not appear and there were no overt references to *Doctor Who*. The creatures were now well capable of life outside the series which had spawned them.

Aimed mainly at children, the play had a fairly straightforward plot. A spaceship, *Starfinder*, en route to Earth makes an emergency landing on Skaro where the Daleks are lying dormant in their city. It transpires that the ship has been sabotaged by a member of the human party, who subsequently reactivates the Daleks in the hope that they will help him to become 'king of the universe'. Instead, they exterminate him. Fortunately, the other humans have joined forces with two Thals, and together they are able to cut off the Daleks' power and return them to a state of inertia.

The script contained a number of wordy scenes intended to illustrate the burgeoning love interest between two of the crew members, Marion (Hilary Tindall) and Rocket (Edward Gardener). A further romantic subplot was then introduced between a prisoner being transported on the *Starfinder*, Ladiver (John Line), and the Thal woman, Ijayna (Suzanne Mockler). Ijayna was described in the script as the daughter of the male Thal Dexion (Nicholas Bennett), but by the time the play opened she had become his sister.

Although some of the plot threads were a little difficult to swallow whole, *The Curse of the Daleks* was a tightly constructed whodunit. Suspicion was thrown first on Ladiver, then on Captain Redway (Nicholas Hawtrey – who later appeared in *Doctor Who* playing Quinn, deputy governor of the human colony in *The Power of the Daleks*) and then on Professor Vanderlyn (John Moore) until, in best Agatha Christie tradition, the traitor was revealed as the first victim, Bob Slater (David Ashford), who had merely feigned death.

Unsurprisingly, the Daleks featured in this show were very similar in appearance to those seen on TV, as they were the fourth and final batch constructed by Shawcraft Models (Uxbridge) Ltd, who had previously supplied the props for the series itself. (The first batch of four was made for *The Daleks*, the second of four for *The Dalek Invasion of Earth*, the third of six for the first Dalek film and the fourth of five for *The Curse of the Daleks*.)

The Curse of the Daleks was originally scheduled to play in London's Strand Theatre, where John Gale Productions were based, but for some unknown reason was switched to the nearby Wyndham's Theatre some two weeks before opening. Despite this disruption, which could not have helped the pre-publicity, it still did reasonably good business, often getting a full house. After its initial run, it was not remounted to go on tour and has not been performed since.

Another publicity photograph for *The Curse of the Daleks*, taken outside the Strand Theatre, London, before the show moved to the Wyndham's Theatre.

CHAPTER SEVENTEEN

Exhibitions: On Display

Every Christmas in the early sixties a *Daily Mail* Boys and Girls Exhibition would be held in London, at the Empire Hall, Olympia. Attractions ranged from opportunities to try out various handicrafts to demonstrations of the Army's latest military hardware.

The highlight of the 1964/65 exhibition was the first major public appearance of *Doctor Who*'s most popular monsters, the Daleks. Two of the Dalek props – the Black Dalek Supreme and one of his silver and blue subordinates – had been loaned by the BBC for the Exhibition's duration, and they glided around with pre-recorded shrieks of 'Exterminate!' while visitors watched in awe from the Brainy Train – an electronically controlled vehicle

adapted from a factory transporter, which ferried people around an invisible track within a special enclosure.

Three years later, the Boys and Girls Exhibition which ran from 27 December 1967 to 9 January 1968 once again brought visitors face to face with the Daleks and with several other of the Doctor's foes. The format on this occasion was rather different, as the monsters were housed in a series of separate enclosures along a darkened corridor, where a continuous loop of *Doctor Who*'s original title sequence played on a monitor screen. A Dalek was the first exhibit, and this was followed by a selection of creatures from the William Hartnell years – an orange/red Mire Beast (described as an 'Octopus' in the Exhibition programme) and some Fungoids

Carole was in dire peril, but with all those young earthlings watching her every move she could not retreat.

What was she to do?

The monsters left her little time to decide.

As Carole herself, a little out of breath, later described:

'They crowded me into a corner. Even though I kept trying to push them back I was pinned against the wall.

'I was screaming and struggling but they held me by the shoulders with their sucker arms. Then finally I got free.

'It was frightening.'

Having thus failed to destroy the earth woman, the Daleks, much to the delight of the enthralled spectators, turned their attention to the Brainy Train.

This is an earth-made device which runs on a track with no rails, no signals and no driver. If no one had heard of the Daleks they would have said it was out of this world.

We regret to say that the Daleks won their fight with this robot marvel.

*From **The Daily Mail** (29 Dec 1964). See photo on page 136.*

The Cybermen stand ready to pounce on any unsuspecting schoolboy who gets too close. (1967/68).

Three exhibits at the ▲ 1967/68 *Daily Mail* Boys and Girls Exhibition, including from the top: a Fungoid from *The Chase*, a Cyberman and a Dalek.

Two Daleks at the *Daily Mail* Boys and Girls Exhibition. In the background can be seen the 'Brainy Train' which took visitors around the 1964/65 exhibition.

from *The Chase*, a Varga plant ('Cactus', according to the programme) from *The Daleks' Master Plan* and, in a glass tank, a group of Rills from *Galaxy 4*. After this came two Cybermen (their costumes made up of parts from a variety of their TV appearances), a Yeti from *The Abominable Snowmen* and an Ice Warrior frozen under a sheet of plastic 'ice'.

Most of the exhibits were simply static props, but a few, such as the Cybermen, were occupied

A Yeti gets to grips with a ▶ visitor to the 1967/68 exhibition.

by actors who would gladly adopt a menacing pose for people wanting photographs. An added attraction was that the exhibition featured the three winning entries in the 'Design a Monster' competition run earlier in the year by the BBC's children's magazine programme *Blue Peter*. These were the Aqua-Man (an angular robot frog wearing polkadot swimming trunks), the Hypnotron (a reptile with a mace-like tail and a head which was one giant eye) and the Steel Octopus. All three of these exhibits were made by the BBC's Visual Effects Department from the competition winners' original drawings.

This was to be the last *Doctor Who*-related exhibition of the sixties, but it established a format and a tradition which were to become very familiar indeed in the years to come.

Carole Ann Ford taunts the Daleks. (1964/65).

CHAPTER EIGHTEEN

Welcome to the Toyshop

Today it is hard to imagine the impact that the Daleks made on the British television-watching population of 1963. Anyone who grew up at that time will recall games of 'Daleks versus Thals' being fought in the school playground, and the child who missed an episode felt left out all week, unable to join in the speculation as to how the Doctor would win through in his latest adventure.

This general enthusiasm led inevitably to a demand for *Doctor Who* merchandise, which nevertheless remained unavailable for the best part of 1964 until this gap in the market came to the attention of the manufacturers. The race was on to get a Dalek model ready in time for Christmas 1964.

The BBC, meanwhile, had been caught completely off guard by the burgeoning popularity of the Daleks – after all, many people in the Corporation secretly felt that this new programme *Doctor Who*, with its young and inexperienced producer, would and should fail. Clearly they were wrong.

The BBC had a department for overseeing merchandise tie-ins to their programmes – *Dixon of Dock Green*, *The Flowerpot Men*, *Z-Cars* and *Andy Pandy* had all spawned spin-offs before *Doctor Who* arrived – but the scale of the Dalek boom defeated them. They decided to give over the job of dealing with all the interested companies to an Australian, Walter Tuckwell, whose organisation, Walter Tuckwell Associates Ltd, already handled several BBC copyright programmes. Tuckwell took responsibility for liaising with the companies and issuing them with licences and the BBC created a new post, Exploitation Manager, to deal with the copyright agreement and clearance procedures. This job was made harder by the fact that Terry Nation, who had created the Daleks, owned part of the copyright and so had to be paid a proportion of all the income generated.

In mid-1965, Tuckwell ran an eighteen-page advertisement feature in *Games and Toys* magazine to promote all the companies producing Dalek-related merchandise. The aim was to get their products into the shops for Christmas, and it worked admirably. Fliers also listing available toys and games were distributed to all the cinemas showing the new film *Dr. Who and the Daleks*, thus raising public awareness of just what could be bought, and Christmas 1965 was a Dalek-ful experience.

This high level of success continued throughout 1966, but by 1967 the bubble seemed to have burst.

◀ **The Dalek Playsuit manufactured by the Berwick Toy Company Ltd.**

Daleks, the space robots which enthralled a million children in Dr. Who, the science fiction serial, are to be marketed by the BBC.

'It is still to be decided whether their will be in the form of finished models or make-it-yourself kits,' a spokesman said.

Made from fibre-glass and wood, the Daleks are 5ft tall and hollow. They move on casters, and a child can control them.

Hundreds of children wrote to ask what would happen to the Daleks when they disappeared from the series.

The BBC finally sent two to Dr Barnardo's Homes, keeping two in case they are needed for TV in future.

The spokesman went on: 'The copyright of the Daleks rests with us. They were created by one of our staff designers, Roy Cusick [*sic*].'
Lionel Clay
From 'If You Want to Buy a Dalek Try the BBC' The Daily Mail (8 February 1964)

The Daleks slipped in popularity, and the BBC were unable to come up with anything which generated the same degree of interest. No one seemed to want to market the Cybermen (a fact which prompted their co-creator and copyright holder Kit Pedler to write several letters to the BBC querying the lack of promotion); and although there was interest expressed in the Quarks, contractual problems prevented the licensing of any products.

Up until the end of the sixties, very little merchandise unconnected with the Daleks was released. In many ways, the Daleks made and broke *Doctor Who* merchandising, as manufacturers and publishers seemed reluctant to produce *Doctor Who*-related as opposed to Dalek-related items. In fact, in the late sixties, the combination of post-Dalek apathy and Patrick Troughton's reluctance to publicise the programme resulted in *Doctor Who* tie-in products all but disappearing from shop shelves.

Terry Nation poses with a ▶ Dalek from *The Dalek Invasion of Earth*.

ACTIVITY BOOKS

The Dalek Painting Book (1965), the first *Doctor Who*-related activity book to be published, was typical of its type. Printed on absorbent – and cheap – paper, it contained numerous black and white line drawings to be coloured in, as well as some maze, dot-to-dot, complete-the-picture and other simple puzzles. Along similar lines was **Paint and draw the film of Dr Who and the Daleks**, although here the 62 drawings told the plot of the film, aided by a paragraph under each explaining what was happening.

In 1966, World Distributors issued a wide range of different titles. The first to appear, in March, were

Doctor Who Sticker Fun Book–Travels in Space and **Doctor Who Sticker Fun Book–Travels in Time**. These were 16-page combination colouring/ sticker books which had little to do with **Doctor Who** apart from the cover illustrations. In May, two **Doctor Who Puzzle Fun** books with the standard mix of material were published. Then came two **Doctor Who Painting Books**, also subtitled **Travels in Space** and **Travels in Time**. Lastly there was **Dr Who on the planet Zactus Painting Book**, which told a single story in 23 black and white line drawings, with a line of text on each page.

None of these World Distributors titles featured the Daleks as that licence had already been granted to Souvenir Press/Panther Books. Instead, they concentrated on the Doctor. Judging from the style of the drawings they contained, **Dr Who on the planet Zactus Painting Book** and the **Puzzle Fun** books were all the work of the same unknown artist.

The only other title to be released in the sixties was Souvenir Press's **Dalek Action Paint 'n Puzzle**, which appeared in March 1966. Not surprisingly, this contained pictures to paint and puzzles to solve.

ANNUALS

One of the first items of *Doctor Who*-related merchandise ever to be produced was **The Dalek Book**, published by Souvenir Press and Panther Books on 30 June 1964. Written by Terry Nation and David Whitaker and illustrated by Richard Jennings, John Woods and A. B. Cornwell, it was a collection of text stories and colour and duo-tone comic strips interspersed with fictional information features about the Daleks. Perhaps the most interesting aspect is that it featured an eight-page photo section of stills from *The Daleks*, arranged to form an original story in which Susan arrives on Skaro and helps the Daleks to decipher a message they have found. She manages to escape when her laughter frightens off her Dalek captors.

On 11 October 1965, the same publishers repeated their successful format with the release of **The Dalek World**, written by Nation and Whitaker and illustrated by Richard Jennings, John Woods, A. B. Cornwell and W. Wiggins. This time, the photo story was based around the first Dalek film, *Dr. Who and the Daleks*, the reader being invited to caption a series of 35 stills.

The third and final Dalek annual from Souvenir Press and Panther Books appeared on 8 September 1966. This was **The Dalek Outer Space Book**, written by Nation and Brad Ashton (with one non-Dalek story by Russ Winterbotham) and illustrated by Richard Jennings, John Woods, Leslie Waller and Art Sansom. There was no photo section on this occasion, but several of the stories featured Sara Kingdom from the TV story *The Daleks' Master Plan*, along with other agents of the Space Security Service (SSS).

World Distributors (Manchester) Ltd entered the fray in September 1965 with **The Dr Who Annual**. This was a mixture of text stories featuring the Doctor (but none of his companions) and factual articles relating to space travel and science. Reputed to have been written by David Whitaker, the text was of a high standard. The cover depicted the Doctor and the TARDIS on the surface of a planet not unlike Vortis, along with a Voord, a Sensorite, a Zarbi and a Menoptra which all featured in the stories inside.

The success of this first annual led World Distributors to produce similar volumes throughout the rest the sixties. The second one was published in September 1966 and it followed the same format, but also included a comic strip. Such strips were in future to remain a staple part of the annual's contents, which would vary little from year to year.

The 1968 volume (published September 1967) contained stories and features by Kevin McGarry, J. L. Morrissey, J. H. Pavey, M. Broadley, J. W. Elliott and Colin Newstead, and illustrations by Walter Howarth, David Brian, Susan Aspey and Peter Limbert. This was the first of the annuals to feature Patrick Troughton's Doctor. In fact, when World Distributors prepared the book they had only a few very early photographs of him available as reference, and consequently he was almost always shown wearing his stove-pipe hat which had actually been quickly dispensed with on TV. Similarly, although this annual was the first to depict any of the Doctor's TV companions, only Ben and Polly were included as Jamie was a relatively late addition to the series. Also of note is the fact that this book featured two publicity stills of the Doctor in an early version of his costume.

The 1969 annual, published in September 1968, featured Jamie and Victoria as the companions, except in one of the strip stories where the drawings were of Victoria but the character was called Polly. The front cover artwork depicted a Cyberman bursting into the TARDIS to confront Jamie and the Doctor, while the back cover bore likenesses of a Cyberman, a Yeti and the Cyber Controller (*The Tomb of the Cybermen*) – although none of these creatures actually appeared in the stories inside.

The 1970 annual (September 1969) featured Jamie and Zoe. It was also the first to have a photographic cover, showing the Doctor leaning on the TARDIS console from *The Power of the Daleks*. By this time, however, readers already knew that the second Doctor, Jamie and Zoe had all left the series and that a new era was just around the corner.

Aside from the regular annuals, World Distributors released one other sixties *Doctor Who* book in a similar format. This was **Doctor Who and the Invasion From Space**, which told just a single text

story and had rather fewer pages than the other annual-type books. Written by J. L. Morrissey and originally entitled *The Diagrams of Power*, the story featured the first Doctor with four travelling companions: the Mortimer family, rescued from a burning hovel during the Great Fire of London. In a note to the publishers, *Doctor Who* story editor Donald Tosh commented at the time that the text was of a higher standard than any other which had been submitted to the production office for approval.

BADGES

Although badges were not to come into their own as a form of *Doctor Who* merchandise until the mid-seventies, Plastoid Ltd did release in 1964 a total of four plastic badges exclusively available through F. W. Woolworth stores.

Two were, predictably enough, of Daleks, and these sold more than one million units. The first was approximately one inch high and showed a Dalek outlined in gold on the black plastic of the badge. The second was of the same design but about three times the size.

The other two were based on characters originating from Bill Strutton's 1965 story *The Web Planet* and were slightly smaller than the large Dalek badge. The first was of a Menoptra and the other showed a Zarbi and a Venom Gun larva standing together.

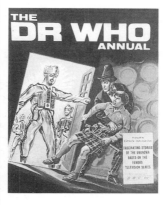

◀ An original advertisement for the Plastoid badges together with the Zarbi and Venom Gun badge, the Menoptra badge, and on their original card backings, the two sizes of Dalek badge.

A selection of *Doctor Who* ▶
and Dalek activity books.

BOXED GAMES

1965 was the year of the *Doctor Who* boxed game, and Bell Toys Ltd led the field with a range of four different games, all featuring the Daleks.

First there was the **Cutta-mastic Doctor Who and the Daleks**. This involved cutting out Dalek shapes from pre-printed sheets of expanded poly-styrene using a heated wire, painting them and then arranging them in front of a provided background. The **Dalek Eraser** was a set of six double-sided cards of Dalek scenes which could be coloured in and then wiped off for reuse. Also reusable was the **Dalek Wonder Slate** which was a basic 'magic slate' consisting of a waxed tracing paper placed on top of a dark shiny card. Drawing on the slate with a blunt 'pen' caused the waxed paper to adhere to the dark lower sheet, leaving dark lines and marks which could be made to vanish by sliding a rule down between the two sheets. The slate came either on a backing card or in a box.

The final game from Bell Toys was **The Dalek Oracle**, a variant of the popular Magic Robot game. The playing board was divided into two adjacent circles, around one of which were dotted several questions. In playing the game, a small Dalek toy was placed in the centre of this first circle and turned to point to a given question. The Dalek was then moved to the second circle, surrounding which were the answers, and placed on a mirror at its centre. When released, it 'magically' spun to point to the correct answer. Operated by magnets, the game contained several question-and-answer sheets.

The **'Dr Who' Dalek Painting By Numbers** contained a set of twelve paints, some brushes and six numbered pictures to complete. Along similar lines was the **Dr Who and the Daleks Stencil Set**, which contained stencils of Daleks, a palette, a brush and five paints.

The **Dalek Shooting Game** was a variant of the standard shooting gallery. The player fired a pop-gun at a cardboard target including four free-standing tin Dalek cutouts. Much more basic was the **Dodge the Daleks Game** – a board game containing dice, plastic Dalek counters and a card-board board.

If a simple dice and counters game did not appeal, an alternative was **Dr Who and the Daleks–The Great Escape Game**. The object of this was to navigate a ball bearing through a plastic maze, avoiding pit-falls along the way. A hand-held game, it was particularly tricky to complete, requiring a lot of eye-to-hand coordination.

Finally in 1965 there was the Chad Valley **Doctor Who Give-A-Show Projector**. This was one of a number of Give-A-Show Projector sets which could be obtained on a variety of different subjects (a basic set was also available through the British Home Stores as the BHS Projector). The battery-powered projector was used to display strips of slides – each containing seven artwork pictures – on to any flat surface (wall, ceiling etc). There were sixteen strips in the *Doctor Who* set, and these could also be purchased separately in four sets of four. The pictures used were particularly noteworthy as they told stories featuring the Zarbi and the Menoptra as well as the Daleks, and even one introducing the TARDIS. Some of the *Doctor Who* slides were also included, along with other subjects, in Chad Valley Projector gift sets.

The final *Doctor Who* boxed game to be released in the Sixties was a smaller version of Bell Toys' Cutta-mastic set, called **Cutta-mastic featuring Daleks**, which appeared in 1966.

CLOTHING

These days, the most common type of promotional clothing is the T-shirt, but it seems that during the sixties this particular marketing device had not yet been thought of.

In 1965 there were just two items of apparel that no fashion-conscious *Doctor Who* fan would be without. The first was a pair of **Dalek Slippers** in red needlecord with the Dalek motif flocked on one side and a circular logo proclaiming 'Daleks are

The reissued Dalek ▶
slippers with the plastic
Dalek 'pockets' on the sides,
and the papier-mâché Dalek
mask.

Three hundred dreaded Daleks were exterminated yesterday.

But it took earthly fire to wipe out the robot monsters from Outer Space.

Dr. Who and his space-time travellers in BBC1's Saturday afternoon science fiction serial had nothing to do with it.

The Daleks died when fire burned down a large part of a two-storey factory where they are made in Northampton.

Fifty were real Daleks. The other 250 were inflatable beach toys.

Mr Howard Bond, managing director of Scorpion Automotives, which hold the BBC licence to make the Daleks, said: 'Fortunately we had not taken delivery of most of the inflatable ones, which we expect will figure largely in the activities of the children on Britain's beaches this summer.

'But our entire stock of components for making the original Dalek suits has been destroyed.'
From 'Blaze wipes out 300 Daleks' The Daily Mail (17 April 1965)

◀ On this page, some of the boxed games available in the sixties.

A selction of Daleks strips ▲ from the back page of *TV Century 21*.

Here' on the other. They were available in children's sizes 2 to 7 and had a sponge rubber sole. The slippers were later reissued without the flocked Dalek and logo, but with a plastic Dalek 'pocket' on one side. If the feet were well covered, so was the head with a 9" by 7" papier-maché **Dalek Mask**. Due to the fragile nature of this headgear, very few examples exist today.

The only other item of *Doctor Who* clothing available in the sixties was a so-called **TARDIS Tie**, which may not have been licensed by the BBC. The only thing known about it is that it featured a picture of the TARDIS printed on to the material.

COMIC STRIPS

The *Doctor Who* comic strip began its long and successful run in Number 674 of TV Publications Ltd's weekly 6d **TV Comic**, dated week ending 14 November 1964. (Its impending arrival had been announced, with a small photograph, in the previous week's edition.)

Initially the strip appeared in black and white on pages 2 and 3 of the comic. It was drawn by Neville Main, and introduced the Doctor's youthful grandchildren John and Gillian as his new travelling companions. This measure was necessary as the licence granted by the BBC did not permit the use of any TV characters apart from the Doctor, although the publishers did get agreement to feature the Zarbi and the Menoptra in Numbers 693–698.

From Number 720, dated week ending 2 October 1965, which saw the start of the tenth story, the strip transferred to the comic's centrespread, pages 8 and 9, where it was printed in full colour. It also gained a new artist, Bill Mevin, who had a more detailed style than Main and produced a more accurate likeness of William Hartnell's Doctor.

After seven four-part stories, Mevin handed over the reins to John Canning, who made his debut with Number 748, dated week ending 16 April 1966. Canning would be responsible for the remainder of the sixties *TV Comic Doctor Who* strips. The last issue to feature William Hartnell's Doctor was Number 783, dated 17 December 1966 (the strip having reverted to black and white printing on pages 2 and 3 from Number 763). The following week, the Patrick Troughton incarnation made his debut – with no explanation whatsoever given for the sudden change of appearance!

The strip continued to present a succession of generally rather ludicrous 'monster' and adventure serials in varying numbers of weekly instalments. The first of these, a four-parter, followed the same format as before, being printed in black and white on pages 2 and 3 of the comic. However, the second (another four-parter) was extended to three pages per issue, including the colour cover. This prominence was due mainly to the presence of the Daleks,

A page from the first ever *Doctor Who* comic strip. Drawn by Neville Main, from *TV Comic* Number 674.

A later Hartnell strip, printed in the *TV Comic Annual* for 1967.

whose run in the rival comic *TV Century 21* had ended the previous week, but also because with Number 788, *TV Comic* was relaunched and its contents revised.

At this point, the name of the strip changed from *Doctor Who* to *Doctor Who and the Daleks*, and those most popular of adversaries were to appear in no fewer than twelve of the nineteen strips from Numbers 788 to 806. By the summer of 1967 Terry Nation had apparently decided to try to sell the idea

A Troughton strip from *TV Comic* number 915 dated June 1969.

The cover of *TV Century 21* number 28 The comic featured heavily the *Dr. Who and the Daleks* film.

of a Dalek television series in America, and he withdrew the rights for them to be used in the strip. The title was immediately changed back to *Doctor Who* (from Number 809), and the following week the strip reverted to being printed in black and white, this time on pages 14 and 15.

A return to colour pages came in Number 824 with the first appearance of the Cybermen. They were to be featured in a number of other serials over the coming months, always in their original design from *The Tenth Planet*, as were another of the Doctor's television foes, the Quarks.

The length of the strip remained at two pages for the remainder of the decade, but reverted to black and white on pages 14 and 15 from Number 877.

The last three instalments featuring Patrick Troughton's Doctor gave an alternative explanation for his impending change of appearance and were printed in Numbers 934–936, dated 8 November–22 November 1969 respectively.

As well as the weekly strip in the comic, there were also one-off *Doctor Who* stories appearing in all the regular *TV Comic* holiday specials and annuals produced during the course of the strip's run in the comic itself. In addition, a colour photographic sticker of William Hartnell's Doctor from *Marco Polo* was given away as a free gift with Number 738 as part of an ongoing promotion. A booklet was available into which the set of stickers could be pasted; the cover of this featured another photograph of Hartnell from the same story. Another photographic sticker, this time of the second Doctor, was given away with Number 789.

One of the problems that *TV Comic* had to contend with in its early years was that the rights to the Daleks had been sold elsewhere, meaning that John Canning had to resort to creating a not entirely dissimiar race, the Trods – a warlike race of robots who hovered around on traction devices wielding ray guns.

The Daleks had been snapped up by City Magazines, who launched a strip entitled simply *The Daleks* in the debut issue of their lavish new 7d comic **TV Century 21**, first published on 23 January 1965. (As a gimmick, the comic purported to originate from the twenty-first century, so the date actually given on the cover was 23 January 2065.)

Throughout the two-year run of *The Daleks* – 104 issues in all – it was printed in full colour on the back page of the magazine. The first 49 instalments were illustrated by Richard Jennings and all but seven of the rest by Ron Turner. The seven exceptions, in issues 52–58, were by Eric Eden. It is unclear who actually wrote the strips as, although most were credited to Terry Nation, some are thought to have been the work of either David Whitaker and/or *TV Century 21* staff writers and artists.

In addition to the comic strip, *TV Century 21* featured a number of full-colour photographic Dalek covers (one from *The Chase*, the rest from the two cinema films), some smaller spoof news items (usually featuring a photo from either *The Dalek Invasion of Earth* or the film *Dr. Who and the Daleks*) and competitions, including one, accompanied by a photo feature, to win three genuine Dalek props from *Dr. Who and the Daleks* (Issue 28, dated 31 July 2065).

▲ The *TV Comic* photo sticker booklet.

Mick Anglo's original ▲
artwork used on the cover
of *TV Tornado* in 1968.

THE COLOUR QUESTION

Many of the Dalek toys released in the sixties had several colour schemes. The Rolykins for example were officially released in three colours – black, silver and red. A definitive guide is difficult to compile, however, as in most cases the toys appeared in other non-official colours as well. There are eight known colours for the various parts of the Cherilea Daleks – grey, light blue, dark blue, black, red, yellow, orange, light green and gold – but others may well exist as the manufacturers produced prototypes from the moulds using whatever plastic they had to hand at the time.

Where colours are given in the text of this chapter, these are the standard ones in which a toy was released. Any other colour variants should therefore be treated as rarities. This applies to the Mechanoid kits as well as to all the plastic Daleks.

One final comic worthy of mention was issue number 59 of *TV Tornado*, dated 4 February 1968. This 7d comic featured a full colour cover painting by Mick Anglo of the second Doctor and an Ice Warrior. Aside from a very brief mention that the cover was of the second Doctor, the issue contained nothing relating to *Doctor Who*.

CONFECTIONERY

The earliest *Doctor Who* sweets were produced in 1965. There were reportedly **Milk Gum Daleks** and a **Dalek Easter Egg**, about which practically nothing is known. There were also **Dalek Jelly Babies** produced in two sizes by Bellamy's Ltd; and a range of **foil-wrapped chocolate Dalek novelties** from Edward Sharpe and Sons Ltd. Cavenham Confectionery produced some **Dalek Chocolate Bars**, at only a penny each, the sales of which had topped 22,000 units before the end of 1967.

Also from Cavenham Confectionery, in their Cadet Sweets range, were **Doctor Who and the Daleks Sweet Cigarettes** which retailed at 2d for ten. Sweet cigarettes were white candy rods, about two and a half inches long, with the end coloured red. What is most interesting about this range is that every box of ten cigarettes contained a picture card from a set of fifty, telling the story of one of the first Doctor's many adventures with the Daleks (*TV Century 21* versions). There was also an album into which the cards could be pasted, available for 1s plus five empty boxes. It is thought that the album was a generic one, not specifically produced for the Dalek promotion. Sales of the sweet cigarettes ceased on 9 November 1969, by which date more than 14,000 units had been bought.

After the boom of 1965/66 there was only one other example of *Doctor Who* confectionery until the seventies. This came in the form of a special promotion for T. Wall and Sons' incredibly successful **Sky Ray** ice lolly. Like the sweet cigarette packs, during the period of the promotion each of these

The set of fifty Cadet ▶
sweet cigarette cards and
one of the boxes the
cigarettes came in.

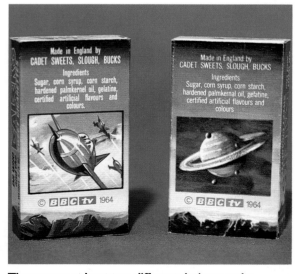

The set of 36 Sky Ray cards and album.

lollies was accompanied by a card inside the wrapper. The story featured the second Doctor battling the Daleks, aided by some Zarbi-like Astro-Beetles. There was also an album entitled **Dr Who's Space Adventure Book** to go with the set of 36 cards. It contained colouring pictures, activity ideas and some text to link together the story told by the cards themselves. All the artwork for the cards and album was by Patrick Williams.

CROCKERY

As more and more manufacturers got drawn into the phenomenon which was the Daleks, so the items being issued became more and more diverse.

One company, J. H. Weatherby & Sons Ltd, which specialised in producing crockery from the Falcon Pottery, obtained a licence to produce several Dalek items in 1965. Their seven-piece range comprised a **Dalek Baby Plate**, a **Dalek Cup**, a **Dalek Saucer** (the kind a cup goes on), a **Dalek Mug**, a **Dalek Porridge Bowl**, a **Dalek Tilly-Tray** (a type of tray which cannot be tipped over) and, strangest of all, a **Dalek Wall Plaque**.

There were at least two different designs on the reverse of the **Cadet** sweet cigarette boxes.

It appears that the artist responsible for these items used as reference the Cowan, de Groot Dalek Money Box rather than photographs of BBC Daleks, hence the likenesses are inferior to those on most other Dalek products of the time.

DALEKS

Although Dalek-related items feature in every other section of this chapter, such was the magnitude of the Dalek boom in the sixties that they merit a section of their own. All the following Dalek-shaped products were released in 1965.

After meeting BBC representatives at a toy fair, American Charles Newfeld was sufficiently impressed with the Daleks and convinced of their market potential – the BBC was then trying to sell *Doctor Who* to America, and the film *Dr. Who and the Daleks* was already on release – that he became keen to add the creatures to his 'Bendy' toy empire. Consequently he produced a **Bendy Dalek** which came in one of three colours – black, grey or white.

Static Dalek toys were also available, with the Herts Plastic Moulders **Dalek** leading the field. Sold exclusively through F. W. Woolworth stores, this silver/grey model stood about seven inches tall and came in a plastic bag.

Selcol Products Ltd brought out a **Dalek Nursery Toy**, a foot-high blue Dalek made from hard plastic. Unfortunately the appendages (eyestalk, sucker arm and gun stick) were all easily removable, casting some doubt on the safety of this toy for nursery use. The packaging consisted of a plastic bag with a header card.

◀ **An original advertisement together with a saucer and plate from J. H. Weatherby & Sons' range of Dalek crockery.**

Dalek toys. L-R, Back Row: 4½" Louis Marx Daleks (grey and black), 6½" Louis Marx Battery Operated Daleks (grey, gold and black), Dalek Nursery Toy, 6½" Louis Marx Friction Drive Daleks (grey and black), Clockwork Daleks (black and blue), Dalek Money Box. Middle Row: Bendy Daleks (grey and white), Herts Plastic Moulders Dalek (grey), Dalek Construction Kit, Herts Plastic Moulders Dalek (black). Front Row: Dalek 'swapits' (12 in assorted colours), Dalek Skittle, Dalek Rolykins (grey, red and ▼ black).

The Cowan, de Groot ▶
Mechanical Daleks.

The original box in which ▶
the smaller Rolykin boxes
were packed, together with
the three standard Rolykins
and an example of a Rolykin
with a domed base (second
from left).

Most functioning Dalek toys, however, were produced by one particular company: Louis Marx & Co. Ltd. From their factory came an excellent selection of models which not only looked good but also worked well. Top of the range were two six-and-a-half-inch Daleks – one operated by battery, the other by friction – both of which were available in either silver (coloured plastic and silver sprayed variants exist) or black. The battery version boasted 'tricky action', which meant that when it hit something it would eventually spin round and head in another direction. The friction drive version was operated in the usual way by pushing it repeatedly over a rough surface and then releasing it. Inside the neck section was a light which sparkled while the toy was moving.

There was also a smaller friction-drive model available. This was four and a half inches high and came in a choice of black or silver.

Smaller still were the **Dalek Rolykins**. Officially available in three colours – black, red and silver – they stood about an inch tall and had detachable appendages. Their most distinctive feature was that they each contained a ball bearing in the base, which meant that they could glide down smooth inclines and be pushed along tabletops. Because of the modest price – only a shilling each – and the size of these toys, seaside arcade machines were filled with them. The Rolykins were amongst the most popular of all Dalek items, with over a million units sold by October 1965. Examples also exist of Rolykins with a heavy domed base, allowing them to sway about in place, but no further information is available on this variant.

FILM MERCHANDISE

A number of items of merchandise were generated by the two *Doctor Who* cinema films. The activity book **Paint and draw the film of Dr Who and the Daleks** and the three record releases (**The Eccentric Dr Who**, **Fugue for Thought** and Roberta Tovey's **Who's Who**) are covered elsewhere in this chapter, but the others were as follows:

Dr. Who and the Daleks was a full colour comic-book adaptation of the first film, using likenesses of all the leading cast. Produced in America by Dell Comics, it was jointly licensed for world rights by Souvenir Press for one year from January 1966.

During the planning stages of the first film, its producer Milton Subotsky approached the BBC with a view to novelising the script. He was a little disappointed when the reply came back that a novel had already been written of the TV story on which the film was based, and that the BBC would not license another.

For the second film, *Daleks' Invasion Earth 2150 A.D.*, a range of promotional items was made

The Clifford Thomas Printing Company produced a **Scotchlite Dalek**, further details of which are unknown, while Cherilea Toys Ltd were responsible for a range of **Dalek 'swapits'**. These were two-and-a-half-inch tall models in three detachable sections – a base, a middle and a top – which came in several different colours. The appendages were also detachable and the top had two variations, slatted and solid. The idea was that children could swap the assorted body parts amongst themselves to create Daleks in a variety of different colour schemes. These toys were sold loose and initially came in three colours – black, light blue and silver – although more were added later.

As for working Dalek models, perhaps the hardest to find today is the **Mechanical Dalek** produced by Cowan, de Groot Ltd. This was constructed from tin and had a blue or black finish. A clockwork toy, it stood about six inches tall and was wound with a key in the side of the base. As it moved about, the head and eyestalk also turned – a unique feature for a Dalek model. These particular toys were so popular that the UK production lines could not keep up with the demand and so they were finally assembled in Hong Kong.

available. Those mentioned in the press handouts of the day are milk-bottle collars, paper bags and paper serviettes.

Posters, front-of-house stills and campaign books were produced for both films, as were many black and white and colour publicity photographs.

One other point worth mentioning is that in 1965 the breakfast cereal Sugar Smacks ran, on the backs of their boxes, a competition to win a Dalek. The entrants had to place in order of importance twelve qualities for fighting Daleks and the winner was ten-year-old John Streeter from Sussex.

◄ A selection of front of house stills, campaign books and poster-fliers for the two Dalek films. On the left the Dell comic adaptation of the first film.

JIGSAWS

In 1965, Thomas Hope and Sankey Hudson produced two sets of *Doctor Who* jigsaws for F W Woolworth.

One set consisted of two very simple 9 3/4" x 13 3/4" 29-piece plywood-backed puzzles. The handsome artwork, reproduced on the box fronts, depicted scenes from a Dalek invasion of London. An added bonus was that the Doctor, the Daleks and the TARDIS were all separate jigsaw pieces and could be erected on small wooden stands within the picture to give a three dimensional effect. Also of note is the fact these puzzles were amongst the few items of sixties *Doctor Who* merchandise actually to include the Doctor!

The other set of jigsaws – cardboard-backed ones this time – also featured the Daleks. Although it officially consisted of four 17" x 11" 187-piece artwork puzzles, there were in fact five produced: *Daleks Attack, Daleks In Westminster, Peace Talks, In The TARDIS* and *In The Laboratory*. The reason for the fifth release is rumoured to be that one of the original four (*In the TARDIS*, which shows the Doctor at the TARDIS controls while a Dalek comes through the doors from outside) was withdrawn at the BBC's request and another (*In The Laboratory* – a similar scene but featuring neither the Doctor nor the TARDIS interior) put in its place.

◄ Ray Brooks as David Campbell standing in front of the Sugar Puffs advertisement seen prominently in the film *Daleks' Invasion Earth 2150 AD.*

NOVELS

Perhaps the most obvious piece of merchandise that can be connected with any television programme or film is a novelisation. In *Doctor Who's* case, there were three produced during the sixties.

The first, **Doctor Who in an exciting adventure with the Daleks**, published in hardback on 12 November 1964, was written by the series' story editor David Whitaker, based on the scripts from Terry Nation's *The Daleks* and with illustrations by Arnold Schwartzman. Rather than making it a straightforward third person narrative, Whitaker chose to tell the story from Ian's point of view, and he radically altered the beginning to give a new

account of the first meeting between the four main characters. In this version, Barbara and Susan are involved in a car crash on a foggy Barnes Common, and Ian, who has stopped in his own car because he is lost, finds them there. Together, Ian and Barbara then try to summon help, and stumble across the TARDIS. Thereafter, events continue pretty much as in the televised version, with allowances made to accommodate those scenes in which Ian, who is telling the story, does not appear.

Doctor Who in an exciting adventure with the Daleks is now widely regarded as one of the best *Doctor Who* novelisations ever written; and when first published it did well enough to warrant a reprint. (The first edition had a pink dust jacket while the reprint had a greeny-grey one).

Following the success of this book over Christmas 1964, the publishers, Frederick Muller, purchased the rights to a further two titles. Bill Strutton was commissioned to novelise his story *The Web Planet*, which became **Doctor Who and the Zarbi**, while Whitaker again did the honours on **Doctor Who and the Crusaders**, adapted from his own story *The Crusade*. The former was published on 16 September 1965 and the latter appeared on the 25 February 1966 (despite the 1965 copyright mark inside). Both books were written in standard third-person narrative and were illustrated by John Wood

▲ A large advertisement for display in shops selling Sugar Smacks during their tie-in promotion with the second Dalek film.

A selection of novels. ▶
Back row: The three British
hardback editions. (The
edition of *Doctor Who in an
exciting adventure with the
Daleks* shown is the reprint.)
L-R, front row: Green
Dragon *Crusaders*, Armada
Daleks, Avon Books'
American edition of the
Dalek novel, *The Dalek
Pocketbook and Space
Traveller's Guide*.

The front of Newton Mills' ▲
Dalek Greetings Card. The
wording is showing through
a hole cut in the front.

A small shop poster ▲
publicising *Who's Who* sung
by Roberta Tovey.

Doctor Who-related ▶
records.

– not to be confused with the designer on *The Web Planet* – and Henry Fox respectively.

The paperback rights to **Doctor Who in an exciting adventure with the Daleks** were sold to Armada Books (an imprint of May Fair Books Ltd) in 1965, and they brought out an edition in October of that year, with new cover and text illustrations by Peter Archer. In addition, the novel was sold to America (Avon books, a division of the Hearst Corporation, released a 50c paperback in July 1967, unillustrated but with a cover photograph by Paul Weller) and to Holland (Uitgeversmij, West-Friesland published a Dutch version in 1966). **Doctor Who and the Crusaders** was also sold to paperback; this time the company picking up the rights was Green Dragon, an imprint of the Atlantic Book Publishing Company. They published their edition in 1967, with new illustrations by an uncredited artist. It has also been reported (although there is no record in BBC documentation) that **Doctor Who in an exciting adventure with the Daleks** was released as a hardback in Canada, and that both this title and **Doctor Who and the Zarbi** were issued as hardback editions from Soccer Books in New York in 1966.

The only other sixties *Doctor Who* book which could loosely be termed a novel, or at least had the basic appearance of one, is **The Dalek Pocketbook and Space Travellers Guide**. This paperback was an illustrated collection of fictional infor-

mation about the Daleks and simple factual material about astronomy and space travel, 'compiled and presented' by Terry Nation.

RECORDS

Like most popular institutions, *Doctor Who* has been spawning record releases ranging from the serious to the cash-in almost since the day it began.

In 1964, Decca, under licence from the BBC, brought out the original version of the series' theme tune, composed by Ron Grainer and realised by the Radiophonic Workshop. The theme was also released in Australia.

Also in 1964 the public were treated to **I'm Gonna Spend My Christmas With A Dalek**, the first single from the Go-Gos, a semiprofessional Newcastle group comprising Mike Johnson (19), Alan Cairns (20), Abe Harrison (20), Bill Davison (22), Les McLeian (19) and Sue Smith (17). Produced and written by Johnny Worth under his pseudonym Les Van Dyke, it featured such bizarre lyrics as: 'I'm gonna spend my Christmas with a Dalek/And hug him underneath the mistletoe/And if he's very nice/I'll feed him sugar spice/And hang a Christmas stocking from his big left toe.' Sue Smith performed the lead vocals in a Shirley Temple-type little girl voice, complete with an inability to pronounce her 'w's. The record also featured a Dalek saying such uncharacteristic things as 'I love you' and 'Please may I have some more plum pudding and custard?'

The Century 21 LP **Favourite Television Themes** (Century 21 Records LA 6) featured a version of the *Doctor Who* theme by the Eric Winston Orchestra, which was also included on the mini-album **TV Century 21 Themes** (MA 105) and released as a single on Pye in 1965.

Another 1965 release was **Landing of the Daleks** (B-side: **March of the Robots**) by The Earthlings. An instrumental, this was initially banned from the airwaves as it contained an SOS morse message. However, it was then reissued without the offending signal. Released the same year was **Dance of the Daleks** by the Jack Dorsey Orchestra, a jazzy instrumental inspired by *Doctor Who* and published by Shadows Music.

The Eccentric Dr Who by the Malcolm Lockyer Orchestra was the theme to the film *Dr. Who and the Daleks*, with some incidental music called **Daleks and Thals** on the B-side. One of the stars of the film, Roberta Tovey, also released a record in 1965. Called **Who's Who**, this was written by Lockyer and contained the following extraordinary lyric: 'Who's Who?/Well Doctor Who of course/He's quite at home in a big spaceship/Or sitting on top of a horse/He's been to the past and future/And whatever he may do/He'll always be a friend of mine/Who?/Doctor Who.'

The record considered by many to be the best

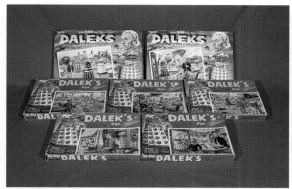

Dalek jigsaws. At the rear are the two wooden stand-up jigsaws and in front are all five of the card jigsaws.

◀ Very few items of merchandise were released which did not feature the Daleks. In the background is Raphael Lipkin's Dr Who Money Box, while in the centre the large Herts Plastic Moulders Mechanoid is flanked by several smaller Cherilea Mechanoids.

Doctor Who-related release of the sixties was the 1966 Century 21 EP **The Daleks**. This contained approximately 21 minutes of dialogue from the final episode of the TV story *The Chase*, with a linking narrative spoken by David Graham (who also played one of the Dalek voices in the story).

In 1967, Bill McGuffie's **Fugue for Thought** was released. This was actually music from the second *Doctor Who* film, *Daleks' Invasion Earth 2150 A.D.*

Perhaps of most interest to the series' fans was a number performed by Frazer Hines, the actor who played Jamie. In 1968 he recorded **Who's Dr Who?**, written by L. Reed and B. Mason and produced by Tommy Scott under the musical direction of Nicky Welsh. This started promisingly, appearing to be an early heavy-metal version of the *Doctor Who* theme, but degenerated into another twee tune in which the following lyrics were heard: 'There's magic in his hands/You ask and he may show it/He simply elevates a stone/Where you or I would throw it/He's been to yesterday/And somehow we all follow/I wonder where we are today/Or where we'll be tomorrow.' Frazer Hines also taped another single, *Jamie's Awae in his Time Machine*, but this was never released due to the intervention of his manager, who had not approved of the first record.

Lastly, it is worth mentioning that a number of TV music compilation albums released during the sixties featured versions of the *Doctor Who* theme. These often bore little relation to the original Radiophonic Workshop version and are of only passing interest to collectors. Also, sheet music for most of the *Doctor Who*-related titles was available.

THE DALEKS EP

There appear to have been three different versions produced of **The Daleks** EP – one for Australia and two for England. All had a photographic sleeve depicting two Daleks from **The Chase**. There were however a number of differences between them.

The Australian release was on the yellow and black Astor label. It featured the original **Doctor Who** theme tune, had pink lettering on the sleeve and a purple background to the photograph of the Daleks. One of the English releases, on the blue C21 label, had the Eric Winston Orchestra version of the theme, red lettering on the sleeve and a blue background to the Dalek photograph. The other English release was identical to this except that it featured Barry Gray's Supermarionation music (from **Thunderbirds**) instead of the **Doctor Who** signature tune.

The anti-Dalek armoury. At the back is the Neutron Exterminator; below that are two Anti-Dalek Jet Immobilisers while left to right at the front are the Twin Rocket Gun, the Sonic Disintegrator and the Fluid Neutraliser.

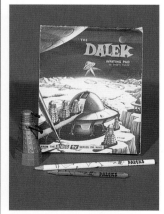

▲ Dalek stationery. The Dalek Writing Pad, Dalek Pencil Sharpener and two Dalek Pencils.

**H & B Plastics' Dalek ▶
Plastic Jar.**

STATIONERY

The first item of *Doctor Who* stationery was reportedly a **Dalek Birthday Card** released in 1964 by the Waldorf Card Company. However, it was 1965 before a fuller range of products became available.

Bailies Agencies took up the challenge with a **Dalek Pencil** which came in several colours, and as a pencil is not much use without something to sharpen it, they also released a small **Dalek Pencil Sharpener**. Newton Mills Ltd, meanwhile, provided something on which to write, in the form of a **Dalek Writing Pad**, an ordinary writing pad with a Dalek cover. The same company also marketed a **Dalek Greetings Card** which bore a full colour artwork picture of a small boy surrounded by Daleks. The wording 'We command you' could be seen through a cut-out hole; when the card was opened, the full message was revealed to be 'We command you to have a happy birthday'.

The following year, Tower Press released a **Dalek Pencil Craft Set**, about which nothing more is known.

TOYS

Almost all the *Doctor Who* toys produced in the sixties were, predictably, Dalek-related. Unless otherwise stated, the date of manufacture of the products described below was 1965.

One thing every child wanted to do was to impersonate a Dalek, and two companies were happy to provide the means. First, in 1964, Scorpion Automotives produced a **Dalek Dressing Up Costume**. This is one of the rarest sixties items today, as in the lead-up to Christmas 1964, the firm's Northampton factory was damaged by fire and the stocks waiting to go to the shops, together with all the components to construct the suits, were destroyed.

BE A REAL
DALEK
THIS
CHRISTMAS

A real working full size
T V Dalek. Be the envy of
your friends as you move
around and control the
lights and probes. The box
is also a super Dr Who
Space Ship to the mysterious land of the Daleks
in the shops now.

NOTE TO MOTHER

Scorpion Automotives

**Comedian Norman ▲
Vaughan poses with a
Scorpion Automotives Dalek
Dressing Up Costume. This
version of the costume does
not have wheels.**

This costume was an excellent representation of a Dalek and, not surprisingly, was in great demand. It had a plastic dome with side lights and a realistic eyestalk, and a neck section (through which the occupant could see out) comprising two rings held in place by vertical rods – just like the real thing. The shoulder section was patterned after the original Dalek design and the sucker arm and gun stick fitted into sockets so that they could be worked from inside. The outfit was finished off with a PVC skirt, printed with the familiar pattern of studs.

There were actually two versions of the costume produced. The first was on wheels but this proved a safety hazard and the second was propelled by foot-power alone. Another safety feature was that if the occupant should trip and fall, the dome automatically came off, thus ensuring that no one could get trapped inside.

Less sophisticated than the Dressing Up Costume, but just as popular, was the **Dalek Playsuit**. This comprised a red PVC skirt printed with a white stud design, which fitted over a silver, cardboard-slatted section topped with a plastic dome. Also provided were an eyestalk which could be fitted into a hole on the dome, and two 'arms' which the child held through suitably positioned holes in the skirt.

If dressing up as a Dalek didn't appeal, there was always the opportunity to be a Dalek killer, as several suitable weapons were on the market.

Lincoln International repackaged their *Dan Dare* water pistol as **Dr Who's Anti-Dalek Fluid Neutraliser**, which came attached to an attractive backing sheet. The same company also produced three other items. The blue and white **Dr Who's Anti-Dalek Sonic Disintegrator** took batteries and emitted a Dalek-killing noise when the trigger was pressed; **Dr Who's Anti-Dalek Jet Immobiliser** was another water pistol, which could fire either single or multiple bursts; and **Dr Who's Anti-Dalek Neutron Exterminator**, or bazooka gun, fired anti-Dalek missiles from its three foot long blue and silver tube. **Doctor Who's Astro Ray Dalek Gun**, made by Bell Toys, was basically a dart gun with a battery-powered torch in the front. This came in a box, while Lone Star Products' red and silver **Dalek Rocket Gun** which fired sucker darts (two were provided) was sold on a backing board featuring a target.

Scorpion Universal Toys Ltd, a subsidiary of Scorpion Automotives (makers of the Dalek Dressing Up Costume), brought out a **Stand Up Inflatable Dalek**. This was an inflatable punch-bag with a Dalek printed on it in blue, white and black.

Not content with producing ready-made Dalek models (covered elsewhere), Louis Marx & Co. Ltd also released their large friction-drive toy as a seven-piece **Dalek Construction Kit**. The friction-drive mechanism was not included, so completion of the kit resulted in a Dalek which could just be rolled

Sundry items. Back: Dalek Bag. L-R: Dalek Plastic Jar, Dalek Candle, Dalek Toilet Soap. They are standing on Dalek Wallpaper.

along. The same company also released three different **Doctor Who and the Daleks Bagatelle** games. There were two circular versions – one large and one small – which utilised identical pictures and cup placings. The large one was ten inches in diameter and contained five coloured balls; the small one was five inches in diameter and had three balls. Both came in boxes. The third Bagatelle was a fifteen-inch-long arch-shaped game, available only from F. W. Woolworth. This contained five balls, and for obvious reasons had different artwork from the other two.

Two **Dalek Balloons** were produced by different manufacturers. Lewis Knight & Co. marketed a large version, exclusively through F. W. Woolworth, while Sto-Rose Toys Ltd were responsible for a smaller type, printed with a two-colour Dalek and available in six different colours.

As well as the Doctor Who Give-a-Show projector (described elsewhere), Chad Valley issued a **Dalek Glove Puppet** with a moulded vinyl head and eyestalk and a fabric body. Bowman Jenkins produced a **Dalek Kite**, a fairly flimsy affair consisting of a polythene face and tail, with two cross-struts made from a lightweight wood. Randall & Wood Ltd added a **Dalek Meteorite Storm** to their 'Linda' range of TV character snowstorms – a small scene inside a clear perspex dome filled with water and tiny red particles which would swirl like snow when it was shaken. The snowstorms are believed to have come boxed, and several variants are known to exist, with differing numbers of Daleks making up the interior scene. Randall & Wood Ltd also brought out some **Dalek Skittles**. Cowan, de Groot manufactured a rather nice **Dalek Money Box**, the dome of which could be removed to retrieve the money inserted through a slot in the back. Selcol Products Ltd, meanwhile, produced an attractive **Dr Who and the Daleks Top**, which was see-through, had moving Daleks inside and whistled as it spun. Hours of fun for all the family.

A different sort of toy was a set of **Dalek**

Transfers from S. Guiterman & Co. Each sheet, which cost 3d, contained forty small pictures featuring not only Daleks but also Mechanoids, a Voord, Menoptra, Zarbi, a Venom Gun, the TARDIS exterior and the TARDIS console. Once cut from the sheet and soaked in water, the images could be slid off their paper backing and on to the skin.

There were also a couple of toys which featured aspects of *Doctor Who* other than the Daleks. With a view to creating another success, two companies brought out Mechanoid models. Cherilea Toys produced a small version to the same scale as their Dalek model, while Herts Plastic Moulders came up with a larger green one. (In later years, Cherilea reused their Mechanoids as components for a lunar landing vehicle toy.)

Lastly, the only licensed TARDIS model to be produced during the sixties was by Raphael Lipkin Ltd, whose blue plastic **Dr Who Money Box** materialised packed in a box.

SUNDRIES

This section collects together all those items which cannot be easily placed in any other category. As such, it forms the strangest collection of sixties products.

In 1965 there appeared on the market a **Dalek Candle** made by Candle Art Ltd, but no details of this are known. There was also something called **Dalek PVC Sheeting** manufactured by Storey's Brothers Ltd, although the mind boggles as to what possible use this could have been. The **Dalek Plastic Jar** from H & B Plastics Ltd was a beaker decorated with transfers, which unfortunately soon rubbed off. There has even been rumour of a **Dalek Firework**, but no examples are known to exist.

▲ The Dalek Candle. It is very similar in shape to the Hi-Ball ice-cream tub, but is not the same. The small bumps representing the studs on the base are perfectly round, not teardrop shaped as on the ice cream container.

◄ Dalek toys. At the rear is the Dalek Kite, in the centre are all three versions of the Dalek Bagatelle (the small circular toy is in its box, while the large circular one is alongside its box) and at the front is a sheet of Dalek Transfers with its original header card, and the Dalek Meteorite Storm.

A surviving example of ▲ the Edwin Hall Dalek Kiddie Ride at an auction in 1991.

Of possibly more practical use was **Dalek Toilet Soap**, made by the Northants Association for the Blind and sold in boxes of three. **Dalek Sponges** are also said to have existed. Apparently there were two sorts: one which you could shove your hand inside, forming a sponge mitten, and another which took the form of a flat sponge shaped like a Dalek. Again, precise details are unknown.

Dalek Wallpaper, showing numerous *TV Century 21*-style Daleks whizzing about on their hoverbouts and firing their guns, was made by The Wall Paper Manufacturers Ltd (Lees Paper Staining Company Branch), a division of Crown Wallpapers. First released in 1965, it was popular enough to remain in the catalogues until the end of 1967, when it was discontinued.

A **Dalek Bag** was also released around this time. This hold-all had a single zipper across the top and transfers of Daleks on either side.

In 1967, Edwin Hall & Co produced a **Dalek Kiddie Ride** for amusement arcades. This stood about eight feet tall and followed the basic Dalek shape, but with a number of modifications to make it less vulnerable to damage by the thousands of children who would use it. The ride included a Dalek voice box as well as flashing lights and a mechanism to produce a rocking movement. Only about forty of these were made.

Even rarer was a **TARDIS Climbing Frame and Playhouse** released in 1969. Only twelve are known to have been supplied to shops (six to Hamleys in London's Regent Street and six to Raggity Anne's in Blackheath village, South London).

There were two promotional items available during the sixties. The first was a booklet to accompany the 1965 stage play *The Curse of the Daleks* (for which an advertising poster was also printed), and the second a glue-it-yourself paper cutout Dalek produced by the *Daily Express* and sent out free in 1965 to every entrant of a 'Name a Dalek' competition.

MISCELLANEOUS

As well as 'official' items licensed by the BBC, unlicensed products were available. These are much harder to track down but the following are known to have been released.

During the sixties, the BBC did not hold any copyright on the police-box design of the TARDIS and so this opened the way for a small free-for-all, with some companies cashing in with new products while others continued what they had always done – Dinky toys had been selling a die-cast metal police box since 1936 and were not about to stop just because the producers of a TV programme had

The Dalek Meteorite Storm. At the top of the two mountains are two tiny Daleks on hoverbouts. The red 'meteorites' can be seen on the floor of the scene. Several variants of the toy are known to exist, with different numbers of Daleks in varying positions.

decided to use the box in a rather unorthodox fashion.

An item which everyone remembers as being connected with the Daleks but which in fact was not, was the 'Dalek' ice cream. Known as a Hi-Ball, this came in a plastic cone with a ball of bubble-gum in the bottom. When turned upside down, the empty cone bore a remarkable resemblance to a Dalek. Whether or not this was intentional is open to debate, but no doubt the similarity did nothing to stunt sales.

There were also a number of products which were suggested to the BBC, but which for various reasons were never produced. Wells Gardner Danton & Co. Ltd's *Doctor Who Dotto Book* (1965) got as far as a signed contract but appears not to have been released; a *Dalek Drawing Book* from the Douglas Paper Company would have featured a Dalek cover around a blank pad; and Young World Productions wanted to run a comic serialisation of *Marco Polo* in one of their magazines but *TV Comic* already had exclusive rights to a *Doctor Who* comic strip. An approach from Allen Davies & Co. Ltd regarding a *Painting by Numbers* set was rejected as there was already one licensed; a set of four colouring books was suggested by Love & Malcolmson; Purnells wanted to release some hardbacked comic-strip books in 1966 while in the same year Mayflower wanted to release something similar in paperback. Some Quark sweet cigarettes were proposed in 1968, as was a calendar, but both fell foul of contractual and copyright problems. Lastly, in 1969 the BBC was approached for permission to release some children's stories involving Dala the Friendly Dalek. Not surprisingly in this case, the suggestion was rejected.

CHAPTER NINETEEN

The Birth of Fandom

The first organised body of *Doctor Who* fans was launched, with full recognition and co-operation from the BBC, barely two years after the series itself got underway. Called the William (Doctor Who) Hartnell Fan Club, it was run by a young fan who lived in Stoke-on-Trent, and was advertised in such places as *Jackie* magazine.

The club periodically produced an A4 duplicated newsletter containing information about the activities of the series' stars and brief details of forthcoming TV stories. Even more appreciated by the club's members was the fact that it distributed, free of charge, autographed BBC publicity photos of regular cast members such as Peter Purves and Maureen O'Brien, who had recently joined *Doctor Who*.

Around the time of William Hartnell's departure from the series, the organisation changed its name to the Official Doctor Who Fan club, and in 1966 or 1967 its format changed slightly as the original organiser handed over to two fellow fans called Larry S. Leake and Philip Jon Oliver, who became the new club secretaries. The club continued to distribute autographed photographs of the series' stars, but its newsletter was revamped, becoming more regular, longer – a few stapled sheets in either A4 or A5 format – and more informative, with more comprehensive previews of the Doctor's TV adventures. Readers' letters and short stories were also included.

The next change came in 1969, when Graham Tattersall took over as secretary of the club. He recalls how this came about:

'My association with the club began, I think, in either 1966 or 1967. I was an avid fan then and used to write to the stars of the show like Anneke Wills, Michael Craze et cetera. As I recall, it was Michael Craze who gave me the address of the club in Hanley, Stoke-on-Trent, which was then run by Larry Leake and Philip Oliver. I enrolled as a member and corresponded regularly for about two years or so. Then in 1969 Larry announced that he and Philip were giving up (though I think by that time Philip had already dropped out) and suggested I might like to take over as club secretary. I readily agreed to do it, but at that point I must admit I had no idea what I was taking on. There was no transfer of funds from the old club or anything like that, so I had to try and re-establish the club as a completely new venture.

'Larry sent me the names and addresses of his current members and I can remember drafting out a letter inviting them to continue as members of the new club. It cost me an absolute fortune in postage! I did have many favourable replies, however, and began to build up a new membership of my own. There were some, though, who weren't happy to carry on and asked for a refund of their subscription. Obviously I could not make any refunds as I hadn't received their money to start with.

'The production secretaries at the BBC were very helpful in supplying publicity photos of the regular cast and information on forthcoming stories and new characters et cetera. I passed this info on to the members in the form of a newsletter which I endeavoured to send out as often as possible.'

Graham Tattersall also produced a couple of issues of a more substantial duplicated magazine entitled simply *Doctor Who*, along the lines of his predecessors' publication. This contained articles and fiction – not all *Doctor Who*-related – and also gave some coverage to the BBC's new imported American series, *Star Trek*, a move which was not universally popular amongst the club's members.

Although *Doctor Who* fandom developed in tandem with the series, it would not be until the middle of the next decade that organised appreciation would really flourish.

▲ One of the early fan club magazines.

▲ The club sent out signed photos of the programme's regulars.

I read with delight that Dr. Who (BBC-1) will be returning next January – only to be horror-struck at the news that he will be TARDIS-less! This 'move' is supposed to give appeal to adult viewers. I can inform you that a spontaneous 'Keep the TARDIS society' will arise throughout the country.
(Mr) H Gardner, Surrey

Steady on, Mr. Gardner - the TARDIS will still be around when Dr. Who returns. As to its role in the new series, well, I'm afraid we must wait and see.
From 'What, no Tardis?'
Radio Times *You Write...*
(10 July 1969)

Jon Pertwee, the comedian and actor, will be the new Dr. Who on BBC television when the programme returns after the summer break next January. He will be the third Dr. Who in the television serial, which has run for six years.
From 'Dr Jon Who' **The Times (21 June 1969)**

Jon Pertwee at his first press photocall, with a Yeti.

CHAPTER TWENTY

End of an Era

There had always been a certain ambivalence towards *Doctor Who* within the upper echelons of the BBC, and by season six there were rumblings that it was perhaps no longer justifying its place in the schedules, this despite the fact that its average ratings had dropped only slightly from the very respectable levels of seasons four and five. Indeed, Terrance Dicks recalls that even as early as the end of season five, when he first joined the series as assistant script editor, there was a feeling that it should be allowed to come to a natural end as soon as Patrick Troughton left:

'Almost the first thing I heard when I came to join as assistant script editor was that the BBC were actually thinking of taking the show off. I thought, that's a great start to my career; three months and that will be the end of it. For a while, they did actually consider ending it, because even then it had been going for a pretty long time in television terms. The viewing figures were okay but they weren't marvellous any more. So I was actually involved in looking around for something to replace the show. We couldn't come up with anything which seemed as good, so eventually it was decided to recast – to get a new Doctor – and to start again.'

Producer Peter Bryant has a slightly different recollection of the situation:

'The BBC were always talking about killing the series off, for some extraordinary reason which I've never been able to understand, but I don't remember anything in particular being said about stopping it when Patrick Troughton left. I mean, there might have been talk of finding a new idea to replace it, but that frequently happened. One was always on the lookout for new ideas. However, I don't recall being specifically briefed to look for a replacement, and I'm sure I would remember if I had been.'

Derrick Sherwin, Bryant's co-producer on the last few Patrick Troughton stories, agrees: 'I certainly wasn't aware of any desire on the part of the BBC hierarchy to finish the series. There was always the possibility at the end of a season that it might not be renewed for another year, but that was the same for any show whatever it might have been.'

A number of new series ideas that Sherwin had himself been involved in developing at that time have generally been assumed to have been intended for the *Doctor Who* slot. Again, however, he denies this:

'One of the reasons Peter and I were so busy on *Doctor Who* at the end was that we were also working on two episodes of a potential new series called *S P Air*, which I wrote and revamped from an original idea called *Highway to Action* by Jon Rollason and Keith Williams. It was about a special body within the RAF which had political authority and investigated things "under the counter" rather than above board – a sort of troubleshooting team – and the RAF offered us some facilities for it. But those episodes were actually made and transmitted, and it wasn't intended for the same slot as *Doctor Who*. It was fairly hard-nosed, and was really for adults.'

Other ideas under discussion at one time or another included a series of Jules Verne-type stories and a remake of the fifties Quatermass serials. However, Sherwin maintains that none of these was considered as a potential replacement for *Doctor Who*:

'You see, as a producer at the BBC, you had to decide what you wanted to do next and then promote it, to try to get it on the road. You were supposed to find your own ideas for new series. The Jules Verne proposal was certainly one that I came up with, but there were a number of others – probably fifteen or twenty ideas – that I developed, which for one reason or another didn't get past the BBC executives.'

Whatever the case may be, one thing which can be said for certain is that a decision was eventually taken to go ahead and make a seventh season of *Doctor Who* for transmission, in colour, and with a greatly reduced number of episodes, in 1970. As Sherwin recalls, he and Bryant agreed from the outset that it would need to be very different from what had gone before:

SALES OF THE DOCTOR

*Most **Doctor Who** stories were packaged for sale abroad by BBC Enterprises. To give some idea of the interest that **Doctor Who** generated globally, the third story, **Inside the Spaceship**, had been sold to the following countries by the end of the sixties: Canada, Malta, Singapore, Bermuda, Nigeria, Gibraltar, Aden, Trinidad, Rhodesia, Cyprus, Barbados, Hong Kong, Ghana, Jamaica, Zambia, Kenya, Thailand, Sierra Leone, Tunisia, Morocco – including all Middle East and Arabic countries – and Far East and South East Asia. By the middle of the seventies, every story transmitted during the sixties, with the sole exceptions of **Mission to the Unknown** and **The Daleks' Master Plan**, had been sold abroad. To facilitate these sales, all **Doctor Who**'s directors had standing instructions that they were to include a fade-to-black either immediately after the opening title sequence, or following the 20-second reprise from the previous episode (which included the episode title and writer credit), and that there was also to be a fade-to-black somewhere towards the middle of each episode. These fades would be used by the overseas television stations to insert commercials.*

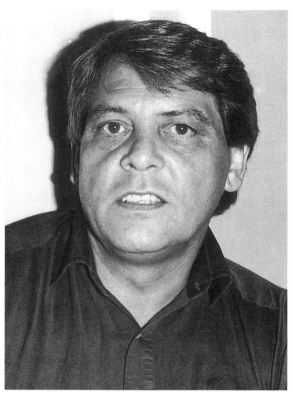

Producer Derrick Sherwin.

'The series had become very fanciful and gone heavily into monsters from outer space, which I found very tedious and unbelievable. The only reason everyone watched was to see what the latest monster was like – whether it had got fur on or a silver head or one eye at the back of its ear, or whatever. The series wasn't going anywhere, the viewing figures were dropping, so I sat down with Peter Bryant to work out what we could do about this. I said the only thing I could think of was to look back, see what had been successful in the past and try to learn from that.

'I went to the BBC's archives and managed to dig out some episodes of *The Quatermass Experiment* (the writer, Nigel Kneale, was my neighbour at the time!). We screened them, and the production was so appalling that we found them hysterically funny. We rolled about laughing! But what the producers had been trying to do – and what ultimately they achieved in *Quatermass and the Pit* – was to get some reality into it. So I said that this was the solution; that what we had got to do with *Doctor Who* was to forget wobbly jellies in outer space and create some reason for bringing the stories down to Earth.

'We couldn't do this with just the Doctor and his two companions, we had to have some other means, so that's why I came up with UNIT, the United Nations Intelligence Taskforce. I sat down and wrote a couple of pages about this special taskforce, specifically with members from all nations, which had been set up to investigate funny things happening in space or the possibility

of UFOs or whatever. It was basically an army intelligence unit – with special powers and, on some occasions, special weapons – which had access to scientists and laboratories and all the kinds of things that Doctor Who might need. It gave us an identifiable group within which to work on special occasions and of course a reason for bringing the Doctor in. It was constructed fairly methodically and thoughtfully in the first instance, to serve a very specific purpose for at least a year's run.'

UNIT made its debut in the season six story *The Invasion* and, as Sherwin tells it, this was always intended as simply the first step in a process of moving towards a more permanent Earth-bound setting – something which he says would have happened even if Patrick Troughton had not been leaving the series:

'The idea was always to bring it down to Earth gently and then to stay there for a long period of time. Quite apart from dramatic considerations, another factor was that budgets were being cut and we were being asked to do more. Don't forget that we were going from black and white into colour, which was an expensive exercise (productions being charged more for using colour studios than for black and white), and we had to have a run of productions that we could afford. We couldn't keep on creating spaceships and monster suits all over the place and going out to the back end of nowhere to film alien planets – it just wasn't on with the financial restrictions which existed.'

Consequently, it was decided that the Doctor should be exiled to Earth at the end of *The War Games*, to provide a reason for him to hook up with UNIT at the start of season seven.

In mid-1969, Sherwin and Terrance Dicks, finally promoted to script editor proper, began to commission scripts for this new season, of which the first story – Robert Holmes's *Spearhead from Space* – began filming in September. On 20 October, Barry Letts arrived to take over from Peter Bryant and Derrick Sherwin as the series' latest producer. And well before this, of course, another important development had occurred with the casting, by Peter Bryant, of a replacement for Patrick Troughton.

The series' new star was first presented to the press at a special photocall held at the BBC Pictorial Publicity premises in Cavendish Place (just across the road from Broadcasting House in London's West End) on Tuesday 17 June 1969, four days after the recording of Patrick Troughton's final episode and four days before its transmission. BBC drama press officer Kevin O'Shea still recalls with some glee the reaction of the assembled newsmen when the door was opened before them to reveal the unexpected figure of the man chosen to portray the third Doctor: well-known comic actor and entertainer Jon Pertwee...

LISTING OF *DOCTOR WHO* MERCHANDISE RELEASED 1963 - 1969

NAME	PUB/MAN	YEAR	PRICE	CATEGORY
Curse of the Daleks, The, stage play programme		1965		Sundries
Cutta-mastic Doctor Who and the Daleks, The	Bell Toys Ltd	1965	29s 11d	Boxed Games
Cutta-mastic featuring Daleks, The	Bell Toys Ltd	1966		Boxed Games
Dalek	Cherilea Toys Ltd	1965	1s	Daleks
Dalek	Herts Plastic Moulders Ltd	1965	4s 11d	Daleks
Dalek (4.5" friction)	Louis Marx & Co. Ltd	1965	5s 11d	Daleks
Dalek (6.5" battery operated with robot action)	Louis Marx & Co. Ltd	1965	17s 11d	Daleks
Dalek (6.5" friction drive with siren and flashing lights)	Louis Marx & Co. Ltd	1965	12s 11d	Daleks
Dalek (bendy)	Newfeld Ltd	1965	10s 6d	Daleks
Dalek (mechanical)	Cowan, de Groot Ltd	1965	15s 11d	Daleks
Dalek (scotchlite)	Clifford Thomas Printing Co. Ltd	1965		Daleks
Dalek (stand-up inflatable)	Scorpion Universal Toys Ltd	1965	21s	Daleks
Dalek Action Paint 'n Puzzle	Souvenir Press	1966	2s 6d	Activity Books
Dalek Baby Plate	J. H. Weatherby & Sons Ltd	1965		Crockery
Dalek Badge (large)	Plastoid Ltd	1964	1s 3d	Badges
Dalek Badge (small)	Plastoid Ltd	1964	9d	Badges
Dalek Bag	Optima Manufacturing Co. Ltd	1965		Sundries
Dalek Balloon (large)	Lewis Knight & Co. Ltd	1965	6d	Toys
Dalek Balloon (small)	Sto-Rose Toys Ltd	1965	3d	Toys
Dalek Birthday Card	Waldorf Card Company	1964		Stationery
Dalek Book, The	Souvenir Press & Panther Books	1964	9s 6d	Annuals
Dalek Candle	Candle Art Ltd	1965		Sundries
Dalek Chocolate Bars	Cavenham Confectionery	1965	1d	Confectionery
Dalek Construction Kit, The	Louis Marx & Co. Ltd	1965	6s 11d	Toys
Dalek Cup	J. H. Weatherby & Sons Ltd	1965		Crockery
Dalek Dressing Up Costume	Scorpion Automotives	1964	£8 15s 6d	Toys
Dalek Easter Egg		1965		Confectionery
Dalek Eraser	Bell Toys Ltd	1965	8s 11d	Boxed Games
Dalek Fireworks		1965		Sundries
Dalek Glove Puppet	The Chad Valley Company Ltd	1965	8s 11d	Toys
Dalek Greetings Cards	Newton Mills Ltd	1965		Stationery
Dalek Jelly Babies (2 sizes)	Bellamy's Ltd	1965		Confectionery
Dalek Jigsaws	Thomas Hope & Sankey Hudson Ltd	1965	2s 9d	Jigsaws
Dalek Kiddie Ride	Edwin Hall & Co.	1967		Sundries
Dalek Kit, Daily Express	Beaverbrook Publishing	1965	free	Sundries
Dalek Kite	Bowman Jenkins	1965	4s 6d	Toys
Dalek Mask	A. Bangham & Co. Ltd	1965	1s 6d	Clothing
Dalek Meteorite Storm	Randall & Wood Ltd	1965	2s 6d	Toys
Dalek Money Box	Cowan, de Groot Ltd	1965	4s 11d	Toys
Dalek Mug	J. H. Weatherby & Sons Ltd	1965		Crockery
Dalek novelties, foil wrapped chocolate	Edward Sharpe & Sons Ltd	1965	1s 6d	Confectionery
Dalek Nursery Toy	Selcol Products Ltd	1965	5s 11d	Daleks
Dalek Oracle, The	Bell Toys Ltd	1965	9s 11d	Boxed Games
Dalek Outer Space Book, The (h/b)	Souvenir Press & Panther Books	1966	10s 6d	Annuals
Dalek Painting Book, The	Panther Books Ltd	1965	2s 6d	Activity Books
Dalek Pencil Craft Set	Tower Press (London) Ltd	1966	9s 11d	Stationery
Dalek Pencil Sharpener	Baileys Agencies	1965		Stationery
Dalek Pencils	Baileys Agencies	1965		Stationery
Dalek Plastic Jar	H & B Plastics Ltd	1965		Sundries
Dalek Playsuit	Berwick Toy Co. Ltd	1965	66s 6d	Toys
Dalek Pocketbook and Space Travellers Guide, The (p/b)	Souvenir Press & Panther Books	1965	2s 6d	Novels
Dalek Porridge Bowl	J. H. Weatherby & Sons Ltd	1965		Crockery
Dalek PVC Sheeting	Storey's Bros Ltd	1965		Sundries
Dalek Rocket Gun	Lone Star Products	1965	5s 11d	Toys
Dalek Saucer	J. H. Weatherby & Sons Ltd	1965		Crockery
Dalek Shooting Game	Louis Marx & Co. Ltd	1965	16s 11d	Boxed Games
Dalek Skittles	Randall & Wood Ltd	1965		Toys
Dalek Slippers	Furness Footwear Ltd	1965		Clothing
Dalek Sponge (fist)		1965		Sundries
Dalek Sponge (shaped)		1965		Sundries
Dalek Stencil Set	Berwick Toy Co. Ltd	1965	4s 11d	Boxed Games
Dalek Tilly-Tray	J. H. Weatherby & Sons Ltd	1965		Crockery
Dalek Toilet Soap	Northants Association for the Blind	1965	5s 11d	Sundries
Dalek Transfers	S. Guiterman & Co. Ltd	1965	3d	Toys
Dalek Wall Plaque	J. H. Weatherby & Sons Ltd	1965		Crockery
Dalek Wallpaper	The Wall Paper Manufacturers Ltd	1965		Sundries
Dalek Wonder Slate	Bell Toys Ltd	1965	2s 11d	Boxed Games
Dalek Wooden Stand-up Jigsaws	Thomas Hope & Sankey Hudson Ltd	1965	5s 11d	Jigsaws
Dalek World, The (h/b)	Souvenir Press & Panther Books	1965	10s 6d	Annuals
Dalek Writing Pad, The	Newton Mills Ltd	1965	1s	Stationery

Daleks, Milk Gum		1965		Confectionery
Daleks, The EP	Century 21 Records (MA 106)	1966		Records
Dance of the Daleks by the Jack Dorsey Orchestra	Polydor (56.020)	1965	5s 11d	Records
Doctor Who and the Crusaders (h/b)	Frederick Muller Ltd	1966	12s 6d	Novels
Doctor Who and the Crusaders (p/b)	Green Dragon	1967	2s 6d	Novels
Doctor Who and the Daleks Bagatelle (large circular)	Louis Marx & Co. Ltd	1965	7s 6d	Toys
Doctor Who and the Daleks Bagatelle (oblong)	Louis Marx & Co. Ltd	1965	7s 11d	Toys
Doctor Who and the Daleks Bagatelle (small circular)	Louis Marx & Co. Ltd	1965		Toys
Doctor Who and the Invasion From Space (h/b)	World Distributors	1966	5s	Annuals
Doctor Who and the Zarbi (h/b)	Frederick Muller Ltd	1965	12s 6d	Novels
Doctor Who Give-a-Show Projector	The Chad Valley Company Ltd	1965	29s 6d	Boxed Games
Doctor Who in an exciting adventure with the Daleks (h/b)	Frederick Muller Ltd	1964	12s 6d	Novels
Doctor Who in an exciting adventure with the Daleks (p/b)	Armada Paperbacks	1965	2s 6d	Novels
Doctor Who on the planet Zactus Painting Book	World Distributors	1966	1s	Activity Books
Doctor Who Painting Book No.1	World Distributors	1966	1s	Activity Books
Doctor Who Painting Book No.2	World Distributors	1966	1s	Activity Books
Doctor Who Puzzle Fun No.1	World Distributors	1966	2s 6d	Activity Books
Doctor Who Puzzle Fun No.2	World Distributors	1966	2s 6d	Activity Books
Doctor Who Theme by the BBC Radiophonic Workshop	Decca (F11837)	1964	5s 11d	Records
Doctor Who Theme by the Eric Winston Orchestra	Pye Records (7N 15603)	1965	5s 11d	Records
Doctor Who's 'Astro Ray' Dalek Gun	Bell Toys Ltd	1965	14s 11d	Toys
Dodge the Daleks Game	Cowan, de Groot Ltd	1965	6s 11d	Boxed Games
Dr Who and the Dalek Rolykins	Louis Marx & Co. Ltd	1965	1s	Daleks
Dr Who and the Daleks Comic	Dell Comics	1966	12 cents	Films
Dr Who and the Daleks Sweet Cigarettes	Cavenham Confectionery Ltd/ Paramount Labs Ltd (Cadet)	1965	2d	Confectionery
Dr Who and the Daleks - The Great Escape Game	Peter Pan Playthings Ltd	1965	7s 11d	Boxed Games
Dr Who and the Daleks Top	Selcol Products Ltd	1965	19s 11d	Toys
Dr Who Annual, The (h/b, 1966)	World Distributors (Manchester) Ltd	1965	9s 6d	Annuals
Dr Who Annual, The (h/b, 1967)	World Distributors (Manchester) Ltd	1966	10s 6d	Annuals
Dr Who Annual, The (h/b, 1968)	World Distributors (Manchester) Ltd	1967	10s 6d	Annuals
Dr Who Annual, The (h/b, 1969)	World Distributors (Manchester) Ltd	1968	12s 6d	Annuals
Dr Who Annual, The (h/b, 1970)	World Distributors (Manchester) Ltd	1969	12s 6d	Annuals
Dr Who Dalek Painting by Numbers, The	Peter Pan Playthings Ltd	1965	9s 11d	Boxed Games
Dr Who Money Box	Raphael Lipkin Ltd	1965	4s 6d	Toys
Dr Who Sticker Fun Book - Travels in Space	World Distributors (Netherlands) Ltd	1966	2s 6d	Activity Books
Dr Who Sticker Fun Book - Travels in Time	World Distributors (Netherlands) Ltd	1966	2s 6d	Activity Books
Dr Who's Anti-Dalek Fluid Neutraliser	Lincoln International (London) Ltd	1965	3s 11d	Toys
Dr Who's Anti-Dalek Jet Immobiliser	Lincoln International (London) Ltd	1965	9s 11d	Toys
Dr Who's Anti-Dalek Neutron Exterminator	Lincoln International (London) Ltd	1965	21s	Toys
Dr Who's Anti-Dalek Sonic Disintegrator	Lincoln International (London) Ltd	1965	12s 11d	Toys
Dr Who's Space Adventure Book	T. Wall & Sons/Sky Ray	1967	free	Confectionery
Eccentric Dr Who, The by the Malcolm Lockyer Orchestra	Columbia (DB 7663)	1965	5s 11d	Records
Front of House Stills		1965/66	-	Films
Fugue For Thought by Bill McGuffie	Philips (BF 1550)	1967	5s 11d	Records
I'm Gonna Spend My Christmas With a Dalek by the Go-Gos	Oriele (CB 1982)	1964	5s 11d	Records
Landing of the Daleks by The Earthlings	The Parlophone Co. Ltd (R5242)	1965	5s 11d	Records
Mechanoid (large)	Herts Plastic Moulders Ltd	1965	4s 11d	Toys
Mechanoid (small)	Cherilea Toys Ltd	1965	1s	Toys
Menoptra Badge	Plastoid Ltd	1965	1s 3d	Badges
Milk bottle collars		1966	free	Films
Paint and draw the film of Dr. Who and the Daleks	Souvenir Press & Panther Books	1965	2s 6d	Activity Books
Paper bags		1966	free	Films
Paper serviettes		1966	free	Films
Photographs		1965/66	-	Films
Posters		1965/66	-	Films
Sugar Puffs Promotion		1966	free	Films
TARDIS Climbing Frame and Playhouse	Furnitubes Associated Products	1968	£5 5s	Sundries
TARDIS Tie	Ergon Tie	1966		Clothing
TV Comic	TV Publications Ltd	1964-69	6d issue	Comics
TV Century 21	City Magazines	1965-66	7d issue	Comics
Who's Dr Who? by Frazer Hines	Major Minor (MM 579)	1968		Records
Who's Who by Roberta Tovey	Polydor (BM 56021)	1965	5s 11d	Records
Zarbi and Venom Gun Badge	Plastoid Ltd	1965	1s 3d	Badges

All the prices quoted for merchandise are in their original (pre-decimalisation) form; one shilling (1s) is equivalent to five new pence. There were twelve old pence in a shilling and twenty shillings in a pound. Thus, for example, an old price of 12s 11d is equivalent to about 64p, and £8 15s 6d to about £8.78. This, of course, makes no allowance for inflation!

AUTHORS' NOTE We have made every effort to ensure that this merchandise listing is as complete as possible, but if you have any further information about any of the items mentioned, or know of any items which are not listed, please contact the authors at the publisher's address at the front of this book.